T0339861

The Sentimental State

The
Sentimental State

⟶∘⟜⟝∘⟵

HOW WOMEN-LED REFORM
BUILT THE AMERICAN
WELFARE STATE

Elizabeth Garner Masarik

The University of Georgia Press
Athens

© 2024 by the University of Georgia Press
Athens, Georgia 30602
www.ugapress.org
All rights reserved
Designed by Kaelin Chappell Broaddus
Set in 9/13.5 Mencken Std Text Regular by Kaelin Chappell Broaddus

Most University of Georgia Press titles are
available from popular e-book vendors.

Printed digitally

Library of Congress Cataloging-in-Publication Data

Names: Masarik, Elizabeth Garner, author.
Title: The sentimental state : how women-led reform built the American
welfare state / Elizabeth Garner Masarik.
Description: Athens : The University of Georgia Press, [2024] | Includes
bibliographical references and index.
Identifiers: LCCN 2023043118 (print) | LCCN 2023043119 (ebook) |
ISBN 9780820366067 (hardback) | ISBN 9780820366050 (paperback) |
ISBN 9780820366074 (epub) | ISBN 9780820366081 (pdf)
Subjects: LCSH: Women—United States—Social conditions. |
Women—Political activity—United States—History. |
Women social reformers—United States—History. |
Public welfare—United States—History. | United States—Social policy.
Classification: LCC HQ1410 .M367 2024 (print) | LCC HQ1410 (ebook) |
DDC 320.082/0973—dc23/eng/20231011
LC record available at https://lccn.loc.gov/2023043118
LC ebook record available at https://lccn.loc.gov/2023043119

FOR *Nüni & Bug*

CONTENTS

ACKNOWLEDGMENTS

I have accumulated many debts while writing this book. I am grateful to advisors, librarians, cohorts, friends, and family who gave generously of their time and attention. Thank you to friends and colleagues at the University at Buffalo (UB) and to my amazing advisor, Susan Cahn. Susan, I can't thank you enough for your help and encouragement along the way. Special thanks to Victoria Wolcott and Gail Radford for extensive readings and comments on early versions of this book. Gail, you talked me off a cliff and I will always appreciate that. Thank you, David Herzberg and Michael Rembis, for outstanding guidance during the early days of the project. I also want to thank the rest of the Department of History at the University at Buffalo for meaningful support, both intellectually and financially. Further thanks to Carole Emberton, Hal Langfur, Erik Seeman, and Jason Young for your help and guidance. Thanks to the UB Gender Institute and the UB Humanities Institute for generous funding and workshop opportunities and special thanks to Carrie Bramen and David Castillo for comments on early versions of this book. I am also thankful for the financial support of the UB Mark Diamond Research Fund, which funded portions of my research travel.

I would not have been able to complete my research without the help and guidance of archivists and librarians. I would like to especially thank Linnea Anderson, archivist at the Social Welfare History Archives, Anderson Library, University of Minnesota. Also special thanks to Tiffany Atwater at the Robert W. Woodruff Library, Atlanta University Center, and Kathy Lafferty from the Kenneth Spencer Research Library, University of Kansas. A special thank you to Genevieve Keeney at the National Museum of Funeral History in Houston, Texas. Additional thanks to staff at the National Archives and the Library of Congress, Washington, D.C. Also, thank you to the Susan B. Anthony Gender and Sexuality Writing Collective at the University of Rochester and for early comments from Jean Pederson.

Warmest thanks to my colleges at SUNY Brockport. I cannot overstate how grateful I am to have found such a welcoming academic home. Thank you Anne Macpherson, Morag Martin, Paul Moyer, John Daly, Michael Kramer, Jose Torre, Katherine Clark Walter, Angela Thompsell, Meredith Roman, James Spiller, Takashi Nishiyama, Carl Davila, Bruce Leslie, and Jose Maliekal. Further thanks to the SUNY Brockport School of Arts and Sciences for generous research funding.

Academic friends, mentors, and colleagues have been instrumental in helping me think through this project. Of course, thank you to my cohorts at *Dig: A History Podcast.* Sarah Handley-Cousins, Marissa Rhodes, and Averill Earls, ya'll have become my best friends and have enriched my life in more ways than I can count. Others who have helped me along this academic journey include Cynthia Orozco, Mary Kelley, Krista Hanypsiak Krause, Katie Darling, Ann Bisantz, Graham Hammill, Lauren Thompson, and Lisa Collin. Thank you, University of Georgia Press, especially Mick Gusinde-Duffy for believing in this project. Thanks to Rachel Van Hart for close reads. I am also grateful to anonymous readers for constructive feedback. I appreciate all the help and take full responsibility for any mistakes in this manuscript.

Deep thanks go to my family for the love and support I have felt through this entire experience. Jane Garner instilled a love of education in me from an early age. Lois Garner and Harlan Garner watched over this project from day one. Richard and Margaret Masarik are the best in-laws one could wish for. Thank you Alice Funderburg for being an awesome sister, friend, and fellow nerd. Thanks to my mom, Francis Garner, who gave me a love of books and taught me how to study. Thank you, O and V. You were just babies when I started this project and are now two of the most mature and smart people I know. I love you. Finally, thank you Jason, my husband, partner, and best friend. You never doubted me.

The Sentimental State

INTRODUCTION

―――――――∽•ᏟᏩᎠ•∼―――――――

It may be, at first, something of a shock to hear of taking the
child out of the realm of poetry and pure sentiment and into
the field of scientific, organized care and protection.[1]

In 1909 women reformers from across the nation met in Chicago, Illinois, to advocate for a federal children's bureau that would oversee matters pertaining to the welfare of women and children living in the United States. Before American women universally had the right to vote, these reformers were working to convince the men elected to the U.S. House and Senate that a bureaucratic agency focused on women and children was of vital importance to the success of the nation.

In support of the new federal agency, Lillian Wald, founder of the New York City Henry Street Settlement house and board member of the National Child Labor Committee, addressed how the role of sentiment was integral to shaping understandings of human welfare. "It may be, at first, something of a shock to hear of taking the child out of the realm of poetry and pure sentiment into the field of scientific, organized care and protection," she began, but added that only to "the superficially sentimental could ... the poetry and purity of childhood ... be sacrificed by using all the fruits of modern thought, study, experience and knowledge to their advantage."[2] While science, not sentiment, was needed to address the United States' high mortality rates for mothers and children, Wald maintained that the "poetry and purity of childhood" would remain intact. Wald's statement acknowledged the power that sentiment had played in pushing reform for women and children up to that point.

This book explores how late nineteenth- and early twentieth-century white and Black women reformers harnessed sentimentality to create political action in the formation of the American welfare state. This is a gendered analysis of state building with special attention to infant mortality, grief, sexuality, and how these seemingly personal elements shaped private and state support for white and Black single mothers and their children. It studies women reformers who worked to bridge private charity for single mothers with state-funded public welfare, while navigating the racial and gendered elements of turn-of-the-century America.

Women expanded their sphere of influence into the realm of social welfare during the nineteenth century through voluntary organizations and women's clubs. In doing so they acted politically—not in party politics *per se*, but in public support of welfare measures for communities larger than their immediate family circle.[3] I argue that grief and sentimentalism were major factors that influenced that political activity. The death of a young child was a very real and emotional experience for many families during the nineteenth century. At the dawn of the twentieth century, many Americans expected a better outcome in the life expectancy of their children. However, in 1910 America ranked tenth among principal nations in infant mortality. The estimated national infant mortality rate was one hundred per one thousand live births, resulting in over 230,000 infant deaths per year.[4] Because of this high death rate, and the real grief those deaths caused in everyday women's lives, the health of mothers and children was at the heart of many Gilded Age and Progressive Era reforms.

This preoccupation with mothers and children was not a new phenomenon but rather one carried over from reform movements of the early nineteenth century. The importance of sentimentalism to the nineteenth century, and the weight that sentimentalism put on the centrality of the mother and child bond to the health of the nation, conditioned white and Black middle-class American women to demand social protections for that bond. I argue that sentimentalism gave middle-class women the language to demand protections of the mother and child connection, particularly when it came to issues of infant and maternal mortality or the sexual "fall" of girls and women.

Government support of social welfare does not happen in a vacuum; it is driven by the needs, decisions, and actions of engaged citizens. Accordingly, this book is an examination of the cultural realities of the women who tapped national, state, and local funds to support the changes they deemed necessary during Gilded Age and Progressive Era America. I seek to understand why everyday women stepped out of their gendered sphere and into the public sphere of state building. Why did middle-class Black and white women concern themselves with "helping" single mothers and illegitimate children? We know the outcome of their movements, but what *pushed* these women to act in the first place? These questions add a fresh perspective to the well-established body of interdisciplinary scholarship in the fields of women's, gender, and sexuality studies, particularly historical studies focused on reform efforts of late nineteenth-, early twentieth-century women. I determine that the modern American welfare state is built upon the back of women's paid and unpaid labor within women-centered reform movements that relied on a sentimental understanding of the primacy of the mother and child bond.

Sentimentalism and emotion were core driving forces behind middle-class women's push into the political realm. Individual responses to catastrophic events that are ostensibly personal, such as the death of a child, colored collective responses that shaped the way the twentieth-century "Progressive spirit" attempted to change society. Sentimentalism gave women who experienced child death and disease an outlet to vent their frustration, anger, and sadness, making sentimentalism an integral part of middle-class women's push to involve government in social welfare reform during the Progressive Era. However, sentimentalism is most often associated with early nineteenth-century literature and culture. Sentimental fiction was a wildly successful literary genre during the nineteenth century and symbiotically shaped, and was shaped, by the culture that many of its readers lived within. Therefore, sentimentalism was not just a literary preference but a cultural phenomenon. The success of sentimental power shaped many aspects of culture, politics, and social movements in nineteenth-century America and played such an important role in everyday society that it carried over well into the twentieth century.[5]

The popularity of sentimental literature corresponds with the rise of women's voluntary organizing, and sentimentalism was the means by which many Americans were exposed to the values of white middle-class women and broad perceptions of right living. As early nineteenth-century changes in the market economy fueled changes in household production, middle-class women began creating associations and clubs to meet their social needs.[6] The sorrow and anger women experienced in their daily lives through either the common fear or reality of losing a child, or through the loneliness of being left behind by grown children, helped fuel this women-centered associational life. Some felt anger at the "slavery of sex" and the unfairness of the moral double standard that relegated all women, regardless of race or class, to second-class citizenship. Middle-class women expressed this anger and sadness in private grief and mourning, through material culture, and increasingly by acting publicly through associative organizations. They joined antislavery societies, they publicly signed petitions, organized moral reform societies, and spoke out in favor of temperance, social purity, and women's rights. All were efforts to combine sentiment and anger at injustice in public efforts to create changes consistent with their own maternal and sentimental feelings.

Contemporary culture presented the deep connection between mother and child as the central bond within a proper childhood. Phrases such as "the mother, who is [a child's] most intimate associate, the sharer of their secret lives," were offered without question or reflection.[7] The sentimental description of a mother's love for her child in early nineteenth-century magazines like *Godey's Lady's Book* was practically indistinguishable from those of late nineteenth-century publications such as *The Outlook*, *The Arena*, *Survey*, and *Ladies Home Journal*, showing the pervasiveness of this cultural phenomenon well into the twentieth century. All used sentimentalism as a means to celebrate the mother and child bond, push social action, and contribute to social commentary.

Women continued to participate in associations throughout the nineteenth century and joined voluntary clubs in droves during the Gilded Age and Progressive Era. These organizations combined gender consciousness with political activity in their work for social welfare. Many scholars refer to these late nineteenth-, early twentieth-century women reformers as maternalists and, as such, part of a political movement by middle-class women that agitated for a range of political and state-sponsored protections for women and children. Maternalists claimed that women needed political power in order to perform the duties inherently gifted to women. They believed that women were especially capable of determining what type of state protection and welfare women and children needed because of their special knowledge and moral qualities by virtue of being women and mothers. Maternalism was therefore a way for some female reformers to gain power both inside and outside official channels of government to improve the welfare of women and children during a time when women were barred from voting at the national level. Arguably, women's exclusion from official channels of government created a political style that found expression in voluntarist politics.[8]

Scholars do not typically use the term "maternalism" as a signifier to describe non-white women's reform work, partly because women of color were barred from official politics by racial exclusion and stigma, and partly because maternalism is known within the historiography of women's reform work as a movement of white, middle-class women. However, historians have done a significant amount of work on non-white women reformers, particularly Black women reformers, who I argue fall under the moniker of maternalist.

Segregation and racism barred Black women from exerting official pressure on white politicians and joining white women's clubs and other voluntary organizations.[9] Therefore, a strong component of Black women's reform grew through other voluntarist means, particularly from within the church. Black churchwomen shaped the church into a space for self-help and spearheaded the building of schools and the creation of welfare services and developed what Evelyn Brooks Higginbotham terms the "politics of respectability" as a way to gain respect in the face of white supremacy but also to combat sexism in the Black church.[10]

Often, middle-class status in Black communities rested on temperance, and morals—not necessarily wealth. Education also represented one step toward Black middle-class status. Activist Sarah Dudley Pettey precisely connected gender, class, and education when she stated that African Americans must rely on "its educated women" as "the potent factors" in "the civilization and enlightenment of the Negro race."[11] According to middle- and working-class respectability adherents, these traits would inspire working-class Blacks to emulate their middle-class behaviors, thus growing the race in a "respectable" way. Often, claims of respectability rested on habits of cleanliness, temperance, education, thrift, self-improvement, and child rearing.[12]

In the eyes of many Black middle-class reformers, the sexuality of young women and potential motherhood held the key to racial pride and uplifting the Black community. Black women of what Michele Mitchell dubs the *aspiring class* concerned themselves with propriety, morality, thrift, and respectability. They maintained that the race had shared interests as a sociopolitical body, ultimately meaning the collective's future—their "racial destiny"—depended on policing Black behavior. Particularly controlling was the oversight it put on Black women's sexuality as the betterment of the race intertwined with reproducing eugenically fit babies. Within this ideological framework, only babies born and raised by respectable Black women would improve the race. This contributed to class stratification among African Americans as middle-class Black reformers focused their fears of Black race suicide on the bodies and sexuality of Black women. Race betterment efforts among the Black middle-class acted as a conservative mechanism of social control over working-class Blacks. Race betterment—better babies, better homes, and better families—depended for these maternalist reformers on the respectability of the Black mother and how well she conformed to middle-class values.[13]

However, many Black reformers understood that women, particularly Black women, worked outside of the home by necessity. In fact, many of the leading female Black reformers had careers of their own.[14] Self-described "race women" built social welfare organizations that addressed issues like delinquency among youths, education, and sanitation. These "social problems," which seemingly had no racial implications, were areas in which Black female reformers could access the state and, alternatively, where white state actors could fund programs that would help solve their "Negro problems."[15] These institutions often received the blessings of white politicians and civic leaders and even received portions of public tax revenue, but the majority of funding came from the fundraising efforts of Black women through bake sales, church events, and even track meets. Social welfare initiatives created by Black female reformers heavily relied on private money for public benefit.[16]

Due to the sheer number of women involved in turn-of-the-century voluntarist politics, women's voluntary associations were able to put external pressure on male policymakers even before women won the right to universal suffrage. The primarily white National Congress of Mother's formed in 1897, and by 1920 it had thousands of branches across the country. Historian Molly Ladd-Taylor labels women who joined this group as *sentimental maternalists* because their ideology was founded on a sentimental understanding of the irreplaceable bond between mother and child that stemmed from the nineteenth century, but their shared consciousness, spurred by popular sentimental culture, drove them to act collectively and ultimately politically. Their goal was to teach mothers how to properly care for their own children and to "awaken their maternal responsibility to improve social conditions affecting all children," particularly in areas of health and childhood mortality.[17] Labeling them *sentimental* should not color these maternalists as ineffective. Mrs. H. V. Davis, head of the Patriotism division of the California Congress of Mothers highlighted the failures of a political sphere operated by men alone, stating, "when the women take the ballot there goes with it an obligation, not merely to do as well as the men have done—for you cannot do worse—but to do very much better."[18] Sentimental maternalists' defense of the domestic sphere was fierce, and they passionately advocated for women's suffrage in order to achieve those goals.

Many maternalist organizations whose main priority was not women's suffrage supported women's enfranchisement as a way to push forward their primary reform goals. Historians have often treated women's voluntary reform work and the fight for suffrage as separate movements, but in reality they were closely related. For example, the Woman's Christian Temperance Union (WCTU) supported women's suffrage in the late nineteenth century while also concerning itself with curtailing society's vices. Even without the vote, the very act of reform work in charitable and voluntary organizations allowed some white and Black women to enter the political sphere, engage in social policy formation, and occasionally cross racial lines.[19]

Concerns over public health and high rates of infant and child mortality rapidly became part of health reform movements that coalesced around illness prevention through segregation and social control. The discovery that germs, not "bad air" or miasmas, carried disease vastly influenced the everyday lives of many Americans and led to an evangelical-type zeal for cleanliness that swept across the country during the Progressive Era. The phenomenon completely transformed the domestic space of the home; the ornate and textile rich Victorian powder room became the sterile, smooth-surfaced bathroom we are familiar with today. Using soaps and sanitizers in the house became priorities for women whose responsibility it became to care for the health of their homes' inhabitants.[20]

Nevertheless, infant mortality was still extremely high. Maternalist activism allowed some white college-educated women to gain official government power and positions within the federal, state, and local government structure, most notably the formation of the federal U.S. Children's Bureau in 1912.[21] A major factor motivating maternalists in the Children's Bureau was the prevalence of infant mortality among the American population, so much so that the first study conducted by the Bureau was a study of infant mortality.

The grief and pain affecting mothers and families is apparent in letters written to the Children's Bureau. These letters written by women from all demographics express the pain, guilt, confusion, and anger over the loss or sickness of a young child. Grassroots organizing and the practical experience of Children's Bureau employees with infant mortality led to a growing federal interest in maternal and child welfare. This activism ultimately culminated with the passage of the Sheppard-Towner Maternity and Infancy Act in 1921. The Act, which provided federal funding for maternal and infant health programs, was passed in response to the high infant mortality rates that the Children's Bureau documented and at the insistence of maternalist voluntarist organizations.[22]

White and Black maternalists who stepped into leadership roles, either in the federal government, state, and local health departments, or private voluntarist organizations, wielded power that allowed them to impact, and sometimes control, the lives of those women whom they desired to help. Often couched in the language of universal motherhood, middle-class reformers tended to penalize women and mothers they deemed unable—or unwilling—to behave according to certain standards, perpetrating what gender studies scholar Laura Wexler terms "tender violence" on those they purported to help.[23] These biases, however, are overlooked when viewing maternalist policies through a strictly political lens, which fails to analyze the elite attitudes and gender-traditionalism that some maternalists promoted and that resulted in welfare programs that, although designed and implemented by women, did not always help the recipients.[24]

My reexamination of maternalism and the exploration of maternalist programs for both women sex workers and child welfare bridges two seemingly disparate American welfare foci and shows how they were intricately related within grassroots women's movements. Many studies of women's reform work and the growth of the welfare state concentrate on either "the girl problem," on child health initiatives through large state entities, or on political machinations. My work bridges these varying studies into a cohesive narrative, while emphasizing sentimentalism as a driving force behind both white and Black middle-class women's activism.[25]

It is important to keep in mind that "women" was not an all-encompassing term. Women's political organizing focused on many different aspects of American life and some women's political organizing did not benefit other women. Nonetheless, a shared identity as women and as mothers rested upon sentimental understandings of gender and nurtured a shared gender-consciousness regarding welfare for women and children. Their efforts resulted in the codification of many women and child-centered reforms and created the foundation of the modern American welfare state.[26]

Undoubtedly, race, gender, and class biases had detrimental effects on the formation of the American welfare system and its recipients. Furthermore, the New Deal codified the biases of Progressive Era social programs into a two-tiered federal policy. One tier became a non-needs-based program meant for white wage-earning men and their dependents, the other a means-tested tier for women and children dependent on the state. Although the parameters of these two channels expanded throughout the twentieth century to include people of color, the basic parameters remained the same.[27]

Classic studies of the American welfare state used a class and political analysis that found the present-day welfare state firmly planted in the policies of the New Deal. This is highly contested and contributes to what William Novak terms the "myth of the New Deal," which downplays state development before the Great Depression. This view overlooks the key role of volunteerism in state formation and the ways that gender shaped the foundations of the American welfare state.[28] Through a pivot in analysis, women and gender historians used not only class but also gender and race as a lens of analysis. By doing so, they dramatically reshaped the historiography of American welfare policy by showing that middle-class white women played an integral part in laying the foundation of the welfare state earlier in the twentieth century. These middle-class, white, female reformers did not question the social underpinnings of motherhood and domesticity or the family wage, but instead venerated these values and fought for programs that would protect motherhood as an exalted status. The gender turn in welfare analysis altered the historiography to show that elements of the current welfare state, like the Social Security Act, were not reactions to the Great Depression of the 1930s but were continuations of a rudimentary welfare state built through the invisible labor of countless female reformers. My study highlights collaborations between private, voluntary organizations and local state apparatus and also incorporates the experiences of African American women into the framework of early twentieth-century maternalism to argue that the grassroots work performed by everyday women made larger maternalist trends social policies to be reckoned with.

The "associative state" is a term first coined by historian Ellis Hawley to describe President Herbert Hoover's ideology of the "American system" of the 1920s that was designed to foster a synthesis between private enterprise, grassroots voluntary organizations, and the national government.[29] It never resulted in a seamless joining, although elements of corporate welfare were encouraged (which subsequently failed miserably during the Great Depression). However, the associative state was not a new phenomenon in the 1920s, but as historian Brian Balogh and others argue, it was instead a continuation of collaborations that had been part and parcel of the national government since the nineteenth century. While I disagree with Balogh's assessment that all Americans share "enduring fears of big government," I do find Balogh's "associational synthesis" a useful tool to analyze early social welfare in the modern American state.[30] This synthesis helps smooth the edges from what modern readers might view as "liberal" or "conservative" actions by reformers and instead allows us to view historical subjects as neither "good" or "bad" but acting within the constraints, privileges, and ideologies of their race, gender, and class. This does not mean we should not critique decisions and actions made in the past, it just allows us to examine that nebulous idea that is "the State" within a framework that offers a more fluid understanding of how state power is formed. Therefore, I engage with the associational synthesis, tracking how formal government power is funneled through private or voluntary groups outside of government agencies.[31] I argue that my subjects created the associative welfare state by creating organizations that eventually became associational arms of local and state governments, which later fed into national government entities such as the U.S. Children's Bureau.

To capture both the growth of these organizations and the cultural sentiment surrounding the movements, I relied on a variety of sources and methods, resulting in both a cultural and political history. Institutional records for the organizations mentioned below were utilized for this study, as well as other peripheral organizations pertinent to the analysis. I also relied on transcripts and minutes from organizational meetings and government hearings. Information from newspapers and periodicals including op-eds, news, and advertisements supplement institutional records. Cultural sentiment is measured through contemporaneous popular fiction and poetry. At the forefront of my analysis is the sentiment and emotion created by the specter of child mortality and how some middle-class Black and white women harnessed that emotion into political action. Therefore, this book does not encapsulate a direct study of the women who were recipients of the social welfare programs these reformers created *per se*, but of the women who organized these programs.

This book is divided into ten chapters and a conclusion. The first section provides a prehistory of Progressivism as related to the primacy of the mother and child bond through the lens of material culture. In this section, I explore how sentimentalism and the culture of sentiment played a role in awakening women to the opportunity to change their lived environments, or those of others, through sentimental writings and mourning practices. I do this through an examination of mourning culture and the sentimentality endemic to nineteenth- and early twentieth-century middle-class women's writings, sentimental literature, and mourning practices. This sentimentalism coincided with the abolition and temperance movements and, later, the social purity movement that looked to control prostitution and other such "vices."

Chapter 1 explores how the shifting American economy in the late eighteenth and early nineteenth century changed middle-class gender dynamics and fostered a cultural preoccupation with the mother and child bond. Cultural perceptions of these changes are explored through an analysis of sentimental fiction and its precursors: seduction and gothic literature. In chapter 2, I focus on infant mortality and an exploration of deathways and material culture, as related to grief and mourning in the nineteenth century, with a particular focus on the mother and child bond. I explore how that bond was expanded to extend sentimental pity to "fallen girls," and how sentimentalism began to lead to the social purity movement. These first two chapters work to lay a groundwork for the actions that middle-class women took on behalf of the domestic sphere later in the century.

Chapters 3 and 4 trace nineteenth-century reform work as it related to the social purity movement and concerns over female sexuality. One of the largest private welfare organizations, the National Florence Crittenton Mission (NFCM), began in the late nineteenth century as a rescue home for sex workers. However, the impetus behind its founding was the death of Florence Crittenton, a four-year-old child who died of scarlet fever and whose father's grief led him to devote his fortune to "rescuing" women from sex work. These chapters weave together sentimental nineteenth-century culture with the social purity movement by exploring the early manifestations of the Crittenton rescue network and its ties with the Woman's Christian Temperance Union (WCTU). The chapters trace both a concern for sexual propriety and protection of the nuclear family alongside the growth of a network of women social reformers.

A note on nomenclature: I often use the term "sex worker," as opposed to "prostitute," which was the term used by social reformers at the time to describe women working in commercialized sex during the nineteenth and twentieth centuries. Borrowing from historian Katie Hemphill's excellent explanation on nomenclature, I choose to use the term "sex worker" to mitigate some of the prejudices against women participating in commercialized sex. The term "sex worker" encompasses women (as well as men and trans people, although not discussed in this book) who periodically engaged in sexual acts for money, food, clothing, or shelter at various times in their lives. I will use the words "prostitute" and "prostitution" only when describing commercial sex as a noun, not as an identifier for a person, unless I am referencing language used by historical actors or other scholars.[32]

The second half of the book explores the interconnectedness between sentimentality and state building in the Gilded Age and Progressive Era, highlighting the early beginnings of the American welfare state through the voluntary work of women reformers who created social welfare organizations that eventually became associative arms of the state. Chapter 5 centers on the NFCM as it became a nationwide private welfare network and the organization's new leader, Kate Waller Barrett. The chapter examines how Waller Barrett led the NFCM through the transition from the social purity movement and a focus on sex workers to one concerned with single motherhood and redemption through "mother love." Chapter 6 shows how Waller Barrett led the NFCM through the transition from an evangelical charity to an associate of the burgeoning welfare state. This close examination of the NFCM shows the complexity of the emergence of the American welfare state and how private organizations laid the groundwork for the associational welfare state of the twentieth century.

The following two chapters chronicle the achievements of Black women reformers working for women and children during the late nineteenth and early twentieth centuries. These chapters are about how racial politics, class status, and sexual morality shaped Black women's methods of social welfare reform and how that reform had a profound impact on the creation of local welfare policies. Despite the racism that disenfranchised Black men, Black women were doing the legwork necessary to build strong social programs in Black communities. Both chapters explore why Black women needed to form their own clubs and organizations and how their goals and reform movements were shaped by race, class, and ideas of morality and sentimentalism.

In chapter 7, I turn my attention to the Colored Florence Crittenton Home in Topeka, Kansas, and its founder Sarah Malone. I use the term "colored" only in identifying the official name of this Crittenton home, which was founded by Black reformers to serve Black women and girls. Within this examination, I demonstrate how the sentimentalism that guided Kate Waller Barrett and the early Florence Crittenton movement fit well with the ideals of the Colored Florence Crittenton Home because it aligned with ideas about Black racial uplift and the moral superiority of middle-class Black women. Additionally, I chronicle how Malone oversaw the integration of the Colored Florence Crittenton Home into the social welfare network of Kansas state.

Chapter 8 considers the Neighborhood Union in Atlanta, Georgia, and its founder Lugenia Burns Hope. Formed in the aftermath of a bloody riot of white citizens against Black citizens and businesses in Atlanta, Burns Hope formed the Neighborhood Union as a way to support Black families in the wake of extreme racial violence. The Neighborhood Union operated within the power dynamic and ideology of social policing while focusing on education, thrift, and middle-class Black propriety, particularly for women and young girls. Burns Hope adeptly steered state financial support toward social welfare programs intended for Black families in Atlanta, while relying on a sentimental understanding of familial bonds and sexual purity.

The preceding chapters explain how collective organizational movements such as the NFCM and the Neighborhood Union operated as hybrid public-private charity organizations reliant on women's unpaid and underpaid labor at the local level. Chapter 9 then explores how middle-class women's engagement with voluntary work and local organization building created a women's welfare network that formed public partnerships and tapped state funding sources and support. This women's welfare network fed into what would become the larger associational welfare state and was integral in creating the federal U.S. Children's Bureau in the twentieth century.

Chapter 10 delves further into the women's domain in the federal government on matters of health and safety for women and children, with a particular focus on curbing infant mortality. Additionally, this chapter highlights how major Children's Bureau resources were devoted to illegitimacy, which relied heavily on the legwork that groups like the NFCM had already started. Because of the earlier work of groups like the NFCM, the Children's Bureau twentieth-century campaigns to "Protect the Babies" included a heavy push to destigmatize illegitimacy, which is a thread that is underexplored within maternalist and Children's Bureau historiography.

I conclude with the passage and later defeat of the Sheppard-Towner Act, a public health bill that provided federal funding for the health and wellbeing of women and children. By this time, women were more engaged in the political process than ever before. In expanding the female domain of the domestic sphere, maternalists created fields of influence in areas of child welfare, labor limits for women and children, prison and institutional reform, education, and other progressive reforms.

The Sentimental State reveals how sentimentalism gave a grassroots movement of middle-class women the language to demand protections of the mother and child bond, particularly when it came to issues of infant and maternal mortality or the social death of "fallen" girls and women. The welfare state grew through the association of private and public organizations that often linked sentimental motherhood, childhood mortality, and sexual morality. Examining the sentimental foundations of grassroots reform efforts in the late nineteenth and early twentieth centuries helps expose the murkiness of the emergence of the American welfare state—how it began in fits and starts during the nineteenth century based on a gendered understanding of sentimentality. Only by understanding the deep emotions inherent in cultural sentimentalism can we understand why average women knitted the threads that connected private reform efforts with public financing.

CHAPTER 1

Take the Sorrows of Others to Your Heart

SENTIMENTAL FICTION
AND CONSCIOUSNESS

Once, as you read the papers, you thought nothing of those
who lost friends; now you notice and feel. Take the sorrows
of others to your heart; they shall widen and deepen it.[1]

In 1857 Harriet Beecher Stowe implored her readers, "Take the sorrows of others to your heart," because not only might one be able to help others but such an
act would "widen and deepen" one's own heart as well.[2] The act of feeling another's emotional pain was a central tenet of nineteenth-century sentimentalism,
which exceeded the limits of literature and permeated every facet of nineteenth-
century culture. Sentimentalism is often understood as a literary genre, which
prioritized feeling and emotion over rationality. However, American sentimentalism in the nineteenth century was more than a literary element; it infused every aspect of culture, finding expression through literature, but also the market
economy, politics, familial relations, philosophy, and deathways. Sentimentality is
a nebulous concept that frustrates the desire for simple definition and must be
looked at within the context of the value system in which it existed.

American sentimental novels gained popularity in the Early Republic through
their precursor the seduction novel, which emerged in England in the mid- to
late eighteenth century. In many seduction novels, the "fall" and abandonment
of young women inevitably led to prostitution and their untimely death. Early
popular seduction novels include Samuel Richardson's 1740 *Pamela: Or, Virtue
Rewarded*, followed by *Clarissa* in 1748, but it was Susanna Rowson's *Charlotte*

Temple: A Tale of Truth that truly unleashed American sentimentality as a cultural phenomenon. Rowson's book was purchased and read continuously from its American debut in 1794, well into the twentieth century.[3]

Charlotte Temple was America's first bestselling novel. It portrays the betrayal of a British fifteen-year-old named Charlotte, who is seduced by a dashing British soldier. He whisks her away to America and then abandons her and her unborn child. With nowhere to turn, Charlotte roams through the winter streets of New York City until she is taken in by a servant. Shortly thereafter, she gives birth and subsequently dies. The book highlights the cruel world that will not allow a betrayed girl like Charlotte any place to thrive. Once she is pregnant and abandoned, her only option is to rely on a man, either a spouse or a sympathetic father. Devoid of these opportunities, the only other option for Charlotte's character is death. *Charlotte Temple* was indicative of the social contradiction that sex-before-marriage embodied. "Falling," or having sex before marriage—literally a fall from grace—was viewed as a moral failing by the individual girl. However, Rowson was very sympathetic to Charlotte, highlighting how society and the sexual double standard severely punished women for sexual transgressions.

The trope of the fallen girl in sentimental literature highlighted the anxiety of the role of young, white women in the Early Republic. Scholar Marion Rust argues that Charlotte's "fall" was not the result of carnal desire, but the result of indecisiveness and lack of self-awareness in the new world order of the Early Republic. Essentially, her lack of decision making brought about her downfall. In the early stages of democratic republican rule it was imperative for young men and women to be engaged citizens. The absence of decision-making by virtuous citizens could be the downfall of the Republic, yet white women of financial means inhabited a precarious role in society as neither full citizen nor full dependents. Rust maintains that Charlotte's "struggle to maintain her chastity was ... not ... a reflection on her ability to regulate lustful impulse, but rather as a marker of her liminal class status."[4] Viewed in this context, it is interesting to analyze Rowson's clear warning to the "dear girls" who are her presumed readers that they must eschew the emotions of love "unless sanctioned by paternal approbation."[5] In this reading, Rowson's hope that other girls might avoid Charlotte's horrible fate by reading her novel is not necessarily a warning to protect one's chastity but a commentary on young women's status in society. Rowson exposes the unfairness of Charlotte's fate after her betrayal but is also careful to point out that her readers will only avoid such a fate if they engage in parentally "sanctioned" sexuality.

Hannah Webster Foster's 1797 novel *The Coquette: Or, The History of Eliza*

Wharton is also a seduction novel that bridges seduction and sentimental novels. *The Coquette* is a fictionalized retelling of the death of Elizabeth Whitman, a white middle-class American woman that died giving birth outside of wedlock. Whitman's story was familiar to late eighteenth and nineteenth-century readers, as her death was soliloquized throughout the nineteenth century as a cautionary "true crime" story. However, in Foster's fictionalized version, Whitman as Eliza Wharton is written sympathetically, again highlighting what literary scholar Cathy N. Davidson argues was the limited "power and authority" women held in the Early Republic.[6] The anxieties over what role women, particularly white middle-class women, would play in the Republic can be viewed in *Charlotte Temple* and *The Coquette*. Both offered up a protagonist's premature death as a sad but justifiable blueprint for how white women should function in the new society, while also subverting this status quo by describing the limited space that women actually held in society.[7]

In the first half of the nineteenth century the seduction novel morphed into sentimental fiction, even as books like *Charlotte Temple* and *The Coquette* continued to be bought and read by scores of American women. Sentimental novels tended to have female protagonists that relied on their moral compass to overcome shortcomings in their own character or in the world at large. The protagonists often found marriage as the righteous and happy outcome after a litany of trials and tribulations in an immoral world, or in the alternative case of "impure" women, the outcome was often death, as in seduction novels. Sentimental stories often entailed punishments and rewards, according to a character's moral constitution.[8]

The rise of sentimentalism was associated with a period of heightened activism and the concern for the suffering of others. This was reflected in the abolition, temperance, and anti-vice movements—all morality-based issues that had the potential to upset the newly emerging middle-class standards of a loving home. These anxieties were heightened by massive changes in the American economy as the growth of the early nineteenth-century market economy changed the way non-enslaved families interacted with the world. Not only were political questions arising, but the nature of work was changing. As a result, family dynamics changed too, particularly the ties between mother and child.

This began with a dramatic shift from a subsistence to a capitalist economy in the late eighteenth and early nineteenth century. Labor that produced goods for the capitalist market moved from home production to the "public sphere" of the factory or other places of business, affecting the gendered nature of work and production. Women were intricately tied to the market economy by producing and supporting the people that performed labor in the capitalist economy, such as bearing children, managing the household, and generally supporting the able and non-able bodied. However, these market changes meant that women and men began performing labor in different social arenas.

This new wage work economy relied heavily on women's domestic labor to support it. Food preparation, cleaning, making and mending clothing, and child-rearing resulting in future workers—the reproductive labor paramount in supporting men's waged work—was provided by wives, female kin, female servants, and slave labor. However, this division of labor created a distinction between productive and reproductive labor and associated independent manhood with waged work, while erasing the visibility of how women's reproductive labor supported wage earning. Women's labor was considered non-income-producing and seen as a labor of love or a biologically determined role as opposed to "real" and necessary wage-earning work. This left many women dependent on male wages but hid the work they did to support it.[9]

America's transition to a market economy coincided with the peculiarly intense and sentimental character of nineteenth-century American domesticity. Historian Jeanne Boydston argues this served to reconcile the increased (but hidden) "reliance on female labor with formal male assertion of economic privilege through a romance of family culture."[10] This specialization in the economy created the imaginary "separate spheres" that men and women theoretically operated within and cast the domestic sphere as the incubator of a properly functioning civilization. Middle-class white women's role in the family morphed from the late eighteenth-century ideology of Republican Motherhood, which championed the education of American women so that they could reproduce virtuous citizens, to one within the *cult of domesticity* that further entrenched the true woman within the home and domestic sphere. Although both roles were congruous, Republican Motherhood was couched in a patriotism unique to the Early Republic Era. As second- and third-generation American middle-class white women began having children of their own, the patriotic zeal gave way to an emphasis on the mother's role as caretaker of the domestic realm. Mothers were still expected to raise good citizens, but the emphasis on a mother's intelligence and patriotism gave way to her nurturing abilities.[11]

Catherine Beecher highlighted this subtle change when discussing the primacy of the mother within the home in the early nineteenth century: "The mother forms the character of the future man," while sisters and wives shaped the hearts of men, "whose energies may turn for good or for evil the destinies of a nation." If American women were "virtuous and intelligent ... the men will certainly be the same."[12] As the domestic sphere became the purview of women, the home became the crucible of both the nation and middle-class morality, purity, and piety.

The cult of domesticity smoothly melded into a cult of motherhood as the ideals of motherhood and womanhood merged into one and the same during the antebellum period. The ideal mother exhibited certain traits such as selflessness and wholehearted care of her family, she was pious, and she was economically dependent on her husband. The ideal mother was a guide and the loving mentor for her children's growing character while her husband was simply a stern passerby in the home. Therefore, children naturally gravitated to their mother because, "her voice is gentlest, her eye beams with fondest affection; she soothes his little sorrows, and bears with his irritability with the tenderest and untiring patience."[13] Mothers and children became an inseparable pair.

Mother and wife became the paragon of true womanhood—the "angel of the house"—by the mid-nineteenth century. However, this idealized image of the domestic sphere was never a reality for most American women. Only a small minority of white middle-class and elite women had the wealth and leisure to be proper "angels" of the home; a status that relied on the reproductive labor of other women who engaged in the marketplace by either selling their time and labor in the form of domestic service (governesses, cooks, maids, servants) or selling their wares (candles, clothing, foodstuffs). Enslaved women performed these same tasks but without the benefit of reaping monetary reward in the growing market economy.[14]

Slave-holding families attempted to create the façade of a tranquil family but ultimately perpetrated brutality upon the Black people they enslaved. As historian Stephanie Jones-Rogers shows, white southern girls "learned how to be mistresses and slave owners through an instructional process that spanned their childhood and adolescence." This education relied on learning how to violently control their "property" from their slave-owning parents.[15] The duties associated with being the angel in the home obviously differed drastically from region to region and even house to house.

Sentimental fiction fused a preoccupation with emotion to storylines that emphasized feelings as the means to develop positive action and outcomes, in the process introducing many white, middle-class women to social ills like slavery and prostitution. Additionally, the evangelical zeal of the Second Great Awakening of the 1820s through 1840s encouraged many white northeasterners to see slavery as a sin against society. The abolitionist movement, along with temperance and anti-prostitution, spread quickly, and by 1838 there were 1,300 antislavery societies in the United States, with memberships consisting overwhelmingly of women. One reason these societies spread so quickly was the large amount of printed material they produced, including sentimental and emotion-filled tracts. In 1838 alone, antislavery societies sent one million pieces of abolitionist literature across the country, including 20,000 pieces directly into the South. Women also signed their names en masse to antislavery petitions throughout the 1830s, asserting their citizenship and their right to have a say in the way society conducted itself.[16]

The sentimental ephemera from antislavery societies played a huge role in spreading abolitionist sentiment to middle-class white women. The Sunday School Union distributed *The Child's Anti-Slavery Book*, which was geared toward children but was undoubtedly read and purchased by mothers. It dramatically recounted stories of enslaved children separated from their parents and mistreated by their masters, playing on readers' heartstrings by highlighting the forced separation of enslaved mothers from their babies.[17] These sentimental writers used emotion to push readers to *feel* anger, sadness, or empathy for the characters that they read about, as well as feel anger or frustration at the social conditions that forced protagonists into horrific situations.

Sentimental fiction reached far into white women's homes and consciousness. Antislavery fiction written by women for a primarily female audience allowed readers to explore "the slavery of sex," drawing analogies between the moral degeneracy of slavery and the predicament of women in patriarchal society. The goal was to make their readers feel such pain and empathy that it would push them into deeper thought and potential action. Literary scholar Karen Sánchez-Eppler argues that sentimental fiction was a "bodily act." The physical tears of the reader were "pledged" to the bodies of the enslaved that they read about in antislavery texts or the betrayed girl in seduction novels.[18] However, even as white readers were asked to feel for enslaved mothers and find their universal motherhood, racial boundaries triumphed. By analyzing sentimental fiction that deals with motherhood and slavery, historian Nora Doyle found that Black enslaved women's bodies were often subjected to bodily violence that white mothers were never subjected to in these writings. Doyle argues that white mothers were depicted as transcendent, their "body disappeared, thus freeing her spiritual influence," whereas "the enslaved mother was firmly bound to her corporality."[19] These types of stories worked to affect white women emotionally but still keep Black women at a distance.

Until recently, the use of sentimentalism by Black writers during the antebellum period was understood as an accommodation to white fragility as a way to avoid upsetting their white audiences. However, revised scholarship suggests a more nuanced understanding of sentimental fiction, one that broadens the theoretical applicability of sentimentalism to encompass the lives of Black women and writers. Harriet Jacobs's *Incidents in the Life of a Slave Girl* updated the slave narrative genre by focusing on the experiences of an enslaved woman and mother, as opposed to the unencumbered male, highlighting not only the cruelty of slavery but also the additional gendered violence that enslaved women faced. Jacobs resisted the sexual advances of her master and assertively resisted his attempt to own her, body and soul. For nearly seven years Jacobs hid in the attic of a shed behind her grandmother's house, stoically enduring the heat and cold, boredom, restlessness, but—most painfully—the knowledge that her children were nearby but she could not let them know she was alive, for their own protection as well as her own.[20] Jacobs's biographer, Jean Fagan Yellin, points out how Jacobs highlighted her defiance, not the torture that she experienced at the hand of her master. Jacobs's trials and tribulations rivaled those of any fictional sentimental heroine, yet her story was autobiographical. Using the tenets of the genre to emotionally tell her story, Jacobs utilized autobiography alongside sentimental fictionalization, making *Incidents in the Life of a Slave Girl* a groundbreaking hybrid text.[21]

First appearing in print as a forty-week serial in the abolitionist newspaper *The National Era*, Harriet Beecher Stowe's 1852 novel *Uncle Tom's Cabin* went on to be the most popular book of the nineteenth century. Stowe used sentimentality to address the evils of slavery and was wildly effective in doing so. In fact, during the American Civil War, President Lincoln greeted Beecher Stowe in 1863 as "the little lady who made this big war," highlighting the profound impact her sentimental novel made on the general public.[22] *Uncle Tom's Cabin* was a huge success; however, Stowe's primary motivation was to show the moral authority that the mothers of the nation had in ending slavery through moral suasion. Stowe beseeched the "mothers of America,—you who have learned, by the cradles of your own children, to love and feel for all mankind." By subjecting her protagonist Eliza to the pain of having her child sold away from her, Stowe implored her readers to "pity those mothers that are constantly made childless by the American slave-trade!"[23]

Using death to further social means was a common theme in nineteenth-century sentimental literature and was used to enforce a host of middle-class Protestant values such as temperance, abolition, charity, chastity, and piety. Fictionalized children's death often took on greater meanings in order to make sense of the cruelty of premature death and became a means to a higher good.

Sentimental culture used the death of an integral character, particularly children or young women, to push a reader toward social action.[24]

Most famously, Stowe used the death of the child Eva St. Claire in *Uncle Tom's Cabin* to protest slavery. Eva's death functioned as something larger within the sentimental narrative by attaining a spiritual power over those who loved her in life. Stowe's depiction of Eva's death in *Uncle Tom's Cabin* is one of the most memorable death scenes in sentimental literature. As she lay dying, Eva sees heaven, showing the living that a just reward waits for them if they live right. Eva "passed from death unto life," thus entering a new state of being in the afterlife, one that will affect those still on earth.[25] Scholar Jane Tompkins argues that Eva's sacrificial death operated as a dramatized victory to "enact a philosophy, as much political as religious, in which the pure and powerless die to save the powerful and corrupt, and thereby show themselves more powerful than those they save."[26] Eva's death operated to invoke the desire for pious and right living among readers, making her death a sacrificial action for the greater good of the abolition movement.

Scenes like little Eva's death are what film scholar Mary Ann Doane labels "maternal melodramas," powerful means of evoking emotional affect to awaken a trauma with which many middle-class women could identify. Thus, death in sentimental fiction functioned as a connective force that tied women together, whether they had experienced the death of their own child or not.[27] This sentimentality did not live in fiction alone. In her famous speech at a woman's rights convention, Sojourner Truth stated, "I have borne thirteen children and seen 'em mos' all sold off into slavery, and when I cried out with a mother's grief, none but Jesus heard—and ar'n't I a woman?"[28] Truth highlights the injustices of slavery by showing how the sentimentality of the mother and child bond was not solely limited to white women. Truth's motherhood was violated by breaking the sacred bond between a mother and child, what literary scholar Gillian Brown describes as "outraged domesticity."[29] Truth asks her white audience to see how *all* mothers have the same maternal bond, prodding her listeners to not sit idly by while crimes against motherhood are committed. In *Uncle Tom's Cabin*, Stowe's Cassey killed her third child with laudanum after her first two were taken from her and sold into slavery. In an example of outraged domesticity, Cassey does not regret her decision but is relieved because "he, at least, is out of pain." Cassey thus protects her child from the violations of slavery by enacting her own violence.[30]

Black women writers crafted their own understandings of sentimentalism in a post-emancipation, yet racially separated, America. In 1865 the newspaper of the African Methodist Episcopal (AME) Church, *The Christian Recorder*, began publishing a serial entitled *The Curse of Caste: Or, The Slave Bride* by writer Julia C. Collins. This rediscovered narrative is innovative because it was written as a completely fictionalized novel and is the earliest known novel written by a Black woman. Previous works by Black women writers such as Sojourner Truth's *Narrative of Sojourner Truth: A Northern Slave* and Harriet Jacobs's *Incidents in the Life of a Slave Girl* were autobiographical, even as Jacobs pushed against the limits of autobiography. Also, most African American autobiographies were presented with a preface by an "upstanding" white person who endorsed the author's character. The fact that *The Curse of Caste* was published in *The Christian Recorder* meant that it would be read by, and reach its target audience of, the growing American Black middle class and thereby forewent the supposed need of a white vouchsafe. Collins portrayed her protagonists, Lina Tracy and her daughter Clair, as respectable women and mothers. These were of course the gendered tropes of sentimentalism, but Collins was not writing for a white audience.[31]

Throughout thirty chapters, Collins wove the tale of Lina Tracy, an enslaved Black woman whose white husband must purchase her to secure her freedom. Lina dies in childbirth and the story picks up with her daughter Claire, who is raised without a mother or a father because he does not know that his child survived. Claire is also unaware of her mixed-race heritage. At the grand climax of whether Claire's racial heritage will not matter to her future (white) husband, or if she too would suffer from the "curse" of caste, readers anxiously awaited the outcome, only to open their papers on September 30, 1865, and read "CORRESPONDENT SICK" where the culminating chapters should be. More than two months later, readers learned of Collins's death from the most sentimental of diseases, consumption.[32]

What this rediscovered text highlights is the ongoing use of sentimentalism as a vehicle for creating a post-Civil War Black womanhood. It is no coincidence, argues literary scholar William Andrews, that only four years later in 1869, Frances Ellen Watkins Harper—who would soon become the preeminent African American woman writer of the nineteenth century—wrote her first serialized novel, *Minnie's Sacrifice*, and published it in *The Christian Recorder* as well.[33] Harper, whose 1898 bestselling novel *Iola Leroy: Or, Shadows Uplifted* would also explore the potential "curse" of caste in the vein of uplift, paints her protagonist as a mediator between white and Black.[34] Collins and Walker both used the AME magazine as a means of publishing sentimental fiction for a Black audience.

Many nineteenth-century readers, both Black and white, followed Beecher Stowe's request to "take the sorrows of others to your heart."[35] Readers delighted in the emotional tug that sentimental stories could produce. But there was also a darker side to these feelings, one found in the real or imagined pain of losing a close loved one to an untimely death. Elizabeth Stuart Phelps began writing *The Gates Ajar* at the end of the Civil War when the "country was dark with sorrowing women."[36] Published in 1868, *The Gates Ajar* was an immediate success, earning Phelps almost instantaneous recognition and becoming the second best-selling novel in the nineteenth century after *Uncle Tom's Cabin*.[37] Phelps hoped to give solace to the thousands of women mourning their lost fathers, husbands, brothers, and sons from the Civil War. The story reads as the journal of Mary Cabot, who learns that her brother Roy has been killed in the war. The platitudes of her pastor do not give her peace. It is only the explanation of death given by her Spiritualist Aunt Winifred that gives her consolation. Aunt Winifred offers Mary the vision of an afterlife filled with the comforts and trappings of the Victorian, white middle-class. This reflects how the culture of sentiment not only affected people's understandings of love and betrayal, just and unjust, pure love and pure evil but also changed the way they understood the afterlife. Phelps went on to write two more books in the *Gates Ajar* series during the 1880s, which also looked toward a Spiritualist, and therefore sentimental, understanding of the afterlife.[38]

Activist, suffragist, and reformer Helen Hamilton Gardener turned the seduction novel on its head in the 1890s, first with her 1890 book *Is This Your Son, My Lord?* and later with *Pray You, Sir, Whose Daughter?*, published in 1892. Both novels railed against the sexual double standard that novels like *Charlotte Temple* (which was still a popular book more than one hundred years later) highlighted. However, in *Is This Your Son, My Lord?* it is not a seduced young woman who finds death after betrayal, but a young man. The story follows Preston Mansfield, a young Harvard graduate who is caught masturbating. Worried about his son's future, Preston's father whisks him off to New York in order to find a woman who will have sex with his son. The father rapes a working-class, fifteen-year-old girl and then blackmails her into becoming his son's mistress. Preston fathers two children with the young woman before becoming overwhelmed with guilt and committing suicide.[39]

Gardener's second novel, *Pray You, Sir, Whose Daughter?* took up the issue of age-of-consent laws for girls, which were abysmally low throughout the country (in 1890 Delaware's age of consent for girls was seven years old).[40] In this second novel Gardener's protagonist is a wealthy young woman, Gertrude Foster, who befriends two working-class girls through her work in a settlement home. One of Gertrude's friends is impregnated by an older man and then subsequently dies while giving birth. Meanwhile, Gertrude's father implores her to stay away from her new friends, lest she be considered guilty of being a "fallen girl" through association. Instead of acquiescing to parental authority, Gertrude rallies support against a bill intended to lower the age of consent for girls in New York state and succeeds in stopping the bill's passage.[41]

Both of Gardener's novels were commercial successes, with some critics going so far as to label her the "Harriet Beecher Stowe of Fallen Women." Gardener turned this success into action, spearheading a campaign in *The Arena* magazine entitled "The Shame of America—The Age of Consent Laws in the United States: A Symposium" to highlight sexual crimes against girls but also to argue that women's suffrage was integral to overcoming the sexual violence perpetrated against all women in America.[42] Gardener and the social purity movement are discussed in more detail in chapter 3. What requires attention here is the commercial popularity of Gardener's melodramatic storylines as well as their call to action.

Sentimentalism produced tears, saccharine sweetness, and melodrama, which made for an extremely popular genre of literature read widely by middle-class men and women alike. However, sentimentalism did not live in novels alone but carried over into popular culture. The "aesthetics of sentiment" appeared in advice books, statues, photography, pamphlets, poetry, and fashion well into the twentieth century. As such, sentimentality was the genre and cultural norm that accompanied American expansion, imperialism, and industrialization through the nineteenth and into the twentieth century. Literary scholar Shirley Samuels goes as far as to say, "sentimentality is literally at the heart of nineteenth-century American culture." Sentimentalism's preference for over feeling marched right alongside the expansion of the market, the expansion of the nation's influence, and the growth of industrial cities.[43]

Because child death was prevalent enough in society and because, through sentimental fiction, women readers could feel empathy for mothers who lost their children, that empathy allowed them to form connections with other mothers. Beecher Stowe highlighted this shared fear and empathy in "The Mourning Veil" when she wrote, "I read this morning of a poor washerwoman, whose house was burned, and all her children consumed, while she was away working for her bread. . . . Ah, this mourning veil has indeed opened my eyes; but it has taught me to add all the sorrows of the world to my own."[44] Even though death was becoming romanticized, mothers were continually reminded that familial bonds could be broken in an instant, and the visceral fear remained. The next chapter examines how sentimentalism reached into the most intimate moments of human existence, as viewed through cultural understandings and performances of death and deathways.

CHAPTER 2

⎯⎯⎯⎯⎯⎯⎯⎯ ∞◦❦∞◦❦ ⎯⎯⎯⎯⎯⎯⎯⎯

Our Little Children Leave Us

DEATHWAYS AND THE AESTHETICS OF SENTIMENT

How could I leave her in the cold, and dampness of the sod—
All crushed beneath the stifling mold—My little one—O God?[1]

In 1796 readers of the *New-York Weekly Magazine* were treated to a three-paragraph figment, a popular short-form writing style of the eighteenth and nineteenth century, entitled "The Dead Infant: Or, The Agonizing Mother." Readers became voyeurs as the main protagonist of the story, the mother, is grief-stricken by the untimely death of her young child. Possessed by bone-deep sadness, she sneaks off to the graveyard in the middle of the night and rips her dead child from its coffin right before burial. She keeps the corpse with her at home. Since her child can no longer eat, she too refuses food and wastes away through grief and starvation. The mid-eighteenth-century English Graveyard school of poetry and prose likened death to sleep and, by the nineteenth century, this language dominated American death culture and influenced American sentimental literature. "The Dead Infant" describes this everlasting "sleep" as a reprieve from the agony of the living world as the mother "once more pressed him with redoubled force to her breast, again kissed his putrid cheek—and slept her final sleep."[2] This story highlights the primacy of the mother and child bond and the expected obsession that mothers have with their children. It epitomized the macabre underpinnings of the domestic sphere, as female authors and readers delighted in its inherent sorrow.[3]

Coinciding with the dramatic changes in the marketplace during the eighteenth century that led to the cult of domesticity in the nineteenth century was a similarly dramatic shift in the way American Protestants understood heaven. According to historian Erik Seeman, the sixteenth- and seventeenth-century post-Reformation beatific vision of the reunion with Christ in Heaven gave way to an eighteenth-century vision focused on reuniting with departed loved ones in the afterlife. As this shift happened, ministers and laypeople increasingly imagined familial reunions in the hereafter. Protestant Anglo-Americans wrote and read literature and poems and read news accounts that imagined, or claimed to describe, aspects of the afterlife.[4] Gothic literature, a genre of fiction that became popular in Britain in the 1760s and in America about thirty years later, as well as sentimental literature, reflected this shifting vision of Heaven through themes of romance, death, and the otherworldly. For example, in 1814 the sentimentalized memoir of Miss Huldah Ann Baldwin depicted her early death as a melancholy event but also an opportunity for Protestant evangelism. Baldwin, lying on her deathbed, begs her family members to "live for" God so that they will enter Heaven and be rejoined with her in the afterlife. Her vision of Heaven entails her family reuniting in the "hereafter" so that they may enjoy a "blessed eternity together."[5]

Child death was not an abstract phenomenon for eighteenth- and nineteenth-century readers. Although infant mortality rates dropped throughout the nineteenth century, the death of children, especially infants, was a visceral reality for many American women. For example, in 1853, 49 percent of the people who died in New York City were children under the age of five.[6] Infant and child death was very much a part of everyday life, and the possibility of a child dying was quite high. Even if a mother did not experience the death of a child firsthand, odds were high that one of her intimate acquaintances lived with that experience. Death most often occurred within the domestic sphere. Before the mid-twentieth century, most people died at home, therefore it was women who cared for the bodies of the ailing and women who cared for the corpses of the deceased. As family dynamics changed in the nineteenth century, women concentrated more of their energies on private relationships, notably the mother and child bond. Historian Mary Ryan notes, "The whole purpose of maternal nurture was to weave tight emotional bonds between women and children, which would, in turn, make an infant's death all the more painful."[7] This cultural reality made women experience death and mourning in distinct ways.

What many consider the flowery, melodramatic language and affect of sentimentalism provided real relief to women and men coming to terms with the death of a child. Mourning is a lived experience and is subject to the social and cultural norms that guide its conduct. Child death was an unfortunate reality for much of human history, but as market shifts changed family structure, particularly among the middle class, the bond between a mother and child became central to familial relationships and the domestic sphere. These changes nurtured a nineteenth-century sentimentalism that encompassed all areas of middle-class life and the "aesthetics of sentiment" appeared in advice books, statues, photographs, pamphlets, poetry, and fashion well into the twentieth century. The aesthetics of sentiment particularly affected American deathways and how middle-class women mourned their children.[8]

Nineteenth-century death practices among middle-class Americans allowed mourners, particularly women, to embody grief and emotion. Middle-class mourning practices entailed an elaborate set of rituals and visual symbols used to enact visible embodiments of private sentiments. Clothing during deep mourning consisted of garments made from flat black silks, black veils, and crepe. In half mourning, a woman dressed in lavender, grey, and purples with perhaps a bit of white trim visible at the wrists. Protocol dictated that both women and men observe a period of bereavement after the death of a loved one with the duration designated by sex and their relationship to the deceased. Typically, women performed acts of bereavement longer than men. While in deep mourning, a woman was mostly restricted to the domestic sphere and her clothing was intended to represent her feelings. Conventionally, a mother mourned for her child one full year, typically in full or deep mourning. Siblings commonly mourned one another for six months. One typically mourned grandparents for six months, aunts and uncles two months, great uncles and aunts six weeks, and first cousins for four weeks. Widows mourned husbands for two and a half years and moved through various stages of deep mourning, full mourning, and half mourning. A widower, on the other hand, typically mourned his wife for three months with a black band either on his hand or on his arm, reinforcing how women overwhelmingly shouldered the cultural burden of mourning.[9]

Through culturally prescribed modes of behavior and dress, women embodied the act of mourning and bereavement. Mary Todd Lincoln spent more than a year in deep mourning after the death of her son, Willie. After the death of her husband, Abraham Lincoln, Mary Todd Lincoln stayed in deep mourning for the rest of her life, just as the matriarch of the British Isles, Queen Victoria, did after the death of her husband, Prince Albert. The two widows shared their sorrows with one another, prompting Lincoln to comment on the Queen's condolences as coming "from a heart which from its own sorrow, can appreciate the intense grief I now endure."[10] The physical act of mourning through wearing black could certainly allow those in mourning a brief reprieve from certain social expectations of the day. Beecher Stowe aptly described how the physical accoutrements of mourning, such as a black veil, could act as comfort or refuge for a grieving mother when she wrote, "The folds of the dark veil seemed a refuge for the mother's sorrow." The veil acted as an "emblem of the shadow which had fallen between her heart and life."[11] Wearing mourning attire was part of a culturally prescribed public performance of proper bereavement, which could offer for many some semblance of comfort during periods of grief.

The rituals of burial also began to take on increasingly sentimental displays in the late eighteenth and early nineteenth centuries. The movement of cemeteries from city centers to suburban outskirts corresponds to a phenomenon known as the Rural Cemetery movement. Rural cemeteries were an attempt to harness a romanticized nature by people who were increasingly living in urban areas. The middle-class turned toward sentimentalism and romanticism to cope with the new urban landscape while indulging in their new vision of Heaven.[12]

Protestant Anglo-American burial practices drastically changed from America's earliest days to the early twentieth century. In colonial New England, many cemeteries were located in the center of town in order to alert people to their own mortality. Carved images on headstones were not intended to memorialize the individual person who was buried beneath but rather served as a sign for the living. Images of winged skulls, hourglasses, crossed bones, or skeletons were often accompanied by Latin phrases such as *memento ete ese mortatum*, remember that you are mortal, or *tempus fugit*, time flies. These images and phrases reminded the community that life was passing like sand through an hourglass, or death could "swoop" down at any time. Nothing on these headstones was romantic or individualized.[13]

Shifting eighteenth- and nineteenth-century ideas about Heaven and Protestant theology brought a change in gravestone iconography and inscriptions. Images of skeletons, reapers, and hourglasses gave way to angels, likenesses of the individual, and sentimental epitaphs. Gravestones no longer displayed dire warnings but instead became symbols of remembrance for the specific deceased person as sentimentalism became a central aspect of how middle-class Americans practiced death and dying.

Death became more individualized. Material culture gives visible clues as to how changing ideas of Heaven as a place for familial reunions coincided with a change in burial styles and literature. Even the naming of burial grounds changed during the late eighteenth and early nineteenth centuries. In the preceding centuries, particularly in Puritan New England, burial grounds were called graveyards. As death took on sentimental trappings, graveyards turned into cemeteries. The word "cemetery" comes from a Greek word meaning "sleeping chamber." This nomenclature reflected the new philosophy surrounding death as an eternal, restful, beautiful, everlasting sleep—an ideology supported by the Graveyard school and later sentimental literature.[14]

The Rural Cemetery movement began with Père Lachaise cemetery in France in 1804 and became the model for other rural cemeteries. It was located on an estate overlooking Paris with a landscape deliberately designed for mourning and contemplation. Père Lachaise incorporated English "picturesque" design theory, which took the natural landscape and attempted to perfect it, balancing nature and art. It allowed civilization to be present without disturbing the power and grandeur of the natural setting. These romantic landscapes included rolling hills, winding drives, classical monuments, and carefully constructed "scenes" that allowed visitors to escape the commotion of the city and retreat into a sentimental pseudo-nature, carefully designed to produce melancholy and pious reflection.[15] Soon the English and Americans began building their own rural cemeteries. Liverpool Cemetery and Kensal Green Cemetery were built in England in 1825 and 1830, respectively. Cambridge's Mount Auburn Cemetery was the first rural cemetery built in the United States in 1831. The next two large rural cemeteries in the United States were Green-Wood in Brooklyn and Mount Hope in Rochester, New York, both founded in 1838. Buffalo's Forest Lawn was founded in 1849.

Rural cemetery designers created spaces for thoughtful contemplation, leisure, and catharsis for many middle- and upper-class families. Phallic obelisks, built to commemorate great men and their families, periodically interrupted the sprawling pastures and rolling hills. However, many graveside monuments highlighted the central place women held in nineteenth-century mourning culture.

The Schulthess monument depicts the life-size relief of a woman in mourning in Forest Lawn Cemetery in Buffalo, New York (fig. 1, pictured right). She is bowed forward, bent low as if in anguish, and her head is covered. She holds a funeral wreath in her right hand but the weight of the moment seems to be too much for her as her arm hangs down, wreath in hand, as if she does not have the strength to reach up and place it upon the coffin. This rendering of a female body in stone is profoundly moving and indicative of how sentimentalism permeated nineteenth-century mourning culture. She engenders grief within the body of a woman. Another example of sentimentality and death is seen in the large marble memorial for Sarah E. Steele (not pictured). It says, "Shed not a tear,

FIG. 1. Obelisk (left); Schulthess monument (right),
Forest Lawn Cemetery, Buffalo, New York. Photo by the author.

nor give the heart to vain regret. Tis but the casket that lies here. The gem that filled it, sparkles yet." This poem is indicative of the change in feelings about death since the seventeenth-century Calvinist preoccupation with corpses and numbered days. Instead, it celebrates the life lived and the promise of a heavenly future where the soul sparkles on.

Cemetery iconography for children was coded and quite uniform across the nineteenth century and into the twentieth. One common motif for children's gravestone iconography was a little lamb, either carved onto the surface of a headstone or fully rendered in stone or marble. Other sentimental children's motifs were wilting flowers or flowers with a broken stalk, representing a life cut too short. The 1866 monument to Tacie Hannah Fargo (fig. 2) is an exceptional example of this type of heart-wrenching iconography. It is a life-sized statue of a female toddler, sitting on a blanket with a bouquet of wilting flowers in her hand. Although the stone image depicts the child as alive, the wilting flowers in her hand tell the viewer that she is not.

A poem from the *Mother's Journal and Family Visitant*, a magazine for mothers that discussed everything from teething to clothing choices, highlighted the real and imagined fear of such a child death. The magazine printed a poem in

FIG. 2. Tacie Hannah Fargo Monument, Forest Lawn
Cemetery, Buffalo, New York. Photo by the author.

which a fictionalized mother asks of her dead child, "How could I leave her in the cold, and dampness of the sod—All crushed beneath the stifling mold—My little one—O God?"[16] Like the mother from "The Dead Infant," this mother too cannot imagine leaving her child in the cold ground. The Fargo gravestone sculpture (fig. 2) captures the need to depict the warmth and life of the deceased child, alluding to the promise of a familial reunion in the afterlife. Upon looking at the monument, one thinks of a familial reunion in Heaven, not of the decay below it. Maternal melodrama played out in imaginations of sentimental fiction readers as well as, in the case of Tacie Hannah Fargo's parents, in their realities.

Material culture and literary tropes of the nineteenth century associated pain, loss, and death with the close relationship between mother and child. However, not only were narratives of this type prolific during the period, but they also served as a means to an end. The pure-hearted religious wisdom of the prematurely dead circulated through nineteenth-century culture, particularly in the common figure of the child-angel who led a recalcitrant family member from a path of sin to one of redemption. In one version of the 1875 sermon "The Child Angel," the Reverend Dwight Lyman Moody replicated the popular narrative. In Moody's example a man's young daughter dies a premature death, leaving him bereft. Later she appears to him in a dream and calls him toward godliness and salvation. Through her spiritual visit, the child-angel overpowers her father's recalcitrance and brings him back to God and salvation through her spiritual presence.[17]

An entire industry grew up around mourning culture in the nineteenth century. Mourners could commission trinkets made from the hair of their loved ones or wear a piece of jewelry with the initials of the beloved on their person. Memento mori are material objects used as a way to keep the memory of a loved one close and date back to classical times. It translates from Latin, "remember that you have to die," and is a solemn reflection on mortality. Memento mori can be depicted in art or literature and varied from the classical period to the modern era. In the eighteenth through the early twentieth century, memento mori took on the trappings of sentimentality and melded with the rise of consumer culture.

A further material example of the melding of sentimentalism and everyday life can be found in nineteenth- and twentieth-century mortuary photography. Photographs of the dead derived from an older tradition of commemorative paintings that depict deceased individuals. Once reserved for the rich and powerful, during the eighteenth and nineteenth centuries commissioning mortuary paintings broadened to the middle classes. Families would also commission posthumous mourning paintings. These would depict the departed as alive but would often provide clues that the subject was deceased. Posthumous paintings of children often displayed a wilted flower in the child's hand or a timepiece in the foreground. These images very much resemble the marble statuary in rural cemeteries, like the Fargo monument in Forest Lawn cemetery.[18]

Postmortem photography, the practice of taking photographs of people after death, became more popular as the medium of photography grew and became cheaper and easier to produce. At first, photographs were made almost exclusively by the daguerreotype process, which displays a small, highly detailed picture on polished silver. When daguerreotype was first invented and introduced as a consumer good, it was an expensive luxury item that only the wealthy could afford. This quickly changed throughout the 1840s as the number of photographers increased and the cost of daguerreotypes decreased. By 1853, there were eighty-six portrait galleries in New York City and roughly three million daguerreotypes were made in America each year. Cheaper modes of photography were introduced in the 1850s, like the ambrotype on glass and tintype, which was printed on thin, cheap metal. Photographs also started being printed on paper in the 1850s as well. By the 1860s most free Americans were able to afford portrait photography.[19]

Postmortem photographs were made for a specific purpose, to commemorate and remember a life lost to death. Photos of a loved one who lived a long and happy life could provide a sense of calm and contentment. Mortuary images of children could also act as a way to keep the sting of death-that-came-too-soon fresh in one's mind. They were a physical reminder of what could have been. These photos would have been carried in a locket or pocket frame or kept in a bedroom hidden from view of the outside world. They were personal keepsakes purchased from the public market, with the purpose of not only reminding one of a lost child but also serving as a reminder of the pain of loss itself.[20]

Instead of a true representation of a life lost, these photos preserve a nineteenth-century *ideal* of childhood. Critic and theorist Roland Barthes contends that in photography, "the power of authentication exceeds the power of representation," which centers the mortuary photo as a reconstruction of the past that cannot be questioned.[21] Small children and infants in postmortem photos are angelic, still, and calm. There is no food or dirt smeared on their faces or white frocks. They are the image of the perfect child—docile, compliant, and peaceful. They have not made a mess; they are not fidgeting or moving, but are

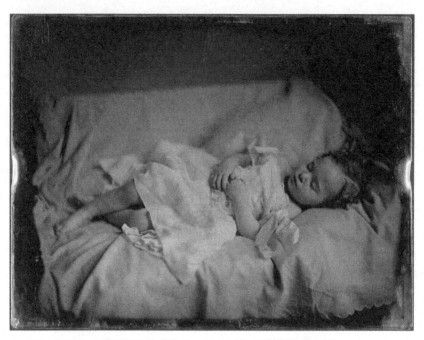

FIG. 3. Southworth & Hawes, postmortem of child, circa 1850,
daguerreotype. Courtesy of George Eastman Museum, Rochester, N.Y.

perfect interpretations of a serene premature death. Figure 3 shows a small female child, roughly two or three years old. Her dress is pristine, with decorative
bows along the off-the-shoulder sleeves. Her flaxen curls rest gently on the pillow,
which holds her lifeless head. Her eyes are closed as if she had just drifted off to
sleep. She is a model of childhood behavior frozen in time forever. The child in
the image will never disobey her parents. She will not grow up and become unruly. She will never develop her own wants and needs. She will not grow up and
leave the protective cocoon of her middle-class home.

These photos helped the observer keep the "wound" of death open. In figure 4
the image helps the observer lament the "could have been" by displaying objects
like a pencil or schoolbooks to mourn a future that will not come to pass. Ultimately, the photos could aid in keeping sadness and loss around by creating a physical response to a material object. Barthes called this feeling *punctum*, where images create not just an image but a sentimental *wound*. He argued sentiment was
grounded in suffering and to view a sentimental photograph produced a physical
response, or *punctum*, of "tiny jubilations, as if they referred to a stilled center, an

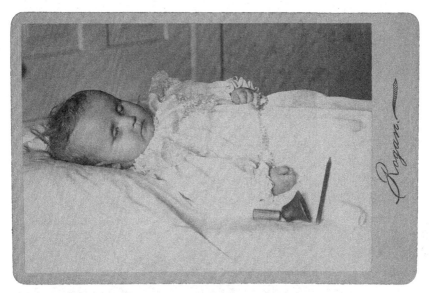

FIG. 4. Rogan, deceased baby with bell, pencil, and rosary, circa 1890.
Courtesy of George Eastman Museum, Rochester, N.Y.

erotic or lacerating value" (emphasis original).[22] The memento mori photograph served as a masochistic reminder of the physical sensations of pain and loss.

These types of photographs also materially captured the primacy of the mother and child bond. Although taken in the early twentieth century, James Van Der Zee's photo (fig. 5), "Future Expectations," captures the expectation that a woman devote her life to the domestic realm and the bond with her children. In this picture, a bride stares directly at the camera while her groom sits to her right looking down at her, bringing the focus of the photograph to the bride. Through early camera magic the photographer has interposed the picture of a little girl playing with a doll near the bride's feet. The child is transparent, not unlike many mortuary photographs or paintings that depicted departed children floating above the portraits of parents or siblings. However, instead of depicting the deceased, this picture depicts the future child of the newly married couple. Because her groom looks away from the camera and the bride looks straight ahead, this image shows the importance of the future mother and her child. The sentimental nature of the image brings a swell of hope and anticipation to the viewer, not unlike the *punctum* that a mortuary photograph could provide.[23]

XII 72/25

g. VanDergee

FIG. 5. Future Expectations (Wedding Day), James Van Der Zee, 1926,
San Francisco Museum of Modern Art, gift of Dr. and Mrs. Barry Ramer,
© James Van Der Zee Archive, The Metropolitan Museum of Art.

However, photographic images and the sentiment they produced also shed light on the multitude of contradictions in nineteenth-century women's lives. A poem from 1901 described a mother so burdened by her daily labors that she wishes she could lay down and die, yet the pangs of the mother and child bond would awaken her from her peaceful slumber:

> I could not sleep within my grassy bed
> For hearing pattering footsteps overhead
> This mother heart, though turned to dust,
> would throb
> Responsive to the baby's lonely sob,
> However faint and low.
>
> And so I could not rest me after all;
> The grasses tall
> And snowy daisies could not bring me peace;
> The aching mother love would never cease.[24]

Another mother may cut out a poem lamenting child death and paste it into her scrapbook, not because she had experienced child death herself, but because she was anticipating the point in which her own baby would grow up and leave her. Mary Clemmer Ames explained this apparent contradiction of nineteenth-century motherhood in her novel *Eirene: Or, A Woman's Right*:

Here is the mother's loneliness which in the country must come to the parental heart with a keener pang than in any other. For it is not the inevitable separation only, which soon or later must come to most every parent and child but it is separation in condition. Someday the father and the mother wake to the consciousness that the children to whom they have given birth belong to another race and time, and come back to them almost as strangers.[25]

In this view, the very act of mothering is in itself a form of continued, bittersweet mourning. Each day as the child gets older, she moves further and further away from her mother.[26]

The symbol of the child's death could evoke a variety of more commonplace and expected events in the female life cycle, in particular the inevitable departure of children when they come of age. Caroline Leslie's poem, printed in 1878 but written in the 1830s, exemplified the pang that some mothers felt as their children grew up and left them:

Yet, when the world our own would claim,
It doth not greatly grieve us;
We calmly see as days go by,
Our little children leave us,
And, smiling, heed not how the swift
Soft-footed years bereave us.
Oh mother hearts! I count you rich
Beyond mere earth possessing,
Whose little babies never grow
Away from your caressing;
Safe-folded in His tender arms
Who gives again with blessing.[27]

Leslie is actually saying to mothers whose children have died that they are the lucky ones because they have the eternal memory of their children as sweet innocents, not unruly teens or inattentive adults.[28] The transition out of childhood was a period where a mother experienced a lack of closeness with her child. Leslie's poem exemplified the extreme pain the split of the mother and child bond could create in women's lives when a child did not grow into the exemplary adult a mother had imagined.

Therefore, two periods of potential danger and grief faced mothers. The first was the potential death of a young child through disease or accident. Second was the period of transition out of childhood where a mother experienced the loss of closeness with her child, even when the transition proceeded normally. This transitional period for mothers and daughters could result in a much more grievous loss. Purity and sentimentality attached to the death of children were akin to the "fall" of girls and young women who were seduced by designing men.

The "fall" or actual death of a daughter led astray would result in a fall from middle-class respectability. In patriarchal American society, property and familial wealth passed through paternal lines. This form of inheritance relied on the chastity of daughters to produce offspring only within the bonds of marriage. After the market changes of the eighteenth and nineteenth centuries, however, a woman's "fall" took on additional meaning. Now, a fallen girl was no longer an affront to a family's wealth or property, she was also an affront to her mother's love and the tight bond between mother and child.

As discussed in chapter 1, in many seduction novels the "fall" and abandonment of young women inevitably led to prostitution and their untimely death. Seduction novels dramatized the loss of middle-class respectability for their tragic heroines, whose actual death almost always followed. Nineteenth-century women readers understood that, yes, this fate could in fact happen to your own daughter; the cooing baby in your arms could grow up in a few short years into a fallen woman. The primacy of the mother and child bond made this kind of sexual betrayal of young women an affront to the prescribed place of women within the domestic realm. If society demanded that women both recede into and rule the domestic realm, the indignity of men's betrayal caused a number of concerned middle-class women to begin acting more overtly to protect the home. One organization, the New York Female Moral Reform Society, began advocating for the elimination of prostitution and the sexual double standard in 1834, even threatening to publish the names of prestigious men who visited brothels. After the Civil War, this larger movement turned into the social purity campaign, which lobbied for "moral reform" through both moral suasion and laws that would put an end to prostitution and, they hoped, the sexual double standard.[29]

Women advocating for social purity operated with an unprecedented level of gender consciousness. They understood that prostitution thrived because of men's sexual freedom and women's limited access to economic opportunity. The social purity campaign attempted to confine sex within the bonds of marriage and to eliminate the double standard that allowed men unlimited sexual experience without any social repercussions, while a woman's "virtue" determined her worth in society. Yet because of their confined place in society themselves, female social purity reformers could only advocate for a single sexual standard, which limited sex for both males and females to the bonds of marriage, instead of advocating for more employment opportunities and more permissive sexual standards for women. Above all else, social purity reformers argued that the sexual double standard fueled the traffic in women's and girl's bodies, thus ravaging the supposedly pure realm of the domestic sphere, their purview.[30]

Sentimental culture captured the anxieties of two periods of danger, death, and grief in mother's lives. One trope celebrated and mourned the purity and innocence of infancy and early childhood, the other warned of and mourned the loss of purity in late girlhood. Both scenarios were threats to a peaceful, safe home where a mother's love was purported to be all-powerful but in fact couldn't solve all problems. The dangers to the family led some women to eventually move beyond sentimental readings to social activism by taking not just their own but "the sorrows of others" to their hearts as well and acting upon those sorrows.[31] Sentimentalism and emotion were core, driving forces behind middle-class women's push into the political realm.

However, our story begins with a *father's* grief and the sentimental vision of a child-angel, which led to the founding of the largest—and eventually women-run—social purity organization in the United States, and arguably, the world. This organization, the National Florence Crittenton Mission, helped form a vast network of women reformers who would go on to build the American welfare state in the twentieth century.

CHAPTER 3

Papa's Baby

ANGELS AND
COMMERCIALIZED SEX
IN THE GILDED AGE

*Truly God had put a wonderful love into my heart for that child, which
I could not understand then, but now I know it was in order that my
thoughts should be drawn Heavenward by her being taken there.*[1]

The culture of sentiment played an important role in the intellectual foundations of the social purity movement. Sentimentalism and protective policy particularly intertwined in the crusade to "rescue" fallen women and girls from perceived debasement. In fact, the origin story of one of the largest social purity and
rescue organizations, the National Florence Crittenton Mission, began with the
sentimental trope of the child-angel. In the depths of despair, New York industri-
alist Charles Crittenton heard the angelic voice of his recently deceased daughter,
Florence. Her celestial voice told Crittenton that if he led a good life, God would
reward him by reuniting them in Heaven. Mirroring Reverend Dwight Lyman
Moody's allegorical sermon, "The Child Angel," Crittenton experienced conversion though the sentimental vision of his heavenly deceased daughter. He went
on to found an evangelical rescue mission in the heart of the commercial sex district in New York City in her honor, the Florence Crittenton Night Mission, which
eventually became the largest American evangelical social purity organization in
support of women and girls.[2]

An increased visibility of prostitution and commercial sex in the nineteenth
century caused the rise of a crusade set to stamp it out. The social purity campaign strove to eradicate or curb sexual promiscuity, sexually transmitted infec-

tions, and prostitution. It attempted to confine sex within the bonds of marriage and to eliminate the sexual double standard that allowed men unlimited sexual experience without any social repercussions, while a woman's virtue determined her worth in society. Above all else, social purity reformers argued that the sexual double standard fueled the traffic in women and girls' bodies and promoted the spread of disease and moral failings. The social purity movement also shifted moral energies away from containing prostitution in red-light districts and toward eliminating it completely.

Crittenton's rescue mission eventually grew into the National Florence Crittenton Mission (NFCM). Although founded by a wealthy businessman, the organization became reliant on the paid and unpaid work of women reformers to drive its operations. The massive wealth that Charles Crittenton had at his disposal was typical of the discrepancy in the availability of money between men and women during the Gilded Age. In a society that still shunned women in the business realm, fortunes such as Crittenton's were by and large the product of male "industry" and were nearly impossible for women to amass. In a bitter irony, Crittenton's massive fortune went towards supporting women who had very few opportunities to earn their own wages. It is worth noting how the funding that supported many philanthropic endeavors was coded male, while the reproductive labor of the day-to-day operations was coded female.

Many women actively participated in the social purity movement and maintained that prostitution could be eradicated by eliminating the sexual double standard that allowed male sexual license and limited women strictly to chastity and monogamy. A new generation of educated women argued that women should have responsibility for creating a single standard of sexual morality. The Woman's Christian Temperance Union (WCTU) president Frances Willard insisted that "we must have such knowledge, conscience, custom and love as will establish an equal standard of purity for boys and girls, youths and maidens, men and women." Many, including Willard, argued that proper child rearing by an empowered and respected mother was the way to achieve this: "The sanctity of motherhood must be respected to such degree as shall make a wife the unquestioned arbiter of her own destiny."[3] As the creators of a future moral society, mothers must raise moral children, particularly moral sons, who would not drink alcohol or visit sex workers.[4] However, the policing and "protection" of daughters became the priority because controlling women's sexuality was already an integral part of middle-class culture. Frankly, it was easier to police America's daughters rather than her sons.

The social purity movement grew up alongside the growth of commercialized sex in American culture. In colonial America and up into the early nineteenth century prostitution was largely relegated to port cities and areas with large transient and working-class populations. By the mid-nineteenth century, however, commercialized sex could be found everywhere. The United States underwent a dramatic economic change as the nation experienced a massive shift from an older, household-centered economy in which apprentices lived within or near their master's homes to capitalism and the wage labor system. This fueled rapid urbanization in major port cities while also increasing the need to push U.S. settlement further and further west. As labor became a commodity, young men, and increasingly women, moved to cities and factory towns to work for wages outside of the paternal supervision that had once been an integral part of the economy. In major cities like New York, Boston, and Philadelphia, houses of prostitution opened in more varied and prosperous areas of town. American westward expansion, coupled with the boom-and-bust economies of western mining towns, also encouraged commercialized sex to seep further into the fabric of American existence. No matter what region, gender, race, or class one belonged to, commercialized sex was available for procurement, employment, or as a means of entrapment to almost any American.[5]

Evangelical reformer Charles Crittenton hailed from the "burned over district" of upstate New York, a region so named because of the antebellum evangelical revivalism of the Second Great Awakening. He arrived in New York City in 1854 as a young twenty-one-year-old and moved in with an older brother near the corners of Broadway and Grand Streets in the heart of the entertainment district. Young Crittenton was part of a mass migration of Americans moving from rural areas to large industrial hubs like New York City during the nineteenth century. During the 1850s Broadway was the center of New York City life. By day, the streets bustled with men and women going to shops and dry goods stores. At night, theaters, shows, saloons, and every kind of amusement were on hand. The new wage labor economy supported a growing entertainment and leisure culture, which inevitably included what some considered unsavory pastimes. Unsupervised youth and a cash culture went hand in hand with the growth of commodified sex and other nineteenth century "vices," such as gambling and drinking alcohol. Crittenton's new neighborhood was, by his own words, "filled with dance halls, dives, and haunts of sin."[6] It was also just five blocks south from where thirty years later he would open the Florence Crittenton Night Mission. Crittenton later wrote about his old neighborhood, "As I looked at these places of sorrow and sin with amazement, yet with a certain kind of boyish interest, I never dreamed that a time would come when I should be interested in the occupants that lived there."[7] In 1854 Crittenton had no inkling that he was to found one of the most long-lasting and far-reaching national rescue missions for women sex workers and single mothers in the country. Instead, the wide-eyed young man of twenty-one commenced his adult life in the bustling commercial and entertainment culture of the city.

Historian Timothy Gilfoyle aptly describes the years between 1850 and 1870 as the "Halcyon Years" for commercialized sex in New York City.[8] Sex workers walked the streets, worked out of brothels and parlor houses, found clients in saloons and dance halls, and were generally visible in many places in the city. In 1857 Walt Whitman wrote, "any man passing along Broadway . . . finds the western sidewalk full of prostitutes, jaunting up and down there, by ones, twos, or threes—on the look-out for customers."[9] Although New York City represented the pinnacle of sexual excess during the time, many American cities experienced similar patterns in the visibility of commodified sex. Sex was for sale in large and small cities alike and was highly visible in certain neighborhoods and streets.[10]

Crittenton's new neighborhood was at the heart of the entertainment and sex district, known as The Bowery.[11] As the commodification of sex in the city grew, the sexual activities that were for sale grew as well. Numerous sexual activities were available for a mass audience and included pornography, model artist striptease shows, masked balls where sex workers freely rubbed elbows with the elite of society, the concert saloon, private "drinking rooms" and "supper rooms" that catered to sex workers and their patrons in otherwise respectable restaurants, and live sex shows within brothels and parlor houses. This sexual entertainment coexisted along streets filled with theaters, large department stores, restaurants, and numerous saloons. No longer was sex work only associated with poverty or working-class culture, like that found in New York's infamous Five Points neighborhood earlier in the century; this new sexual culture served as an increasingly important leisure economy in the nineteenth-century metropolitan city.[12]

The increased visibility of sex in the city emerged with the rise of the male "sporting" culture and was part of a larger commodification of leisure activities in the nineteenth century. Sporting men engaged in numerous forms of gaming such as horseracing, pugilism (boxing), rat baiting, and cockfighting. Sporting culture promoted aggressiveness, male comradery, and sexual promiscuity. Older patterns of social deference broke down, engendering affability based along lines of gender as opposed to class. There were social stratifications among sporting men, however. The "Bowery b'hoy" was a younger, working-class youth who played in the area of The Bowery and prized brawn and comradery, whereas other "fancy men" like the "Broadway dandy" reveled in leisure, fine art, and sexual pleasure. A male-centered egalitarianism bridged the gap between the working-class "Bowery b'hoy" and the "upper-tendom b'hoys" and dandies, which allowed young middle-class men working as clerks and accountants to rub elbows with working-class men from The Bowery.[13]

Sporting culture associated monogamous, heterosexual intercourse with femininity and the domestic sphere, and they associated prostitution and erotic entertainment coupled with blood sports and communal drinking with male youth culture. This went hand in hand with the Victorian ideal of women as sexless and devoid of passion while men "naturally" had an insatiable sexual appetite. Therefore, many sympathizers deemed extramarital sex with sex workers as essential to the regulation of human society. From the 1830s and continuing throughout the nineteenth century, males, both married and unmarried, increasingly engaged in commodified sex outside of marriage. One sporting newspaper wrote that brothels were "as essential to the well-being of society as churches."[14] Prostitution became deeply ingrained within the youth culture of the nineteenth-century city, leading Whitman to write that frequenting sex workers was "an ordinary thing. Nothing is thought of it—or rather the wonder is, how there can be any 'fun' without it."[15] Alternatively, women were held to a strict standard of chastity and, after marriage, monogamy with their husbands. This double standard allowed men to experience sex outside of marriage with impunity while a woman's entire reputation relied on her strict adherence to Victorian standards of sexual propriety.

By all accounts, young Crittenton participated in the New York City sporting culture. It is impossible to know if he partook in the sexual liberties that many sporting men enjoyed, but he did admit to visiting the theaters and opera, "gambling and drinking, dancing and traveling."[16] Prostitution and other commodified sexual activities flourished in theaters and dance halls and most anywhere gambling was allowed. Theaters acted as an invaluable link between prostitution and sporting culture. The dark, semisecluded third-tier balconies were reserved for sex workers and their clients. Even "respectable" theaters like the Park Theater, sponsored by John Jacob Astor IV, was known for prostitution in its third tier. There were also "sub-theaters" that did not restrict prostitution to the third tier and were "little better than a brothel turned inside out," wrote one commentator.[17] The adjoining streets near theaters always housed numerous brothels and parlor houses. Needless to say, Crittenton and his brother enjoyed the pleasures of being young, aspiring men in the heart of the city.

Crittenton eventually married Josephine Slosson in 1858, but, by his own account, did not leave the sporting life after becoming a husband. He continued to stay out with "old associates" until late at night and frequently returned home quite drunk. He admitted that this put a strain on his marriage to Josephine and was the source of "many tears and heartaches" in the early years of their marriage.[18] Nevertheless, Charles and Josephine Crittenton were soon to become part of the New York City nouveau riche. In 1861, right before the start of the Civil War, Crittenton opened his own business as a supplier of sundries and wholesale drugs to local pharmacists. After a slow start, Crittenton & Co. grew exponentially in the postwar years. By all accounts Crittenton was a fair and enterprising businessman who reaped the benefits of the burgeoning Gilded Age.[19]

The Crittentons had their first child, a son, in 1862. A city-wide scarlet fever outbreak in 1863 tragically took his life at just under two years old. Crittenton contracted the fever too, leaving Josephine and her sister to care for him and their dying baby, performing the gendered duties of nurse and mortician that hundreds of other women across the city were also performing. He later wrote, "my wife, with only the help of her sister, was left to care for both of us. When the little one passed away, I was so near death myself that I did not realize it."[20] Crittenton never mentions how Josephine felt after the death of her baby boy, only that the "house was desolate." Josephine did, however, convince Crittenton to join her at a local evangelical revival meeting shortly thereafter, perhaps as a way to ease her suffering. Crittenton admitted that he was touched by the preaching and was "weeping like a child" by the end of the sermon. He later wrote of how, at that moment, he was ripe for Christian conversion, being so distraught over the death of his only child, but no one came and ministered to him that day, so he shortly thereafter settled back into his normal everyday life. The death of his son and his fleeting religious revival experience did not instigate any drastic changes in Crittenton's social life. He admitted a preference for social drinking over gospel meetings.[21]

The Crittentons had a second child in 1865 and named her Adeline, whom they called Addie. By the next year Crittenton's business was booming and he conducted himself as a typical New York captain of industry, carousing with business associates in the most fashionable restaurants and saloons. Success and Crittenton's love for excess put continued strain on his marriage. At Josephine's behest, the Crittentons joined Saint Clement's Episcopal Church in 1874. Crittenton was the quintessential Gilded Age captain of industry. He lived the high life, spent money freely, smoked the best cigars, and wore the latest fashions. Part of that lifestyle included belonging to a Protestant church located in the right neighborhood. Like all "good" nineteenth-century gentlemen and their families, the Crittentons attended church, but it was not a major part of their life. Although Crittenton mentions that he was "in a constant state of reformation" since joining the church, there was no real religious conversion, just a guilty conscience.[22]

In 1877 the Crittentons welcomed a late-in-life baby girl that they named Florence, whom they affectionately called Flossie. Soon afterward, the family moved from their house on Sixth Avenue to the fashionable Fifth Avenue, a move that Crittenton says he and his wife had "looked to so longingly for many years." By that time Crittenton's business was immensely successful, and he was at a point in his life where he could step away from its daily operations and spend more time with his family. By his account he spent a large amount of time with little Florence and insisted they were constant companions. They enjoyed hours together at the nearby Mount Morris Park, often staying until Florence's bedtime. Father and daughter were so close that Florence would often only answer to the moniker "Papa's Baby" instead of Florence.[23]

Often, Crittenton's business responsibilities required him to travel, and while on a trip to Rochester, New York, Crittenton received a telegram stating, "Flossie very ill—scarlet fever—come home immediately."[24] He recounted his terror upon reading the words, *scarlet fever* because his only son had died from the same disease fifteen years earlier. Once the onset of symptoms began, usually sore throat and fever, children could succumb to the disease in as little as forty-eight hours. Between 1830–1883 scarlet fever was the most infectious childhood disease that caused death, and it accounted for 30 percent of childhood deaths in many large cities.[25] Crittenton commenced the sixteen-hour train ride back to New York City and made it to Flossie's bedside just before she died. Florence Crittenton died on March 16, 1882, at the age of four years, four months, and four days old. As her body laid in the casket in their front parlor, Crittenton said that "all that remained of my heart's delight was contained in that box." Writing about it many years later, Crittenton lamented that he could not hear the toll of a cemetery bell "without its bringing back to me the remembrance of that awful, dark hour." They buried Florence in the fashionable Woodlawn Cemetery. "Papas Baby—Flossie" is engraved on the marble stone that marks her grave in the Crittenton plot, which still stands.[26]

After Florence died, Crittenton spent seven months in a deep and debilitating depression. He braved snow and rain to visit her gravesite daily. His sorrow negatively affected his marriage with Josephine who—in his view—accepted Florence's death "in the spirit of resignation." We don't have a record of Josephine's thoughts and feelings on the death of her youngest child—the second child she had to bury. It is probably safe to assume Josephine's resignation to the death of her child reflected the commonality of such tragedies. The loss made her no different than any other of the thousands of women experiencing the same trauma throughout the city. Additionally, their surviving daughter, Addie, was seventeen years old and spent a great deal of time with her mother throughout her young adult life. However, Crittenton experienced a crisis of self. He neglected his business and wondered, "what was the good of making money if I did not have my child to lavish it upon?" He questioned why God would rip his beloved child away from him, a man who could lavish all the love and material possessions on the child, while there were unwanted children playing in the gutters of New York City?[27]

However, true to the trope of the sentimental child death, Florence's passing would not be in vain. While on a Third Avenue train heading uptown in the midst of his depression, Crittenton was overwhelmed with sadness and began to cry. He pressed his face against the glass window, hoping that other passengers would not notice the well-dressed man crying in the back of the train car. At that moment, Crittenton experienced his sentimental conversion. Florence spoke to him clearly, saying, "Papa I can't come to you, but you can come to me." All of Crittenton's fears that he would not be reunited with his daughter in heaven vanished when he heard Florence's voice. For the first time since Florence's death, he felt "that possibly God did love me and that He was going to reunite me with my precious child in heaven."[28] From that moment on, Florence's gravesite in Woodlawn Cemetery held no more meaning for him; "there was a meaningless handful of dust under the green sod that covered her grave," he wrote. After experiencing Florence's angel, Crittenton believed that he would reunite with her in Heaven.[29]

When writing his autobiography many years later, Crittenton understood Florence's death as a sign from God. It was only through Florence's death that he could be brought back to Christ to evangelize and work on behalf of others. His love for Florence had been so strong that he could hardly understand his love and grief, but once he heard her angelic voice, he understood. He wrote, "Truly God had put a wonderful love into my heart for that child, which I could not understand then, but now I know it was in order that my thoughts should be drawn Heavenward by her being taken there." It was not until a sentimental spiritual conversion that Crittenton understood the meaning of her death.[30]

After his life-changing episode, Crittenton started attending noonday prayer meetings, admittedly something that he previously thought were a bit silly. Soon, however, he enmeshed himself in the Protestant evangelical community and volunteered at the Cremorne Mission in the Tenderloin district. The Cremorne was located just a few blocks from one of the most notorious brothels in the city, The House of All Nations. Run by well-known madam Kate Woods, the brothel was renowned for housing well-known sex workers from all over the world. Each room was decorated with furnishings from a different country. The brothel was notorious because many women who worked there specialized in the "French" style, or oral sex. Social purity reformers often blamed immigrants for these "unnatural acts," leading one reformer to lament that women working in "French" houses "stoop to practices that the ordinary American girl could not be induced to do." However, numerous contemporary studies found that a majority of women sex workers were native-born women.[31]

The Cremorne Mission was one of many religious missions in the city that aimed to help destitute men and women with food, clothing, and medical care along with offering prayer and Bible study. After Crittenton's first visit to the Cremorne, a well-known evangelical reformer named Smith Allen asked Crittenton to join him in rescue work. Crittenton accompanied Allen through the "saloon district" and distinguished this trip as the moment that he began truly caring for the well-being of "fallen" women and girls. Crittenton wrote, "We reached Baxter Street where we went up into a little room where there were two girls to whom [Allen] introduced me. Soon we began to sing . . . After completing the hymn we knelt in prayer . . . not only that God would save these two girls, but also the tens of thousands of girls that were in the city." After Allen completed a prayer, he asked Crittenton to pray and talk with the girls alone.[32]

Unsure of what to say, Crittenton told the two girls about his grief and depression over losing Florence. He recounted his love for his little girl and how she was taken from him too soon. He told the girls how his world had fallen apart at her death. Crittenton continued kneeling with the "fallen girls" and they all cried as he recounted his story and expressed how his grief for his dead daughter led to his religious conversion. Apparently the two girls were so moved by his story and his love for his dead baby girl that "the girls were weeping as if their hearts would break, and both of them expressed a desire to lead a Christian life."[33] One must wonder how many deaths these two "fallen girls" had experienced in their short lifetimes.

This melodramatic recounting was, according to Crittenton, his first experience with rescue work and using the story of Florence's death, and the profound change that it had created in his life, to proselytize and convert. As Allen and Crittenton left the room, Crittenton told the girls to "go and sin no more." He immediately realized that they had no other place to go, that "there is no door open to them from the Battery to Harlem unless similar to the ones they have been going in and out for the past several years."[34] As a result, the idea came to him to start a rescue mission in which fallen girls and women could go, find God, and reclaim a "moral" existence where their sexual past could not haunt them. Soon thereafter Crittenton, Allen, and "several other gentlemen" started the Florence Crittenton Night Mission, funded almost entirely by Crittenton's large fortune. Thus, Crittenton became part of the larger social purity movement that worked to control and outlaw vice in American cities.[35]

The social purity movement of the nineteenth century had its roots in the antebellum reform movements and sentimental understandings of the mother and child bond. In New York, the Female Moral Reform Society began advocating for the elimination of prostitution and the sexual double standard in 1834. Catholics founded the Sisters of Mercy in 1843, which ran a foundling asylum and hospital for single mothers. The Sisters of the Good Shepherd was founded in 1846 as a Magdalene society for "repentant" sex workers. The American Female Guardian Society opened a home for "friendless" or abandoned women in 1848. The Five Points Mission opened in 1850 and the House of Industry in 1854, both operating as places where women engaged in sex work could go if pregnant or too sick to work.[36] Antebellum reformers viewed prostitution as a form of slavery for women, and after the Civil War they increasingly devoted time and resources to the purity, or "new abolition," cause. It is hard to separate many social purity advocates from early feminists as many purity reformers argued that women must have control over their own bodies.[37]

In 1858 William W. Sanger, the resident physician on New York City's Blackwell's Island, published a book entitled *The History of Prostitution: Its Extent, Causes and Effects Throughout the World*. Sanger provided a detailed study of prostitution in New York City and vehemently argued that prostitution was allowed to flourish only because people were too prudish and uptight to talk about it. He felt that such silence caused "the most stupid indifference" to the "social problem," a contemporaneous term for prostitution.[38] Sanger went on to argue that prostitution was expensive for society to maintain. He calculated that the state paid over seven million dollars of taxpayer money in New York City alone to fund city hospitals for the treatment of sexually transmitted infections, reformatory asylums and institutions, and increased police and judiciary expenses related to prostitution and vice. To curb the tide, Sanger proposed that mothers better fulfill their parental duties by teaching their children social hygiene—meaning chastity—and rudimentary sex education for when they married. He also blamed widespread prostitution on the sexual double standard that kept women in "the trade" once they had fallen. However, Sanger did not believe prostitution could be eradicated. Instead, he believed, along with many physicians of the mid-nineteenth century, that prostitution was a necessary evil as it was an outlet for men's perceived excessive sexual desires and proposed regulation of "the trade" over eradication.[39]

Health officials, in an attempt to curb the spread of venereal disease, and city officials trying to relegate prostitution to specific areas of town both considered numerous plans to regulate prostitution in the nineteenth century. They proposed plans such as licensing sex workers and places of prostitution, zoning red-light districts, and testing women suspected of prostitution for venereal disease. They never seriously considered forcing men who frequented sex workers to be tested. Sanger believed a medical bureau under the direction of the police department should regulate prostitution in New York City. The bureau would inspect brothels and other places of prostitution and would have the power to commit women found to have sexually transmitted infections to the hospital, where they would be imprisoned until cured. Also, known sex workers would be restricted to red-light districts with the idea that if they were confined to certain areas, "upright" society would be spared from their vice. Sanger was part of a larger movement among men of medicine, like the American Medical Association and the New York Society for the Prevention of Contagious Diseases, that wanted to regulate prostitution for the public health benefits they believed it would produce.[40]

Experiments with regulation were active in continental Europe throughout the nineteenth century. In England, lawmakers passed a series of regulations known as the Contagious Diseases Acts intended to regulate prostitution as a means to stop the spread of venereal disease. The Acts were controversial from the start because they allowed police to arrest women merely suspected of prostitution. Accused sex workers were taken to a local hospital and forcibly inspected for disease. If a doctor found symptoms of venereal disease, the woman would be interned in a locked hospital for up to three months. The amended 1869 Act allowed for internment up to one year. In opposition, a group of British men formed the National Association for the Repeal of the Contagious Diseases Acts to protest and lobby against the legislation. Those men excluded women from their organization because they deemed the subject matter too unseemly for women to participate in. This prompted reformer Josephine Butler to create the Ladies National Association (LNA), which took up the cause from a woman's perspective. The National Association and LNA aroused the sentiment of those who might have moral qualms about government-sanctioned prostitution, as well as those concerned with the lack of civil liberties the Acts afforded women, with great effect.[41]

Butler demanded that authorities stop the "instrumental rape" of suspected sex workers, a shockingly modern analysis that she used to describe the forced speculum-assisted inspection for venereal disease. She was a fierce advocate for women's rights and the sovereign right of women over their own bodies. However, Butler attributed her drive for reform work to the profound heartbreak she experienced when her young daughter Eva died by falling off the top-floor banister of her home. It is impossible to know whether Butler would have become such a fierce advocate for women and girls had her youngest daughter not died. Regardless, Butler fulfilled the sentimental trope of action-in-the-face-of-premature-death and attributed her turn toward social reform to Eva's death; the sense of grief and loss she felt could only be filled by service to others.[42]

Americans were keenly aware of the battles over the Contagious Diseases Acts, fueling opposition to regulated prostitution in the United States. As more women were exposed to the ideas of the women's rights movement through sentimental fiction that questioned the double standard, like *Charlotte Temple* or Lillie Devereux Blake's 1874 *Fettered for Life* that depicted the sexual exploitation of working-class women by upper-class men, they began rejecting the common understanding of prostitution as a "necessary evil." Historically, many men and some women viewed prostitution as a necessary release for men's supposedly greater sexual needs. However, as sex work became more visible in American cities, and as women became more cognizant to their second-tier status in society, women began organizing against regulation and what they viewed as state-sponsored slavery of women. A new generation of educated women, such as doctors Elizabeth Blackwell and Caroline Winslow, railed against regulation and the double moral standard while still relying on sentimental understandings of the transformation from girlhood to womanhood.[43]

Most social purity reformers were wholeheartedly against regulation measures and organized into groups such as the New York Committee for the Prevention of State Regulation of Vice. Former abolitionists Abby Hooper Gibbons and Aaron Macy Powell formed the New York Committee for the Prevention of State Regulation in 1876, which later became the American Purity Alliance, in response to proposed measures to regulate prostitution in New York. They argued that regulating vice was not the moral way to curb the spread of disease or crime. Instead, they maintained that a single standard of sexual morality should be used for both men and women. That would, in return, stop the trade in women's bodies that led to so many "fallen girls."[44]

Social purity crusaders that rallied against regulating legalized prostitution commonly argued that regulation represented an "Old-World system of licensed and state-regulated vice."[45] Samuel Blackwell informed readers of the pro-suffrage *Woman's Journal* about the defeat of a bill to outlaw licensed prostitution in Geneva, Switzerland. To clearly mark businesses where prostitution was legal, licensed brothels were required to hang a red lantern above the door. Thus, inhabitants were call *lampes rouges*, or "red lamps." After the proposed abolition bill was defeated, the "red lamps" made a procession through the streets and into a church where they placed a red lantern on the communion table and sang a popular hymn, which began with "Source divine of light and life."[46] Blackwell's readers took this act as an indication of the sinfulness inherent in prostitution. Social purity reformer Kate Waller Barrett embellished Blackwell's recounting, writing that the red lamps carried banners with the words, "'Down with God,''Down with Morality,' upon them." She continued that they "drove away the police and took possession of a church, where a consecration service to the Devil was held."[47] As evidenced by Waller Barret's hyperbole, many social purity reformers believed the moral fabric of America was tied up in the fight against regulating prostitution.

Protecting the moral soul of the nation meant policing the streets of America's growing cities. The mid-1870s also saw the formation of Anthony Comstock's Society for the Suppression of Vice (SSV), which operated well into the twentieth century. The SSV claimed under its jurisdiction "the enforcement of laws for the suppression of the trade in, and circulation of obscene literature and illustrations, advertisements, and articles of indecent or immoral use."[48] Comstock successfully lobbied for legislation banning "obscene" literature from the mail in 1873 and became an agent of the U.S. Postal Service to enforce such restrictions. He was not just concerned with mailable paraphernalia. He also, along with other social purity reformers, physically raided dance halls, brothels, gambling houses, and rat pits.[49]

Social purity reformers' attempts to police morality was an uphill battle, as there was money to be made from vice. Brothels and "public houses" integrated into many cities' tax structure. High revenues from brothels offered property owners large profits, which in turn benefited municipal tax collectors. Brothels linked an underground economy full of sex, alcohol, and gambling to the growing real estate industry, and ultimately to the municipal government. Everyone involved made money, and graft and corruption frequently lined the pockets of individuals of every level of the hierarchy: property owners and lessees, municipal tax collectors, police, and the owners and workers themselves.[50]

Many social purity campaigns, especially those in New York City, formed in reaction to the municipal government's complicity in this informal economy. Journalist Edward Crapsey found that New York City police would raid brothels and gambling houses and then demand payment for "protection" in the form of a dismissal or lighter sentence. In 1894, at the conclusion of one of the largest examinations of law enforcement in nineteenth-century New York City, the Lexow Committee concluded that prostitution was "fostered and protected by the police of the city."[51] Social purity reformers were well aware of the connections between the informal economy and municipal government and used the cycle that sex workers found themselves in as a reason for rescue work. One article detailed the "hard lot" of the trade. Once a sex worker was sentenced to pay a fine, the "procurist" (either a madam or pimp) paid the fine for her. Then she was told to go back out on the street to repay the debt. If she was not able to repay, the "procurist" would turn her back over to the police.[52] Josie Washburn, a woman who performed sex work around the turn of the twentieth century, chronicled how women often paid monthly fees between fourteen dollars and up to one hundred dollars to avoid jail time and even higher fines. Washburn described the system as a "hold-up," where women had no legal or social protection and were thus easily taken advantage of. She recounted angrily the system that accepted and validated "the oath of every man, no matter how depraved" but did not accept the word of women accused of prostitution in the court of law.[53]

Overwhelmingly it was women who bore the brunt of fines and prosecutions dealing with sexual matters. If a woman wound up in prison, for either repeat prostitution or other charges, she experienced horrible treatment. These women were viewed as "outside" of womanhood, unnatural, and well past redemption. Women prisoners languished in the worst, most neglected corners of the prison, were raped by male guards, or were put to work as sex workers within the prison.[54] Responding to the danger that women prisoners faced, many social purity and other reformers focused on prison reform. They found abuse and illicit sex in prisons, guards sexually assaulting female inmates, and prisons where inmates were not separated by age, sex, or criminality.[55] These situations pushed many reformers to call for female oversight in the courts and prisons, which began to create a new category of professional women workers in the penal and judicial system.

Reformers argued that police matrons were better suited to protect women and girls within the court system and would be there to intervene if the woman or girl was a potential candidate for a reform organization. The WCTU supported the use of police matrons, arguing they were an excellent way to intervene in the lives of women arrested for prostitution or public drunkenness. They succeeded in having police matrons hired in several cities between 1876 and 1888.[56] However, for many women sex work was worth the risk. A female sex worker could earn between one and five dollars a "trick," amounting in one evening to more than most working women made in a week. This "informal economy" made money for and provided work for many people, particularly poor and working-class women, who otherwise might not have an opportunity to work for adequate wages.[57]

Some laws intended to curb prostitution actually made it expand. The New York Raines Law, which attempted to keep working-class saloons closed on Sundays, allowed hotels with ten or more beds to serve alcohol on Sunday. Therefore, instead of shutting down sales of alcohol in saloons, the saloons simply converted their back rooms and upper floors into small bedrooms for rent. These Raines Law hotels turned high profits. Some operated as hotels, some as rooms for rent by the hour, and others became houses of assignation. The Raines Law also had an unintended consequence of making brothels obsolete and less in the control of women. On the Raines Law, Emma Goldman said it "relieved the keeper of responsibility towards the inmates and increased their revenue from prostitution." No longer was a madam in charge of women in a brothel. Using Baltimore brothels as evidence, historian Katie Hemphill demonstrated how madams, who often began their careers as sex workers, could provide a sense of community and comradery for the women that worked for them. However, after the Raines Law was passed in New York City, the interconnected economy of madams, sex workers, landlords, and providers of goods shifted as freelance sex workers began renting rooms in Raines Law hotels.[58]

There were no easy answers to the social issues that arose around commercialized sex work. Most solutions ignored the economic disadvantages women faced within an economic patriarchy, making sex work one of the few lucrative avenues where women could earn a living wage. For the most part these systemic issues were addressed through voluntary and piecemeal programs, like Crittenton's Florence Crittenton Night Mission, and addressed individual women instead of system-wide issues of inequality. Nevertheless, little Florence's angel continued to lead her father toward evangelism, social purity, and the growth of the future NFCM.

CHAPTER 4

———— ⊶०ℭ⌒⊅०⊶ ————

Little Lambs Waiting for
the Slaughter's Knife

SOCIAL PURITY AND
THE MOTHER MISSION

*To-day [sic] as never before, magnificent opportunities are open for
women to help their fallen sisters. The awakening of womanhood
to the needs of women was one of the greatest movements of
the nineteenth century, and it shall continue to be one of the
forward movements of the twentieth. On every hand will the work
open up, and educated, refined women will dominate it.*[1]

The "fall" that young women were expected to experience when they entered
sex work took on meanings beyond the fall from grace that characterized original sin. Nineteenth-century sentimental understandings of the mother and child
bond, and the manner in which girls *should* transition into women, meant that
any deviation from a sexually pure childhood and legally sanctioned sexuality in
marriage was anathema. Therefore, social purity reformers were not just lamenting the rise of sex work on city streets but also the affront to middle-class standards of sexuality in young adulthood.

By 1883, when Crittenton began the Florence Crittenton Night Mission, the
brothel was on the decline in New York City. As land-use changed and the furnished room became a more popular alternative, many female sex workers began working out of hotels instead of brothels. In this way they escaped the control of a madam and the high prices charged to live and work within a brothel.
This agency and change of living conditions, coupled with increasing repression

from social purity campaigns, made the brothel less and less a place where commercialized sex occurred. It also meant that many women and girls were "walking the streets" to procure clients, particularly in The Bowery district.[2]

In addition to changing patterns of where prostitution operated, The Bowery was giving way as the premier environment for commercial sex to more upscale areas further north, like the Tenderloin district. The antebellum sporting culture was giving way to the mass entertainment culture of the late Gilded Age and Progressive Era. With this being said, however, the saloons, brothels, houses of assignation, dance halls, public houses, and theaters were still popular forms of entertainment and business in The Bowery, if perhaps looking a little shabbier than in previous years. They also catered to a more working-class clientele.

Nevertheless, The Bowery still played a large part in New York City nightlife. Saloons of every caliber lined the streets around Broadway, from what reformer Helen Campbell described as "gin-palaces to bucket-shops." Interspersed between the myriad of bars were theaters and lavish concert halls, offering the opportunities to view a variety of entertainments, from Shakespearean plays to the performance of bawdy songs and dancing women. Those looking for cheap entertainment could walk into small "dime museums"—made famous in midcentury by the flashiest of New Yorkers, P. T. Barnum—and view the latest "oddities" on the circuit. The bravest of pleasure seekers could try their luck at any number of carnivalesque shooting galleries that lined the streets. Young men and women crowded the sidewalks, where a cacophony of laughter and music could be heard spilling out into the night air. What some viewed as a cheap escape from the humdrum of a hard, working-class life, others viewed as a den of sinfulness and debauchery.[3]

In the midst of this rowdy neighborhood Crittenton opened the Florence Crittenton Night Mission, later affectionately known as the Mother Mission, in April of 1883 at 29 Bleecker Street in an old brownstone home and former brothel. It housed a kitchen and a dining room, a large meeting room made from two smaller living areas, and an upstairs fitted with beds for women who wanted a reprieve from the street. Demand for beds was so high that within a short time Crittenton needed additional space. He purchased the larger 21 Bleecker Street, another former brothel owned by "Madam Rose, who had kept it as a disreputable house for over twenty years." The home's reputation was infamous, and it was "said that a large dark stain on the dining-room floor was the blood of the man who had been murdered there."[4] Soon thereafter, Crittenton purchased 23 Bleecker Street and combined the two houses together.

The Florence Crittenton Night Mission operated in a prime location within the working-class entertainment district. As Crittenton described it:

> Both sides were filled with dance halls, saloons and sporting houses. You could meet from fifty to one hundred girls any night going the few short blocks from Broadway to the Bowery and many more men. Butt Allen's famous dance and concert hall, with gambling den attached, was there. Harry Hill's noted dive was one block below on Houston Street. In Mulberry Street, a short distance away, were the sub-cellar dives, two stories below ground under the control of Italians, where for a few cents degraded men and women could go in out of the cold and remain over night, sleeping on the damp, dirty floors, or else sitting in the broken, rickety chairs.[5]

Many of the Mother Mission's inhabitants came from the "sub-cellar dives" described by Crittenton.

Before the Florence Crittenton Night Mission opened, Crittenton referred to two unnamed homes in the city where fallen girls could go. He lamented, "the rules for their admittance were so strict that it was almost impossible to get a girl in." One of the homes he was likely referring to was the Girls Temporary Home run by the Children's Aid Society and located on Saint Marks Place. This home actively resisted being a "Magdalen Asylum," a place that took in sex workers with the goal of reformation. Instead, it was set up as an industrial mission where homeless girls received free meals and in turn learned how to sew. The strict entrance criteria meant that many girls who participated in commodified sex were turned away.[6]

In fact, this was one of the selling points for the Florence Crittenton Mission, at least in the eyes of its proponents. The Florence Crittenton Night Mission prided itself on being a place of refuge. Crittenton wrote, "I very soon discovered that if we were really going to reach the girls we would have to use different methods from those already in vogue, and from the first it was our unanimous opinion that everything pertaining to prison methods should be strictly avoided."[7] Ideally, the women who needed the services of the mission could come and go as they pleased. Some years later, Crittenton superintendent Kate Waller Barrett referred to this freedom of movement as a type of catholic plan, perhaps alluding to the open-door policy of Catholic foundling institutions.[8] Women who came to the Mission were given food, clothing, and medicine or treatment by a doctor if needed, and a place to sleep. Women could stay at the Mission until they found "respectable" employment, had relatives located, or were sent to the hospital if they had a detectable venereal disease. There were no entrance criteria according to supportive contemporaries, but women were not anonymous. Upon entry a woman's name, age, denomination, nationality, place of residence, and father and mother (if known) were recorded.[9] Undoubtedly, some women found even the simple recording of their names too restrictive. One of the Florence Crittenton Mission's early and most famous converts gave an assumed name upon entering the home. It took many months, but after Crittenton workers gained her trust, Nellie Conroy experienced a religious transformation and went on to proselytize for the Florence Crittenton Night Mission, temperance societies, and social purity organizations; she even spoke to a crowd of three thousand at Cooper Union in New York City. Although many women who engaged in sex work conducted business under one or more pseudonyms, many women gave the Crittenton rescuers their name, whether given at birth or assumed later.[10]

The Florence Crittenton Night Mission operated as an evangelical Protestant rescue home, assisting twice as many Protestants as Catholics and only a fraction of Jewish women.[11] Prayer meetings were held nightly and passersby on the street could hear hymns pouring out of the meeting room. Religious services lasted from roughly nine o'clock at night until the early hours of the morning, when the supposed bad influences were put to bed. Historian Timothy Gilfoyle argues that by the 1870s anti-prostitution measures "had come full circle" and had abandoned efforts to salvage the moral souls of prostitutes. However, this is exactly what the Florence Crittenton Night Mission of the 1880s endeavored to do. Crittenton workers wanted to give women working in commercialized sex a place to stay in order to leave their bad surroundings and give them a chance to rebuild their lives. This was thoroughly embedded in an evangelical message of Christian salvation. Although conversion was never demanded, it nevertheless structured the entire rescue operation.[12]

The sentimentalized death of four-year-old Florence Crittenton was always at the forefront of the movement. A picture of little Florence and a vase of white flowers operated as the focal point of the mission's main room, reminding patrons and volunteers of the child-angel that started it all. One observer noted that the women who came to services varied widely in age, one woman coming in with her small daughter, both dressed in rags. "Florence girls," or the saved, ranging in ages from fifteen to fifty, sat in the front and one by one told their stories and how others could join them in their redemption. These tales of sorrow and grace were interspersed with scripture readings, hymns, and exhortations to return to their mothers' loving arms.[13]

Florence Crittenton Night Mission volunteers organized a "Rescue Band" to go out into the streets to find girls to bring back to the mission. Crittenton volunteers spread out into the night, entering "low concert halls and stale beer dives" to find women who needed and wanted their help. These establishments often occupied basement rooms that could only be reached by narrow wooden stairs or dark hallways. As social reformer Helen Campbell found them, "the rooms are small, the ceiling low, and the air is always full of the fumes of tobacco and beer."[14] The Rescue Band included a small group of volunteers, usually both men and women, consisting of a mixture of middle-class evangelists and previously rescued women.

Routinely, the group would leave the Florence Crittenton Night Mission around one or two in the morning, after the "regular service" of hymns and salvation stories was over for the evening. The group of about eight to ten would split off into twos and threes and proceed down The Bowery, speaking with anyone they encountered. Often, the "Band," as they called themselves, would enter the "bar rooms" and head to the back where young people would congregate around a piano, the low ceilings and dim lights exacerbating the smokey air and scent of stale beer. According to Crittenton, the Band would return to the Mission around four in the morning, "frequently having one or two girls to bring back with us as trophies of our labors."[15]

The voices of women who sought shelter at the Mother Mission, were approached by rescue workers, or who interacted with reformers during the period are not readily available. Unfortunately, the voices of the working-class, of the misbehaved, or of the morally shamed are not the voices that are typically recorded for prosperity. One of the rare voices that we do have did not think very highly of reform workers. Josie Washburn, a brothel owner and sex worker in Nebraska, did not have positive things to say about the rescue workers she encountered, saying reformers "talk twaddle" and were "inferior to us in intellect, and even in the knowledge of biblical history." She emphasized the dichotomy between rescuer and rescued, saying how if rescuers were successful, "They recommend the rescued woman to their friends as a 'poor, lost creature' whom they have saved from shame." Washburn highlighted the dichotomy of rescue work and how a woman "must accept the brand" of being a "fallen" woman in order to receive help or aid from rescuers.[16] Being "rescued" gave up a woman's sense of self-determination. In order to get help, she must relinquish her agency. Rescuers could feel a sense of superiority when the women they were helping could be infantilized or cast as lost and in need of guidance.

Rescue work was couched in middle-class sentimentality. Although advice literature written for reformers preached against any kind of condescension, it was nevertheless built into the language of the movement. Reformers often portrayed girls as bobbing in rough waters, waiting with "patient suffering and mute lips" for the rescuers' hand to pull them to safety before they sunk below the waves of shame and degradation.[17] Women and girls were infantilized, cast as children needing guidance. True to the sentimental and maternal drive behind the Mother Mission, Crittenton rescue workers styled themselves as mothers, there to take care of the "mother's girls" who were abandoned or lost. Volunteers passed out cards that read:

ANY MOTHER'S GIRL WISHING TO LEAVE A CROOKED LIFE,

MAY FIND FRIENDS, FOOD, SHELTER, AND A HELPING HAND BY

COMING JUST AS SHE IS, TO THE FLORENCE NIGHT MISSION.[18]

True to middle-class sentimentality, a mother's love was depicted as the salve for all of the world's troubles.

Not all women were passively rescued; some wanted help and actively sought it from the rescue mission. One twenty-year-old woman in New Orleans wrote to the New York City Mother Mission, asking if they would come and rescue her from her life of prostitution.[19] Other women wrote to the home after their stay, expressing deep gratitude and appreciation for their rescue. One woman wrote, "I am working hard and no matter when any of you hear from me from the Home, you will know that I am doing right."[20] Women and girls had many reasons to want to stay in rescue missions. As historian Linda Gordon points out in her study of the Massachusetts Society to Protect Children from Cruelty, reformers often found a direct correlation between "incestuous molestation in childhood and subsequent sexual misbehavior." Late nineteenth-century reformers had a limited vocabulary when it came to describing molestation and abuse. However, many were also well aware of the abuse, neglect, and molestation inflicted on the girls and women in their care.[21]

Not all women who stayed at the Mother Mission were sex workers. Crittenton recalled a young woman who was turned out on the streets by her mother because she lost her job as a bookbinder. She could not afford to pay her mother rent any longer, so the mother "turned her out after dark." A police officer found the girl on the street and took her to the Mother Mission, where she lived for four months. Crittenton boasted that after her rescue, she is "now a married woman, and working for her Master." Her marriage meant that she had entered respectable womanhood and she was working "for her Master," hence leading a "saved," Christian life. The Mission functioned as both a place to reform but also to prevent women from engaging in sex work.[22]

Crittenton spent most of his time and money running the Mother Mission, to the detriment of his marriage. Josephine's feelings, at least initially, were unsympathetic to the women Crittenton was devoted to helping, and there seems to have been many tears and arguments over his rescue work. She complained that he did not care about his family anymore. Instead, she accused him of being "out all night among those harlots who are not fit to live and ought to be cast off the face of the earth."[23] According to Crittenton, Josephine came around eventually and actually did some Mission work with him. However, superficially it seems the couple led separate lives. When their daughter Addie was admitted to a university in Leipzig, Germany, Josephine went with her. She stayed in Leipzig until Addie finished her studies. Josephine was back in America for only a short time before she died in 1886.

As work at the Mother Mission continued, Crittenton began to envision using his fortune to create a nationwide Crittenton rescue organization with one or two missions, or homes, in each state. The homes would make a network that allowed women to travel from one home to another in order to escape bad environments or situations. He commented on what we would call today domestic abuse and how women found it hard to escape men that hurt them or sold their bodies. The ability to change cities, or even states, would help women escape dangerous situations. He began to create the national network in 1889, opening Florence Crittenton homes in San Francisco and San Jose, California. Both homes were completely funded by his large fortune and relied on paid female matrons' reproductive labor for daily operations.[24]

In 1892 Crittenton met Frances Willard, the president and firebrand of the Woman's Christian Temperance Union (WCTU). The WCTU was an enormous organization that joined Protestant religion with social reforms intended to raise the status of women and the family. Temperance societies, or organizations that advocated against the production and consumption of alcohol, existed for decades before the formation of the WCTU, but women always played secondary or auxiliary roles in those organizations. What made the WCTU different, and arguably more successful, was its structure of female authority. The abstention from alcohol served as the base of the movement, but the organization championed a variety of concerns that affected women, including sexual exploitation, domestic violence, labor concerns, social reform, and women's political empowerment. The WCTU was the largest women's organization in the United States during the nineteenth century, growing to over two hundred thousand members by 1892.[25]

Willard became president of the WCTU in 1879 and the attention of the organization shifted from one primarily focused on closing saloons to an ambitious "Do Everything" campaign. Within ten years of Willard's presidency, the WCTU sponsored more than thirty-five areas of public activism such as prison reform, public health, and improved working conditions for laborers. Because of the decentralized structure of the organization, individual chapters were able to focus their efforts on causes of their choosing. The WCTU's push for social purity was second only to that of temperance. The WCTU was the most important organization for extending the social purity movement into everyday women's homes, causing Willard to marvel that no WCTU department grew as rapidly as that for social purity work.[26] Most WCTU supporters believed that alcohol and prostitution went hand in hand. Most Crittenton workers agreed. Within hours of their meeting, Crittenton pledged five thousand dollars to assist in opening five Florence Crittenton homes under WCTU auspices and in the cities of Willard's choosing.[27] The collaboration between Charles Crittenton's Florence Crittenton Mission and Frances Willard's WCTU only spread the social purity movement that much further, reaching middle-class women within and without the WCTU organization who otherwise might not engage in political or social movements. These networks of mostly women reformers would prove integral to building the foundations of the American welfare state.

The Social Purity movement in the WCTU focused on combating the sexual double standard, which they argued hurt women and families. The WCTU Committee for Work with Fallen Women strove to "save" sex workers through Protestant Christianity and temperance. By 1885, the name and emphasis of the committee changed to the Department for Social Purity. The Department stressed preventative measures including providing temporary housing for women fleeing prostitution and domestic violence, "life-saving stations" for young girls entering the city for the first time, and mothers' associations designed to encourage sex education for children. Social Purity Department members also advocated for raising the age-of-consent laws across America. These laws determined the age at which a girl could consent to sexual intercourse. Lower age-of-consent laws meant that a man only had to "prove" that a girl above the age had consented to sexual intercourse. Social purity reformers argued that these laws only protected men from charges of rape and fueled the traffic of young girls into prostitution.[28] By insisting that age-of-consent laws change, reformers demanded that state power be used to protect vulnerable girls.

Many WCTU members and social purity reformers turned their focus to rescue work when William Stead, a British journalist, published a series in the *Pall Mall Gazette* in 1885 entitled, "The Maiden Tribute of Modern Babylon." It was a scathing expose of "vice" in the London underworld. To expose the inhumanity, Stead himself purchased a thirteen-year-old girl from her mother, supposedly for "immoral purposes," to prove to his readers that London was "the greatest market in human flesh in the whole world." Stead's stunt actually landed him in jail for three months, but the exposé also ignited public interest in prostitution in both England and the United States.[29] It was not until Stead's claim that English gentlemen could easily procure the virginities of young girls in the London underground that the WCTU social purity department took up the campaign to raise the age of consent in America. Stead's exposé showed that English law set the age of consent at thirteen years old. The WCTU launched a shocking campaign showing that the age of consent was just ten years old in most states. Concurrently, the WCTU social purity department also launched campaigns to revise prostitution, rape, and seduction laws.

Advocates for raising the age of consent pointed out that girls could not marry or sell property at such a young age, therefore they should not be vulnerable to men who would rape them or make them sex workers. Women's rights advocate and author of Is This Your Son, Oh Lord? and Pray You, Sir, Whose Daughter? Helen Gardener summed it up thusly: "What good can it do any human being to have the age of consent below that at which honorable marriage or the right to sell property comes to a girl?" She went on to answer her own question, remarking, "It is a law in the interest of the brothel, in the interest of the grade of men who prey upon the ignorance and helplessness of childhood."[30] Reformers like Gardener maintained that trickery, ignorance, or abuse could lure or trap young girls into prostitution.

Mary Grace Edholm, social purity advocate and superintendent of press work for the WCTU, melodramatically alerted readers to the dangers of low age-of-consent laws, writing, "The unsuspecting child followed him, carried away with the dream of the promised presents. The door opened; the bolt turned; the screams of the child availed not. She left the room robbed of her virginity and started on the path of prostitution."[31] Edholm continued, "the man would swear that she had accompanied him of her own free will, hoping to get the jewelry; and even though she did not understand what he wanted with her, the judge and jury, themselves fathers of little girls, would hold the child guilty and the man innocent."[32] Edholm grossly highlighted how the double standard operated in a system with low age-of-consent laws. The girl was raped and no longer a virgin, making her "spoiled" in the marriage market while the low age-of-consent law prevented her from having any redress in court. Even if a charge of rape could be brought, "unless a girl dies in the attempt to defend her honor, her innocence must be proved to the satisfaction of a jury of men."[33] Age-of-consent laws operated within a penal system that did not weigh a woman's testimony to be as credible as a man's. Thus, in the mind of middle-class social purity reformers, if a girl was raped (or in the parlance of the period, "seduced"), no self-respecting man would lower himself to marry a defiled woman, leaving her only option to support herself: prostitution.

In reality, most women elected to enter sex work either to escape a broken home or to earn a living wage. Overwhelmingly, women engaged with sex work were native-born and were from working-class backgrounds.[34] Nevertheless, reformers continually attempted to paint sex workers and fallen girls as victims, "young, credulous, ignorant country girls," or immigrants fresh off the boat.[35] Class bias made it impossible for many middle-class reformers to recognize the agency of women sex workers, even while many of them believed the consent by a women to sell herself sexually while living in poverty was not a just trade. Reformers could be as patronizing as they were helpful; the line between help and control was always shaky. Reformers demanded that their charges adopt middle-class notions of temperance and chastity while understanding that an unequal moral standard between men and women left women economically and sexually vulnerable.[36]

The infantilization of young girls in need of rescue rallied middle-class women to their cause and perhaps filled a need for women who felt compassion in a different way, through their love of their own daughters both living and dead. In language reminiscent of the sentimental literature so common at the time, Edholm relayed her experience doing outreach work for the Mother Mission:

> One evening we visited an aristocratic house of shame, and, as I stood in the doorway of that parlor, such a sight met my gaze as froze my heart with horror. There sat eight or ten of the most beautiful little girls I ever saw, and not one of them over sixteen years of age. There they sat, dressed in their little short dresses, just as mother dressed them, with their hair braided down their back, just as mother braided it to send them to school. And as I looked at them, I could think of nothing but a lot of little lambs waiting for the slaughter's knife. And if some man had taken a knife and drawn it across the throat of every one and left her weltering in her blood on that splendid carpet, it would not have been one ten-thousandth as bad as the fate she was waiting for.[37]

The gothic image of little girls scattered across a sumptuous carpet, their throats slit from ear to ear, seems quite melodramatic. Yet, the affect was one intended to pull the heartstrings of readers and to get women to act in defense of girlhood and motherhood.

Sentimentalism and the fear of death, both physical and social, always had a heavy hand in the social purity movement. The child-angel loomed quietly over the movement, propelling parents towards a more just society. Edholm channeled her grief over the death of her own daughter into her rescue work: "As I looked into the eyes of these beautiful girls, I thought of a little girl I have up in heaven waiting for me, and I pressed my hands across my throbbing heart and said, 'Oh God! what if it were my little girl!'"[38] In fact, Crittenton never mitigated the original impetus for creating his national network of rescue homes. Whenever he spoke to a crowd, he usually referenced his spiritual conversion in response to his sentimental experience with Florence's angel. His conversion story, wrote one commentator, "always produces a noticeable effect on a congregation."[39] The specter of reunification in Heaven with deceased children continued to be a driving force of social purity reform.

Reformers like Dr. Elizabeth Blackwell advocated for a "theology of action," encouraging women to engage in reshaping entrenched systems detrimental to the female sex. However, this was to be done while maintaining their status as angels of the home. One integral solution came back to mothers and their assumed ability to shape the moral natures of their children, particularly the moral nature of boys. Frances E. W. Harper, Black reformer, WCTU leader, and author stated, "no woman loves social purity as it deserves to be loved if she only cares for the purity of her daughters and not her sons."[40] Shaping a new moral sensibility entailed molding the moral compass of children. Reformers emphasized the importance of teaching boys to be better, more moral men.[41]

Nowhere was the need to impose moral purity on boys more clearly laid out than among the National Purity Congress. Raising moral boys was imperative to changing the status quo. Additionally, astute reformers argued that it was also a way to curb the sexual violence white men committed against Black women. Martha Schofield, a white northern reformer who ran a school for Black people in the South after the Civil War articulated this fact well, stating, "The still greater need and only safe building for the future is to teach boys—yes boys— the danger and the wrong, and lift men to the responsibility of nobleness of fatherhood and to respect *all* women" (emphasis added).[42] Schofield unabashedly highlighted the constant danger that some white men posed to Black girls and women, noting that white people were aware of this threat and did nothing.

Harper went further, highlighting the absurdity of white middle-class mothers in only protecting the virtue of white girls, and "not for the servant girl beneath the shadow of her home."[43] She chastised white women for looking the other way when white men abused Black domestic workers in their households.

Harper astutely pointed out that the women who "are leaving the impress of their hands upon your children during the impressible and formative period of their young lives" were in constant danger of sexual assault in white households. Reminding white women that "the degradation of one class is a menace to the peace and welfare of the other," Harper admonished her audience that "no mistress of a home should be morally indifferent to the safety of any inmate beneath her roof, however humble her position may be."[44] Harper exposed the hypocrisy of allowing Black women to raise white, middle-class children but not be worried about Black women's safety or moral cleanliness. Not only should white mothers be the angel in the home, but they must also be the protector of *all* who inhabited their domestic sphere. The entitlement white men assumed toward Black and working-class female bodies would only abate when white mothers taught their sons morality and sobriety. The fate of the moral fabric of America rested on the work of mothers in the home.

Although most social purity reformers operated under the often false assumption that the only reason women and girls would enter sex work was because of trickery or abduction, they still were advocating for laws that would protect women and girls from men. This often met fierce resistance, as what protected women and girls often endangered male privilege. For example, in Iowa in 1888, in response to pressure from the WCTU and others, the Iowa assembly raised the age of consent from ten to thirteen years of age. Those against the measure argued that the increased age made men "liable to imprisonment for life for yielding to the solicitation of a prostitute."[45] In another instance, men argued, "wild and ... perverted girls" would "lay traps for inexperienced boys" and blackmail them into marriage.[46] After all, raising the age of consent would curtail men's freedom when it came to having sex with whomever they wished. Reformers such as Helen Gardener always pointed out that these protestations were not really to protect men from designing women, but instead to protect the prerogatives of men. Quite poignantly yet melodramatically, Gardener pointed out the fact that these laws were made by men "to cater to crime against the baby girls of the lower and middle classes of the race."[47] Historian Kimberly Hamlin establishes that Gardener was much more of a radical and free thinker than other social purity reformers like Powell or Willard.[48] Nevertheless, the battle over the age of consent caused a variety of reformers with different backgrounds to come together and argue that women had to be the maternal protectors and shields of the home. Many social purity reformers' outspokenness was always couched in the understanding that these reforms were for the *protection* of the home, and particularly for the children that inhabited it. Social purity's ultimate goal was to buttress the angel in the home; when women and mothers had control over the domestic sphere, they would extend their purview to the world at large. Only through doing their sentimental duty would the moral soul of the nation be saved.

The collaboration between the Florence Crittenton Night Mission and the WCTU buoyed the social purity movement and recruited women to work closely with the growing national Crittenton Mission. Through partnerships with local organizers Crittenton opened the afore mentioned homes in San Francisco and San Jose, California, and a short-lived home in New Brunswick, New Jersey, in 1890. More homes were opened, in Sacramento in 1890; Norfolk, Virginia, in 1891; Los Angeles in 1892; and four homes through the WCTU in Denver, Portland, Chicago, and Fargo, North Dakota.[49] As more women got involved in the Crittenton work, individual Crittenton homes began to play a role in how the Crittenton operation moved forward. A movement toward the primacy of the child-mother bond began to overtake the objective to save individual sex workers' souls. That is the subject of the next chapter.

CHAPTER 5

A Little Child Shall
Lead Them

KATE WALLER BARRETT
AND THE NATIONAL
FLORENCE CRITTENTON MISSION

Let us remember that very often their babes are as dear to these
forsaken, betrayed mothers as our little ones are dear to us; that
the child is often their all, and that it is also a means of salvation,
for the Christ has said, "A little child shall lead them." [1]

Charles Crittenton founded the Florence Crittenton network, but it was women reformers across the country who ran the homes that made the Crittenton organization a household name by the early twentieth century. As news of Crittenton's sentimental rescue work spread, particularly through the WCTU and his travels proselytizing his vision of redemption, reformers began asking the "millionaire evangelist" for guidance and monetary help with their own local organizations.[2] Dr. Kate Waller Barrett was one woman reformer who was well aware of Crittenton's activism and, while in the process of running her own rescue mission in Atlanta, she reached out to Crittenton in 1893 to ask for advice and assistance. This instigated a lifelong partnership between Crittenton and Waller Barrett. They began working together, and within three years Crittenton hired her to run the entire Crittenton organization. Through Waller Barrett's guidance and organizing acumen, she took the privately funded collection of Crittenton rescue homes and turned them into a sentimental yet scientifically oriented organization that acted as a separate, but complementary, arm to the budding American welfare state.

Waller Barrett guided the Crittenton organization through the transition from the social purity and religious zeal of the nineteenth-century Mother Mission to the social science and maternalist-led organization of the twentieth century. However, she did not abandon elements of sentimentalism and evangelical Christianity but bridged the two with components of scientific motherhood and public action. In a period where the institution of motherhood was romanticized while the unrestrained sexuality of young women was feared, Waller Barrett steered money and resources to the ambiguous cultural boundary between two areas of reform—the efforts to rescue fallen women and the efforts to curb America's high rates of infant mortality through an intervention in the social and economic issue of single motherhood.[3]

Dr. Kate Waller Barrett was born in Virginia in 1857 to a wealthy slave-owning family, whose plantation on the Potomac River was less than thirty miles from Washington, D.C. When war broke out in 1861, Barrett's father enlisted as a Confederate soldier under General Robert E. Lee to fight, and potentially die, for his right to profit from the enslaved people his family held in bondage. Waller Barrett's upbringing as a slaveholder in Virginia undoubtedly shaped her racial views. Historian Stephanie Jones-Rogers has clearly documented how slaveholding families raised their daughters to be future slave-owning mistresses, and how that education shaped how white women understood their relationship to the people they held in bondage. Looking back on her childhood, Waller Barrett was ashamed of her early years as a slaveholder, writing that as a young girl she "absorbed the worst features of the [slave] mistress . . . and looked upon them [enslaved people] as mine by 'divine right.'"[4] Her limited racial enlightenment later in life was tempered by her advocacy of "states' rights" and the power that individual localities should have when it came to self-governance and race relations.[5]

After the Civil War the Waller family recovered much of their land, wealth, and status, and life for the household settled into a comfortable routine. Kate Waller studied with private tutors as a child and took classes at the Arlington Institute for Girls in Alexandria, Virginia, as an adolescent. At the age of nineteen she married Episcopal minister Reverend Robert South Barrett and together they had six children throughout their twenty-year marriage. Shortly after their marriage the Barretts moved to Richmond, Virginia, where Robert served as Rector of Christ Church in a working-class neighborhood called "Butchertown." Poor and working-class Black and white people lived in close quarters among the tenements and battered cottages dotting the hilly terrain. Christ Church was nestled in the valley between two of Richmond's seven hills and in the heart of the "slum"

FIG. 6. Dilapidated housing in Butchertown. The White House of the
Confederacy is in background. In Gustavas A. Werber, *Report on Housing
and Living Conditions in the Neglected Sections of Richmond, Virginia*,
Vol. 439. Richmond, Va.: Whittet & Shepperson Printers, 1913, p. 33.

district in the former capital of the Confederacy. Churches and dilapidated man-
sions neighbored saloons, brothels, and tobacco factories up and down the steep
graveled streets.[6]

Post-Civil War Richmond was a rapidly industrializing city and one of the
few southern cities that quickly transitioned from the slavery-based agricultural
South to a modern, industrial city. However, Richmond had one of the highest
mortality rates of large American cities during the period. The overall death rate
was roughly 24.27 per 1,000 in 1893, making it the fourth deadliest city in the
nation. A little over a decade later, in 1911, Richmond had the second-highest
mortality rate in the nation with a death rate of 21 per 1,000. In comparison,
New York City had an overall death rate of 15.2 per 1,000 the same year.[7] Officials blamed disease and high mortality on Richmond's Black population and attempted to publish reports with mortality statistics that excluded the Black population in order to make the city seem healthier and more enticing for investors.
Like other growing "New South" cities such as Baltimore and Atlanta, Richmond
struggled with its history of slavery and white supremacy. White public health officials in Richmond ignored substandard living conditions in many of the city's
poorer areas, including Butchertown, and diverted resources away from areas
with high populations of Black people to areas inhabited primarily by middle-

and upper-class white residents. Increasing industrialization, population growth, and public health concerns contributed to increased mortality and prostitution in areas like Butchertown.[8]

As parish leaders, the Barretts set up help stations in Butchertown and organized aid for women sex workers, both white and Black, offering them warm clothes, food, and prayer. Waller Barrett described the area as teeming with "sin, and wickedness, and want upon every side," and despite perceiving much of what she saw in Butchertown as "vice," she also developed a true concern for women sex workers who, in her eyes, were caught in an endless web of exploitation.[9] Although they were not completely free from sin, Waller Barrett came to believe that sex workers were simply women led astray and cast aside by an unsympathetic society. Much in line with the gender consciousness of many social purity reformers, she began to see prostitution and the sexual double standard as elements of women's second-class status in society, not only as a moral failing of the individual. Waller Barrett's experience with sex workers in Richmond changed her perception of "scarlet women." Instead of the vipers of wickedness she had been brought up fearing, most of the women she encountered were working to survive in whatever ways they could, and society's scorn kept them in a cycle of exploitation and poverty. This sex consciousness shaped her reform efforts for the rest of her life.[10]

Motherhood became the touchstone for Waller Barrett's reform work, and she often described the moment when she resolved to devote her life to fallen women and girls. While living in Richmond, a woman with an infant came to the Barrett's home begging for food and clothing. The mother told the Barretts she was a country girl who fell in love with a man who promised to marry her. She followed him to the city, succumbed to his charms, and became pregnant. Once she told her "gentleman" about the pregnancy he abandoned her, leaving her on the streets of Richmond with a fatherless child. This was a familiar story to many social purity reformers, who often painted fallen women as ignorant country girls, beguiled by the machinations of cunning men. Waller Barrett's origin story seems to be no exception. It is impossible to know if the abandoned mother was an amalgam of numerous women Waller Barrett encountered, a pitiful figure recognizable to sentimental culture designed to pluck the heartstrings of like-minded or skeptical readers, or if the episode actually took place the way she described.[11]

Whatever the case, Waller Barrett relayed the intimate connection she felt with the young mother through their shared motherhood, as her own firstborn was only a few months older than the woman's baby. She later wrote, "The man who had come and wooed me had been honorable and good: the man who had wooed her had been dishonorable and unfaithful, and to this fact more than anything else, possibly, was due the great difference in our lives from that time on."[12] According to Waller Barrett, although the mother's sexual indiscretion had resulted in pregnancy and left her and her child homeless, her unfortunate situation was not created by her sexual missteps alone but from the way society treated her after a man had not upheld his patriarchal duty. It was acceptable to cast shame on a single mother, as "good men and bad men, good women and bad women stood shoulder to shoulder to keep her down and out, to make it almost impossible for her to be an honest woman and true mother," Waller Barrett wrote.[13] They both experienced the pain of childbirth, and both faced death when they brought their sons into the world, but Waller Barrett lived a life of comfort within a sphere of married domesticity, while her abandoned "sister" wandered the streets in shame. She positioned the chance meeting as the moment she decided to dedicate her life to fighting the sexual double standard that left single mothers homeless and betrayed, while their seducers continued to live life with abandon.

Not unlike Crittenton's experience with Florence's child-angel, Waller Barrett heard "with startling distinctness" God's voice in that moment, and she vowed that her "voice would always be lifted in behalf of this outcast class."[14] This origin story was not unlike the child death of sentimental novels, or the tragic unfairness of seduction novels. The fallen-girl-turned-mother character was destined to a life of hardship, but through her ordeal, Waller Barrett and the reformers she led would carry inspiration and change to the larger society. Evangelical zeal intertwined with the centrality of the sentimental mother and child bond to create a scenario where motherhood had to be protected, even in the face of perceived sin or shame. Love for one's child—not sexual purity—became the source of "true" motherhood.[15]

As Waller Barrett became more interested in aiding fallen women, the growing Barrett family moved to Atlanta, Georgia, in 1891 when Reverend Barrett was promoted to dean of Saint Luke's Cathedral. During this period, Waller Barrett often accompanied Reverend Barrett on trips to Europe, where he acted as a tour guide for Episcopal parishioners. Not unlike Jane Addams and her study of poverty in East London, while on these trips Waller Barrett studied prostitution in large European cities and learned about European movements to both eradicate and legalize prostitution.[16] Wishing to further her reform work with fallen women and single mothers, she studied "everything pertaining to the social evil." Soon, however, she felt that her "lack of technical medical training was a great disadvantage" to being an authority on the issue. She determined that formal medical training would establish her as a professional on the subject of prostitution, rescue homes, venereal disease, and obstetrical issues, so she enrolled in medical school at the newly formed Women's Medical College of Georgia. She graduated with her MD in 1892 and later received an honorary doctor of science from the same college in 1894.[17]

Waller Barrett wanted to be an expert, and she pursued her medical education with the same zeal that a growing number of women entering medical schools did. Her medical education was an extreme achievement and set her apart from the majority of her fellow reformers, both male and female. The 1890s proved a boon for women entering medical schools, with numbers peaking in 1910 at six percent of all physicians in the United States. However, that number rapidly declined in subsequent decades as increasing professionalization and gatekeeping practices tied prestigious medical schools to philanthropic largesse while schools that accepted women and African Americans were forced to close their doors. It wasn't until the 1970s that numbers of female medical students began to rise again.[18]

The Barretts were both from wealthy families, and Reverend Barrett's salary as the dean of Saint Luke's Cathedral provided the family with a comfortable income. This allowed Waller Barrett the ability to pursue her education while paying domestic servants to take care of her home and children. She often took her oldest children with her to classes while leaving the youngest in the care of nannies, primarily Black women.[19] Waller Barrett's duties as the wife of a prominent Episcopal minister often took precedence over her personal projects and kept her extremely busy. She accompanied her husband on another extended trip to Europe during the summer of 1892, where Reverend Barrett contracted an extreme case of typhoid. Waller Barrett took advantage of the extended delay by taking advanced postgraduate nursing courses while Reverend Barrett recuperated in Saint Thomas' Hospital in London.[20]

That same year she collaborated with a network of women in Atlanta and opened a rescue home, putting her reform work and medical degree to task. Almost at once, the home came under fire from local residents who complained that unsavory women would be getting aid in their neighborhood. Waller Barrett and her co-reformers had to move the home to four different rental properties before area residents convinced the Atlanta City Council to outlaw rescue homes within the city limits entirely. This was not the first time Atlanta residents and the city council thwarted social purity reform efforts. One year earlier a proposed rescue home faced stiff opposition when property owners feared that property rates near the rescue home would drop or that the women of the neighborhood might somehow be mistaken for one of the "fallen" women living in the home. Detractors felt so threatened that they promised to tear down by hand any rescue missions that were built in their neighborhood.[21]

Like Richmond, Atlanta was also transforming into a modern New South city with increased urbanization, industrialization, and emigration of rural white and Black Americans into the city. Within this charged environment, women's bodies became a central flashpoint in determining the future image of Atlanta. Prominent Atlanta citizens viewed women as either the city's "best hope" for future progress as respectable mothers raising prosperous citizens, or as the city's "greatest threat," by embodying sin and vice. As residents became hyperaware of their city's urban growth, prostitution, and unaccompanied women, both white and Black, became increasingly important to police.[22]

Waller Barrett used her class, race, and connections to garner support for her rescue home from local white clergy members. She implored the Ministerial Union, of which most ministers from all denominations in Atlanta were members, to support her efforts. Although Waller Barrett was the primary organizer of the home, Reverend Barrett enabled her appearance in front of the Ministerial Union. His role as dean of Saint Luke's Cathedral lent him sway among clergy in the city, and she managed to become the first woman to speak in front of this all-male body. Even though some clergy in Atlanta engaged in charity work, Waller Barrett received lukewarm support for the home, prompting her to mockingly comment on how earnestly Ministerial members agreed rescue work was important, but nevertheless with "remarkable unanimity of spirit they contented themselves with telling it to God instead of also telling it to the public, who needed to be educated upon these points."[23] Regardless, she persevered until she convinced one of the local newspapers to support her efforts. The publicity prompted the city council to appoint a committee to examine the work at the home. Upon realizing the rescue home was managed by Waller Barrett and other well-connected white women in Atlanta, and was *not* the rumored den of vice that they feared, the city council agreed to donate five acres of city-owned land to build a new home, along with two hundred dollars a month for expenses.[24]

Even though the city council offered monetary assistance, the Atlanta rescue home still had difficulty raising the necessary funds to operate. At the behest of mutual friends, Waller Barrett wrote to Charles Crittenton in 1893 asking him for help and advice on building and running the home. Crittenton was traveling in Europe at the time but sent the manager of the San Francisco Florence Crittenton Home, Reverend J. W. Ellsworth, to Atlanta in his stead. The visit was brief but fruitful. Shortly after Ellsworth returned to California, Waller Barrett received a $3,500 check from Crittenton to complete construction of the new rescue home on the land donated by the city council. By this time Waller Barrett had attracted many well-connected, white Atlanta citizens to be part of the project. The mayor agreed to be the treasurer of the organization, and both a matron and superintendent were hired to run the day-to-day operations.[25]

Later in the year Crittenton traveled to Atlanta for the Christian Workers' Convention, a large conference of over two thousand "leading Christian people, ministers, business men, legislators, law makers, judges, officials" where he was a keynote speaker.[26] Waller Barrett attended Crittenton's keynote address and admitted that his speech touched her deeply. Crittenton had railed against the negative connotations that clouded public opinion regarding rescue work, lamenting that many felt that women who assisted the fallen would themselves be tainted or that helping would encourage the proliferation of "vice." The difficult experiences in Atlanta with the Waller Barrett rescue home, but also previous homes, were still sorely felt among social purity reformers in the community. However, Crittenton had a way of inspiring his followers, and Waller Barrett recalled that his words made her draw "a breath of real freedom— freedom from dread of public opinion." She wrote that after hearing Crittenton speak, she committed herself more fervently to rescue work than ever before.[27]

After only three years in Atlanta, the growing Barrett family moved to Washington, D.C., in 1894, where Reverend Barrett filled the job of general missioner of the Protestant Episcopal Church of the United States. Waller Barrett quickly ingrained herself into the religious and charity-minded social fabric of the capital city and became a staple at philanthropic events in Washington.[28] She also devoted more of her time to working with Charles Crittenton and the existing network of Florence Crittenton homes. The years 1894 to 1896 proved momentous to Waller Barrett, Crittenton, and the growing Florence Crittenton organization. On Crittenton's invitation, Waller Barrett visited the Mother Mission in New York City in 1894. She also visited private rescue homes in Nashville and Little Rock that were preparing to operate under the auspices of the Florence Crittenton network. She began assisting Crittenton in transitioning four other private rescue organizations into Florence Crittenton homes in Topeka and in Williamsport, Harrisburg, and Erie, Pennsylvania.[29] Then, in 1896 Crittenton hired Waller Barrett as superintendent of the entire organization, and together they incorporated the Florence Crittenton homes into a national entity, the National Florence Crittenton Mission (NFCM). They established the national headquarters in Washington,

FIG. 7. Charles N. Crittenton standing outside the railcar "Good News." n.d,
courtesy of the University of Minnesota, Anderson Special Collections.

D.C., in the Hope and Help Mission, a rescue home previously established by the
WCTU.[30]

When Waller Barrett assumed the role of NFCM superintendent, it allowed
Crittenton to devote all his time to evangelical proselytizing and traveling across
the United States, speaking at revival meetings, churches, and individual Florence Crittenton homes while living out of his personal railcar, the "Good News."
He spoke to packed revival meetings, often with audiences of over 2,500 people,
about the duty of Christians to look after the less fortunate, particularly fallen
women and girls. Often, he would venture out to dives and brothels near the railroad tracks where his railcar was parked, searching for souls to convert. He carried an evangelical message of salvation and redemption to "lost" girls along the
way, whether they were interested in his message or not. Much of his time was
devoted to soliciting volunteers to organize clubs—or "circles" as the organization called them—to aid and support local Crittenton homes.[31]

Simultaneously, Reverend Barrett suffered from rapidly declining health and
died in September 1896, leaving Waller Barrett a widow with six children at the
age of 39. She never remarried, professing that the sacrament of marriage was
between one man and one woman not until death, but for eternity.[32] As a widow,
she began a lifelong career of professional reform work devoted to the NFCM

and numerous other women's organizations. Much of her activism derived from her religious convictions and her belief in the redeeming and innate qualities of the mother and child bond. Her own birth experiences of being on the divide between living and dying, "standing at the portals of life and death" was, in her words, what strengthened her religious convictions and instilled a feeling of mutual respect for all mothers, regardless of circumstance.[33] She felt a connection to them through their shared experience of motherhood and wanted fallen women to have the same opportunities and respect that married women received. The act of mothering brought one closer to God in Waller Barrett's view, and unmarried mothers achieved respect *through* motherhood, not in spite of it.

Under Waller Barrett's guidance, the NFCM transformed from a rescue home for women sex workers into an organization more keenly focused on supporting "wayward" young women and unmarried, pregnant mothers. Organization leaders still lamented the ideology of the sexual double standard, but they also began focusing on expectant mothers in the hopes of preventing them from giving their children up for adoption, which often resulted in the child's death, and then going into sex work. Waller Barrett often professed how the power of maternity could help a woman who had gone astray, saying, "We believe most profoundly in the redeeming influence of mother love and I have known it to succeed in softening and converting women whose hearts seem absolutely calloused."[34] This idea of "mother love" fit squarely into accepted understandings of male and female gender roles. As one contemporary ladies' advice manual proclaimed, a child "is the source of a mother's greatest and purest enjoyment."[35] Sentimental understandings that mother love solved any moral failings an unmarried mother had in her past led Waller Barrett to believe the "natural" love a mother developed for her child negated prior mistakes. If an unmarried woman embraced her role as mother and worked hard to provide for her child, she was worthy of respect in Waller Barrett's eyes. In her view, motherhood was the ultimate human connection and should be protected for the well-being of society.[36]

This viewpoint was progressive in the late nineteenth century, as it granted respectability to a fallen woman without erasing her past sexual transgression. However, in order to gain this respectable status, a single mother must completely devote herself to a life of temperance, piety, and devotion to her child. In NFCM philosophy, fallen unmarried mothers could live under the umbrella of respectable motherhood, functioning in society as working single mothers, but *only* if they devoted themselves to middle-class notions of sentimental motherhood and respectability.[37]

Crittenton workers professed that most single pregnant women wanted to keep their babies, they just needed a means to do so and the comfort to know that they would not be shunned. Charles Crittenton soothed one worried woman's mind by reminding her that most people surrounding a fallen girl knew that she was pregnant, sometimes before her own family did, therefore why not have her keep her child and raise it with a mother's love. He suggested that the Crittenton system provided single mothers a network of Christian women for friendship, aid, and help finding employment for women after they left the Crittenton home. He wrote, "most of the girls when they first come to us, feel like giving up their children, and it is only after the mother love has asserted itself, and they have become converted and want to do their full duty, that they want to retain their children."[38] His view highlighted how Crittenton philosophy created a space for single, working mothers within society while also adhering to a language of sentimentalism and maternal duty. They converted fallen women to mother love, not unlike a conversion to Christianity. Although religious conversion was never a requirement at any Crittenton home, the language of conversion, Protestant Christianity, and the sentimental power of the mother and child bond pervaded much of the Crittenton experience.

The organizational shift from a focus on rescuing sex workers to helping single mothers is exemplified through the Hope and Help Mission in Washington, D.C. When the NFCM took the mission over from the WCTU they began to focus on unmarried mothers over all else. Waller Barrett indicated that the original intent of the Washington house was to rescue sex workers and matter-of-factly noted that that "class" of women simply did not look for help in the numbers needed to support a rescue home. Instead, reformers at the rescue home found themselves catering to "betrayed and deserted girls" and those that could be prevented from yielding to temptations as opposed to a focus on women already participating in sex work.[39] Waller Barrett and other Crittenton reformers felt that a mother's love for her child could often provide a motivation for change that was lacking in sex workers.

It is entirely possible that women entered the Hope and Help Mission under the auspices of a betrayed girl, skewing Waller Barrett's numbers. Young women may have felt shame or wanted to avoid the patronizing and sermonizing that might come along with being "rescued" from prostitution. They may have wanted to seem more deserving and thus changed their life stories to elicit sympathy, not pity or scorn from reformers at the mission. Surely many women sought shelter at the home who had received money in exchange for sex but did not consider themselves hardened prostitutes. Not unlike Josie Washburn's earlier critique of purity reformers who insisted that women wear "the brand" of shame in order to receive help from their rescue missions, some women may have made themselves into a more sympathetic figure in the eyes of middle-class reformers in order to gain admission to the Hope and Help Mission. In order to gain admittance to the mission, women had to exhibit real or feigned vulnerability from the "hands of wicked and designing persons" to be worthy of assistance. On the other hand, Waller Barrett was keenly aware of public scrutiny and the ability to get private donations and voluntary assistance from the community. "Betrayed and deserted girls" garnered more sympathy, attention, and money than unrepentant streetwalkers, perhaps prompting her to make such statements.[40]

Waller Barrett became a key figure in creating early ties between private charity and public support of social welfare programs. When the NFCM formed, all organizations calling themselves Crittenton homes came under the auspices of the National. Thereafter, Waller Barrett used her connections in D.C. to secure a congressional charter for the NFCM in 1898. A congressional charter provided acceptance and prestige to an organization and was normally given to entities that operated in the public interest.[41] The NFCM charter was granted, much to the chagrin of some social reformers who believed the state and charity should remain entirely separate. The superintendent of charities for the District of Columbia publicly chastised Waller Barrett and the NFCM for seeking the charter and for requesting appropriations from the District of Columbia for the D.C. Hope and Help Mission, which it received. The D.C. superintendent went on to say, "This is woman's work for woman. It should be left untouched by the hand of officialdom ... To subsidize every agency which is 'doing good work' would rob charity of its peculiar virtue and place it on the level of politics."[42] As much as some officials wished for charity work to stay in the realm of selfless love and women's devotion, Waller Barrett pushed back against notions that women's reform work should be unofficial, unrecognized, and unpaid labors of love. She used her Washington connections to strengthen the NFCM by securing congressional support and public funding through other means besides the franchise.[43]

Maternalists like Waller Barrett were very aware of the fine line they had to tow when entering the political realm, a space historically off-limits to women. They were stepping out of the Victorian home and into the turn-of-the-century public sphere by extending a woman's capacity to mother, care, and nurture from her own family to the vulnerable of society. The self-awareness of women entering political discussion, particularly when it concerned women and children, is evident in a poem from the *Florence Crittenton Magazine* from 1899:

Women's Sphere

They talk about a woman's sphere,
As though it had a limit;
There's not a place on earth or heaven,
There's not a task to mankind given,
There's not a blessing nor a woe
There's not a whisper, Yes or No,
There's not a life or death or birth,
That has a feather's weight of worth
  Without a woman in it.[44]

The poem's first lines summed up the maternalist movement in one stanza, mockingly pointing out that the "private" or "women's" sphere had no limit. The very impetus behind the maternalist movement was the idea that women made and mothered everything. They were the mothers that birthed the men that inhabited the public sphere. Therefore, if women were wise enough to raise men that ruled, they were wise enough (or perhaps wiser) to help mold and shape the public sphere, especially when it governed the lives of women and children. Maternalists like Waller Barret stressed how women's sentimental reform work, if translated into efficient, nonpartisan, and tough-minded public action, could bring social progress.

CHAPTER 6

Redemption through
Mother Love

SENTIMENTALITY MARCHES
INTO THE PROGRESSIVE ERA

Charles N. Crittenton, the founder of our House, and Kate Waller Barrett,
his successor, knew what it was to love and sacrifice for their flesh and
blood; and today our Florence Crittenton Homes should mean to us an
extension of that love and sacrifice; for they are the sanctuaries where
nameless little children may come into their heritage of mother love.[1]

Kate Waller Barrett proved an adept organizer and even though each Florence
Crittenton home was technically an entity unto itself, there were certain expectations a home had to maintain in order to keep the moniker of "Florence Crittenton." The most important was that babies must be kept with their mothers, with
rare exceptions.[2] This was a particular movement away from most other rescue
homes, asylums, or maternity homes where babies were adopted out or lived in
an institution under the assumption it was better for the child to be raised away
from the bad influence of its mother.[3] Part of Waller Barrett's job entailed con-
vincing the public and other charity workers that the NFCM's focus on keeping mother and child together was a worthwhile endeavor. One way she did this
was through the *Florence Crittenton Magazine*, a monthly periodical designed to
keep homes abreast of what was going on nationally but also a means of soliciting interest and donations from the general public. The cherubic faces of fat
and happy babies accompanied stories meant to tug at the heartstrings and encourage those who wished to create "a better class of men and women" to give
freely to the Florence Crittenton homes. Article writers ensured that those Chris-

tians who wanted to "hasten the millennium," would surely do so by helping the Crittenton babies and their redeemed mothers.[4] Most importantly, the magazine provided a means for the NFCM to show how fallen women could be redeemed through the power of mother love and how important the Crittenton homes were in fostering the bond between mother and child.

In addition to fostering the sentimental power of motherhood, the NFCM emphasized the scientific benefits of keeping mother and baby together. NFCM records revealed low infant mortality rates among babies born out of wedlock in Crittenton homes, which they attributed to good medical care and breastfeeding for at least six months.[5] Nationally, babies born out of wedlock had a mortality rate up to three times higher, approximately 200–300 deaths per 1,000, than those born to married parents with an average of 95 deaths per 1,000 births.[6] Individual NFCM homes published their monthly reports in the *Florence Crittenton Magazine*, including deaths of mothers and infants. This number was typically very low, between one and five per home, per year. Some homes were able to brag they had no infant deaths for an entire year, which they attributed to breastfeeding and keeping babies with their mothers.[7]

Waller Barrett used breastfeeding as a way to position the NFCM as experts on the social issues of illegitimate children and infant mortality and highlighted how the NFCM was a leading authority on infant mortality prevention. In a speech delivered to the 1910 meeting of the National Conference of Charities and Correction in Saint Louis, she chastised charity organizations that separated mother and child, going so far as to call one Saint Louis maternity hospital's board of managers guilty of murder by "robbing these children of their rightful food." Of the ninety-six babies born there the previous year, three were stillborn and three were adopted. Ten babies were boarded in institutions, of which six died, while the remaining seventy-nine babies who stayed with their mothers in the home and were nursed survived. Channeling the righteous indignation so familiar in sentimental novels, Waller Barrett lamented, "The voices of thousands of these helpless little ones who have been condemned to death by starvation cry unto high Heaven for vengeance."[8] Repeatedly, she forcefully pointed out that separating mother and child resulted in higher rates of infant mortality. She situated the NFCM as experts who knew how best to deal with single mothers and illegitimate children in the most humanitarian and practical way possible.

Articles frequently reassured the curious public that Crittenton homes were clean, safe, and expertly run, while other articles outlined the day-to-day operations of the home. These highlighted the expert, qualified care that the babies received from NFCM doctors and nurses. One early Crittenton article walked a reader through the daily operations of a home and highlighted the centrality of breastfeeding to the workday. Mothers spent the majority of their day either learning skills for future employment, doing chores, or taking classes in literacy or Bible study. Babies and toddlers stayed in the supervised nursery. Mothers visited the nursery at designated times throughout the day to nurse their babies. At the end of the workday, the babies slept with their mothers in their room. The article touted the scientific methods that Crittenton matrons and nurses followed, like scheduled breastfeeding, but stressed that they took the individual needs of each mother and child into account.[9]

The Crittenton daily schedule was designed to allow mother and child ample time to breastfeed and spend time with one another. Even many married working-class mothers did not have the time or opportunity to breastfeed and bond with their children because the financial demands on their labor often forced them to forgo breastfeeding in lieu of unpasteurized cow's milk or subpar baby formulas, making the Crittenton focus on breastfeeding quite extraordinary. The bonding time was imperative to reducing the number of single mothers who gave their children up for adoption and lessened the number of babies that died from lack of proper nutrition. However, single mothers staying in Crittenton homes did not have a choice as to whether they would breastfeed or not. They were expected to nurse their own child in addition to wet nursing orphaned or abandoned babies in the home if they were physically able to do so. Waller Barrett and Crittenton workers told mothers that they must nurse their babies because the milk produced naturally "is absolutely necessary for starting that child properly in life." Only diseases like tuberculosis or syphilis were acceptable excuses not to breastfeed.[10]

In addition to keeping babies with their mothers, Crittenton homes had to provide a pseudo family for occupants, surrounding "a girl with strong, self-reliant Christian women, who can make her understand that a respectable life is available for her, if she labours faithfully."[11] Women and girls who stayed in the home were instructed by a wise but stern matron on lessons in domesticity, reading, writing, simple nursing, and Bible study. As Superintendent, Waller Barrett insisted that missions have a home-like feel and be devoid of any institutional features if possible. Of course, "home-like" was fraught with racism and classism, as the term meant many things to many people. Occupants' power to control their daily activities was virtually nonexistent as Crittenton matrons and other employees, like nurses, demanded a strict schedule of organized activities. Even reading choices were curated by well-meaning matrons to shape girls' minds into

FIG. 8. "Mary 1 yr., breastfed." Picture taken at the Florence
Crittenton San Francisco Home, 1917, Library of Congress.

vessels capable of "wholesome subjects of conversation." Women staying in the
home were advised not to speak of their past transgressions while there but instead to focus on loving their baby, learning proper decorum, and gaining a skill
or trade so that they might be able to support themselves and their child when
they left.[12] Some homes did not teach a trade specifically but taught the girls useful skills such as millinery and basic "industrial training" like cooking, cleaning,
simple nursing, and laundry. Homes also acted as *ad hoc* employment agencies,
helping mothers find paid work in homes and businesses that allowed them to
bring their baby with them.[13]

Crittenton officials recommended a woman stay for at least six months in
the home, maintaining that women and girls who came to the homes for help
needed to distance themselves from their former lives and acquaintances. By im-
mersing themselves in the day-to-day operations of the Crittenton home, matrons and Crittenton workers argued that occupants would entirely separate
themselves from the negative influences that colored their past and possibly led
them to need the Crittenton home in the first place. They also argued that staying at least six months allowed new mothers a substantial opportunity to fully
bond with their baby and learn "right living."[14] Many women who came to Crittenton homes between 1883 and 1910 stayed the entire time asked of them.[15]
However, not all homes could afford to keep girls for a full six months. Many were

overcrowded and had waiting lists to get in. Even though Crittenton aided individual homes with his personal funds, and some homes received municipal or state funding assistance, most homes still relied on fundraising for the bulk of their operating expenses.[16]

Crittenton matrons and workers sought to mold occupants into model citizens through motherhood, but the social control element could be too restrictive for some women and girls. Reformer Helen Campbell often heard comments such as, "I want to do better; but, oh, I can't be shut up in one of those places," when referring to such rescue homes.[17] Even though NFCM policy dictated that homes should be warm and inviting, there was a constant element of surveillance and uneven power balances inside Crittenton homes. What seemed scientific, loving, and moral to maternalist reformers negated the rights of self-determination for occupants.[18]

Waller Barrett's tenure as head of the NFCM corresponded with a shift in the ways that adolescent girls experimented with their sexuality and experienced relationships with men outside of Victorian standards of propriety. Single, wage-earning women wanted to experience the fun and, as historian Kathy Peiss chronicled, the "cheap amusements" that the new century had to offer.[19] The low wages women earned made the custom of "treating" inviting, where men treated women to the evening's entertainment, and, in return, women repaid them with companionship or sexual favors. One salesgirl commented that, "If [girls] are agreeable they are invited out a good deal, and they are not allowed to pay anything."[20] This form of reciprocal entertainment led Jane Addams to caution that a girl's "love of pleasure ... turns into all sorts of malignant and vicious appetites," when she does not have a good outlet of expression. Too much "pleasure" could get a girl into trouble.[21]

Even so, the NFCM continued to rehash the prescriptive literature of the tricked or fallen girl. "Little Jane Smith" was one of the earliest such stories told in the pages of the *Florence Crittenton Magazine*. It was the story of Jane, a teen-aged schoolgirl who fell in love with a handsome gentleman who seduced her. She thought the two were engaged to be married, but after impregnating her, Jane's dashing gentleman disappeared and continued unencumbered while "little Jane" wound up working as a sex worker in a brothel. When her beauty faded and alcohol became her only solace, Jane committed suicide by drinking a bottle of poison. This seduction story followed the same sentimental seduction trope as *Charlotte Temple*, which remained popular throughout the nineteenth century. A rakish man took advantage of a girl's naiveté and then left her to her fate of becoming a sex worker and/or an early death. However, "Little Jane Smith" promised readers that Florence Crittenton homes offered another path for a betrayed girl like Jane. She could redeem herself and become respectable through the power of her own motherhood, under the direct tutelage of dutiful Christian Crittenton women of course.[22]

Understandings of adolescent female sexuality between the founding of the NFCM in 1896 and the beginning of the 1910s still relied on the seduction narrative and elements of social purity to a large extent. Waller Barrett described Crittenton work as a critical reaction to the unfairness of the sexual double standard and claimed in 1908 that the majority of girls coming to their homes had been "betrayed." Adhering to the seduction narrative, she wrote, "how often woman's extremity is man's opportunity, and if it were not for our homes they would invariably become inmates of haunts of sin and the seduced very soon become the seducer."[23] In reality, women did not become sex workers as the result of giving birth to illegitimate children in the numbers that social reformers claimed. Additionally, women who did exchange sex for money, particularly within brothels, often had access to knowledge about contraception and abortion, negating their need for a maternity home. Nevertheless, Crittenton work was touted as benefiting girls, and the rest of society, by making productive, wage-earning members of society as opposed to prostitutes.[24]

As the Victorian nineteenth century gave way to the Progressive Era of the early twentieth, ideas about betrayed and fallen women took on more biological meanings, and a transition in the way reformers and social workers understood female sexuality took place. The betrayed or "tricked" girl of the nineteenth century began to turn into the delinquent or "feebleminded" girl of the twentieth. Feebleminded was a term used, especially in the case of women, as a category of mental deficiency that held the potential to undermine society by reproducing other defective or feebleminded children. The term "feebleminded" was a fundamental part of eugenic discourse that postulated deviancy was inherent in certain bodies. If those bodies could be prevented from reproducing, social ills like poverty, immorality, and disability would cease to exist. This in turn increased the desire by some reformers, doctors, lawmakers, and scientists to police the bodies of fertile-age women who acted outside the bounds of sexual propriety. Historian Michael Rembis found that cultural fears over the rise of an underclass of girls who did not conform to *proper* sexual morality, who lived in poverty, and who theoretically reproduced these traits in generation after generation led early twentieth-century maternalists and social reformers to segregate "deviant" fertile-age women inside state reformatories. Increasingly these so-called sex delinquents were deemed feebleminded and segregated from general society so that they could not reproduce their reputed deficiencies. In general, social workers slowly started to view adolescent girls' sexuality not as a byproduct of men's lust but the manifestation of deliberate and dangerous acts of immorality, deviant enough to warrant rehabilitation and incarceration.[25]

Eugenic discourse played a large role in determining who was deemed dangerous enough for rehabilitative incarceration. In 1903 Waller Barrett wrote, "If any girl is so incompetent that after two years' training, such as we give, she is not able to earn her living, she should be kept indefinitely, instead of being turned adrift in the world to be preyed upon by the vicious." This statement shows this transformation in thinking, as there is an acknowledgment that male lust will take advantage of a girls' incompetence, yet her body is perceived as dangerous because she could "bring into the world a number of children to be cursed in inherited disease, and to be a burden upon the State to support."[26] However, the Crittenton line maintained that most single mothers were not feebleminded but suffered at the hands of an unsympathetic society. The NFCM bragged that their compassionate yet scientific methods of dealing with illegitimacy benefited society *and* saved the taxpayer money by keeping mothers and children off local poor relief, arguing their method of keeping mother and child together gave a single mother a powerful incentive to right living.[27]

This viewpoint acknowledged a popular understanding that illegitimacy was the result of bad behavior but, in opposition to eugenic thinking, positioned the bond between mother and child as a redeeming quality. The NFCM taught single mothers how to be self-sufficient by teaching them a trade or helped them find work in domestic service because it was a job to which they could bring their children. This allowed women to keep their babies while also earning an income, thus staying free of local poor relief roles. This assertion strengthened the NFCM's argument that mother and child should stay together, even if the child was illegitimate. Their foundational belief, that illegitimacy did not trump motherhood, meant that women could work, lack a male breadwinner, yet still regain *and* retain respectability and their child.[28]

Professional opinions began to have more sway over the day-to-day decisions in evangelical organizations like the NFCM after the 1910s. Waller Barrett took pride in keeping the NFCM as clued in to modern scientific concepts as possible, while maintaining the organization's particular focus on the sentimental mother and child bond. This resulted in a period of transition and inconsistency, where girls in Crittenton homes drifted between being perceived as tricked girls and helpless incompetents, with both monikers relying on a lack of agency. NFCM homes were reserved for first time "offenders" and only rarely did a girl get a second chance in a Crittenton home. In 1910 Waller Barrett highlighted how the NFCM used "professional" services in deciding whether to admit a girl with a second unwed pregnancy. If a pregnant girl came for admittance to a home, Crittenton officials examined the girl's previous pregnancy experience. If there were questions about the adequacy of the girl's care or situation, such as if she had access to counseling services, the diagnosis of a psychiatrist was requested. Or, in the case of referral by a community agency, the case worker was consulted. This reliance on the opinions of professional "experts" operated to further define certain young women as deviant, and in the case of the NFCM, unfit for admission to a Crittenton home.[29]

A crucial step in the development of private charities working as arms of the state happened as many Florence Crittenton homes established liaisons within the local courts who referred or brought young pregnant or wayward girls to the local mission. If a Crittenton home had a strong relationship with the local court system, it often operated as a juvenile reform organization as well as a maternity home. For example, the home in Denver, Colorado, began cooperating with the state and local government early in the home's existence. The matron of the home, Mrs. Coton, was appointed in 1906 as a probation officer by the city court system. She guided juvenile girls through the court when they were arrested for suspected sex work and sent many girls to the Denver Crittenton home. Additionally, Denver's mayor appointed a special female officer to surveil saloons and dance halls in order to send wayward girls to the Crittenton home for a mandatory period of time.[30]

Underage girls were not always pregnant when sent to a Crittenton home by authorities; they might merely be acting outside the bounds of acceptable female behavior. Police officers sometimes brought girls to a Florence Crittenton home without a court order. One Florence Crittenton matron in Boise, Idaho, had a fifteen-year-old girl brought to her by local police. The girl was not pregnant nor a sex worker, but was an "incorrigible girl" and they hoped the Crittenton home could set her on a better path.[31] In other circumstances, the courts themselves might call in reform organizations to address women and girls arrested for crimes such as prostitution or public drunkenness. A 1908 raid on known houses of prostitution in Pittsburgh resulted in the arrest of eighty-eight women. The police court solicited the help of local charity organizations in order to "assist some of the girls retained at the Central Police Station. A list of the women showing their age, nationality, and condition was sent to all the charitable institutions in the city, with the request that they call at the Police Court and consult as to what should be done with the girls." The Crittenton home viewed their role in these mass raids as a form of "civic cleanliness" or social hygiene, giving them the opportunity to mold young women into an ideal image of respectable womanhood.[32]

Some Crittenton homes began operating as arms of the state and in many ways functioned as small reformatories for adolescent girls. By 1914 a quarter of all NFCM inhabitants were sent to the homes by a court order. Barrett argued that this demonstrated "the judges and officers of the courts, which always represent the highest degree of intelligence in a community," saw the value that Crittenton homes provided to the community.[33] Girls were clothed, housed, fed, taught a trade, given medical treatment, and offered maternity care if needed. In turn, the homes received some state money while operating largely on private funds. Thus, the NCFM operated as a loose system of pseudo-public welfare and penal system intertwined.

By the 1920s, many social workers and psychological professionals came to label any girl who had sexual experiences, even forced or incestual, as a "sex delinquent."[34] However, the NFCM held onto the idea of the betrayed girl longer than eugenically minded reformers and did not fully support the eugenic discourse that pushed to segregate and or sterilize young women deemed feebleminded. Putting her belief that mother love was all powerful to task, the director of the white Topeka Crittenton home, Mrs. R. F. DeArmond, admitted an eighteen-year-old Edna Waldren to the home. Two weeks prior Waldren had abandoned her seven-month-old baby at the Union Pacific train depot and then fled to Kansas City. When the baby was found and Waldren discovered, the truth came out. Waldren's uncle was the father and had instructed her to get rid of the baby to hide his criminality. As locals followed the story of the foundling baby and its teenaged mother, it became a news sensation. Despite abandoning her baby, Waldren garnered sympathy from the Crittenton matron and was admitted to the Crittenton home.[35]

Many Crittenton workers treated girls throughout the 1910s and into the 1920s sent to Crittenton homes as sexually ignorant or lacking in moral fortitude, not as genetic or biological defectives.[36] Overall, there was a lack of "feeblemindedness" discourse going on within the NFCM between the years 1900 to 1920, the period when other social science reformers were coming to rely on the concept. Even in the 1930s, the NFCM still relied on older notions of the sentimental mother and child bond as opposed to automatically labeling a fallen girl a sex delinquent. To many NFCM workers, the homes were still "sanctuaries where nameless little children may come into their heritage of mother-love."[37] Additionally, much depended on the matron of the particular Crittenton home and how the girl was admitted, through her own volition, court ordered, or referred by another charity organization. There seems to be no evidence that individual homes or the NFCM did much to find girls that left homes without permission, even when court ordered.[38]

A girl's experience in a Crittenton home depended on individual circumstances, particularly if she was willing to adhere to the rules of the Crittenton mission in which she stayed. As the superintendent of the NFCM, Waller Barrett acted in a supervisory role and made suggestions to satellite homes, but she did not dictate policy. Therefore, homes operated through diverse means and in response to local needs, customs, and available resources. Many homes developed policies that did not include the original mission of rescuing sex workers. Some homes only took court cases, other homes did not take any girls involved with the police or court system. Some homes refused to administer to girls labeled feebleminded by local authorities, while other homes dealt with them extensively.[39]

This satellite policy allowed individual homes to choose whether they would accept Black women and girls. Many northern homes admitted Black women and girls on a limited basis while most southern homes did not.[40] There were two Black-governed Florence Crittenton homes in operation under Waller Barrett's leadership, one in Alexandria, Virginia, which opened in 1899, and a home in Topeka, Kansas, opened in 1905. Black women operated both segregated homes. A husband-and-wife team managed the Virginia home. Mr. William Johnson was the home's superintendent, and his wife was in charge of the Mothers' Class and the Sewing Circle. This home not only provided a safe space for pregnant young women but also operated a day nursery and kindergarten for the surrounding neighborhood.[41] Sarah Malone founded the Black Topeka home and became an integral part of the NFCM, attending numerous NFCM annual meetings and working closely with Waller Barrett throughout the early twentieth century.[42] A third home opened under Black leadership in Kansas City, Missouri, in 1925, after Waller Barrett's death. The NFCM did not officially desegregate until forced to do so after *Brown v. Board of Education* in 1954, and even then, local attitudes toward race dictated how many Black women a home would admit.[43] This disparity in aid for Black women and girls was not lost on reformers like Frances E. W. Harper, who likened the discrepancy to two women drowning in quicksand while women on the shore "threw out their ropes of deliverance" to one, while "for the other there was not one strand of salvation."[44] White supremacist ideology was endemic during the period in question and Crittenton workers were not immune to the racist prejudices of the day. Waller Barrett's own views on race were complicated but also indicative of the period where blue-and-gray reconciliation reunions promised renewed brotherhood between northern and southern white men while Jim Crow was codified across the country.[45]

However, the legacy of the NFCM in regard to race is not as clear as some historians suggest.[46] Waller Barrett often lamented the lack of homes available for Black women and assisted Black women, directing her field secretary, Mrs. Hazzard, to help Black women reformers in their outreach to fallen girls.[47] Pictorial evidence highlighted by historian Katherine Aiken indicates that homes in New York City; Detroit; Trenton, New Jersey; Boston; Fargo, North Dakota; and Los Angeles were all integrated in the early twentieth century. The white Topeka home admitted at least one Black girl, even as Malone's "colored" home was in operation. Early accounts of the New York City Mother Mission promised that women of "whatever caste, creed, or colour" were welcome in the rescue mission. Additionally, the Crittenton organization accepted Black-run Crittenton missions, such as those in Topeka and Alexandria, on the same terms as other satellite homes.[48] However, as strong as Waller Barrett was in leading the National Florence Crittenton Mission organization, local organizers and customs shaped what individual homes would look like.

Women's organizing and footwork made the individual homes run and ensured that each home had its own culture and focal point. The Scranton, Pennsylvania, home focused on sex workers well into the twentieth century, after many other homes abandoned the practice. The Denver Florence Crittenton home focused on wayward girls and worked closely with the court system. The Boston home was often at odds with the national organization over funds and salaries for matrons. Some of the homes operated on a strict color line basis while others were integrated. As the NFCM grew and more homes joined the national organization, individual homes operated through a variety of funding channels. Until his death in 1909, and then for many years afterward through a trust, all Florence Crittenton homes received money from Charles Crittenton's personal fortune. Most homes also relied in some part on private charity, particularly through donations garnered by the female voluntary work of a local Florence Crittenton Circle. Other homes, like the one in Los Angeles, received a portion of their budget directly from the city to help defray operating costs.[49] The type of funding received depended very much on the local home, the women and men who ran its operations board, the willingness and ability of the local Circle to tap the network of local women's clubs to raise sufficient operating funds, and the willingness of local and state governments to fund such work.

Members of women's voluntary organizations learned about the work that the NFCM did, as well as political and reform movements oriented around protection for women and children, through women's clubs. Some groups like the National Congress of Mothers had their own magazine that spread information, while other groups created reading lists and book clubs for members to discuss the political and social ramifications of proposed laws, reform movements, and other current events. Popular magazines like *Ladies Home Journal, The Outlook*, and local newspapers also ran stories of interest to women's clubs. Members of women's voluntary organizations inserted themselves into political conversations and provided their input, wrote to their political representatives, and contributed their labor to both state and charitable associations in ever-growing numbers.

Additionally, the increasing connections between private charity and public welfare created spaces for women to hold positions of authority. Although Waller Barrett tended to overemphasize the Victorian sentimentality of the "naturalness" of a mother's love and management of her children and home, she truly believed that those motherly qualities made a woman specifically adept at operating and managing organizations. She argued that the most efficient state boards of charity were those that had both men and women because each sex brought unique perspectives to the table. According to Waller Barrett, "many undesirable things in institutions have not been uncovered because of the fact that there was no woman on the State Board." She argued that women performed most of the labor within charities while men overwhelmingly sat on oversight boards and did not know what was happening within the organization. Because women did most of the labor in such charities, they simply knew best how the organization should run. Therefore, she argued that women should be on the boards and have positions of power and authority within the organizations.[50] This network of reform-minded women's clubs was part of the Progressive Era movement toward an expanding state and federal apparatus in support of social benefits. However, this network largely maintained vestiges of nineteenth-century sentimental ideas about family and motherhood, and their romanticized views worked their way into public policy.

Waller Barrett held prominent positions in many voluntary women's clubs and had working relationships with hundreds of politically minded woman reformers of the period. She cultivated relationships with Progressive luminaries such as Jane Addams and Julia Lathrop. She was an important member of the National Council of Women (NCW). This organization along with its affiliate organization, the International Council of Women, was founded in Washington, D.C., in 1888 as a means to promote the family and the community in public and private capacities. Both groups developed from a conference called by the National Woman Suffrage Association to commemorate the fortieth anniversary of the 1848 women's rights convention held in Seneca Falls, New York. In 1895 the Florence Crittenton organization became an official affiliate of the NCW. Waller Barrett spoke at the NCW annual meeting alongside speakers such as Susan B. Anthony, Clara Barton, and Frances Willard. In 1899 Waller Barrett spearheaded the NCW's "Committee to Inquire into the Proper Training and Care of Dependent and Delinquent Children," which led the organization toward a larger focus on dependent children. Barrett became president of the NCW in 1912 and presided over official partnerships with numerous women's clubs, including the National Congress of Mothers and Parent-Teacher Associations, the Daughters of the American Revolution, and the General Federation of Women's Clubs with the NCW.[51]

In 1909 Waller Barrett helped found the Equal Suffrage League of Virginia and assisted it in growing to over thirty thousand members by 1919. Although pro suffrage, Waller Barrett did not encourage women to get involved in politics for the sole reason of being political. Instead, she urged women to participate in legislative matters because it was their duty to engage in political and social housekeeping. She stressed that women were the natural protectors of the home, emphasizing, "It is not politics but the proper protection of our homes and education of our children that is involved."[52] Through this maternalist movement, middle-class women pushed into the public sphere to take on issues typically left to private endeavors by arguing that matters of the home and private sphere were also matters of the state.[53]

Waller Barrett continued to emphasize the empowering role of motherhood within the NFCM but also in her broader network of reform groups and activism. While superintendent of the NFCM, Waller Barrett was also president of the NCW and established ties between the NFCM and many women's clubs. In fact, Barrett encouraged local Florence Crittenton homes to form Mothers Clubs through the National Congress of Mothers for all expecting and new mothers in their homes. Barrett was an active member of the National Congress of Mothers and spoke at many of the national meetings.[54] Additionally, she was the president of the Virginia state chapter of the Daughters of the American Revolution, further tying all of these women's groups into a tighter web. When she traveled to thirty-two states on behalf of the Daughters of the American Revolution, each state auxiliary cooperated with the local Florence Crittenton home to accommodate Barrett, hold mutual meetings, and provide entertainment for Waller Barrett and other traveling NFCM employees.[55] Thus, Waller Barrett's integration within these women's organizations makes clear that her ideas about "fallen" women and single motherhood were not outside of the theoretical parameters placed on motherhood by many middle-class women. Her prominent role in national women's clubs highlights how widely known and accepted the work of the NFCM was during the early twentieth century.

Kate Waller Barrett was a leading figure in the transition from the sentimental social purity movement of the nineteenth century to the increasing publicly funded welfare state of the early twentieth century Progressive Era. When she accepted the superintendent position of the NFCM in 1896, she began the transition of the Florence Crittenton network of homes from an evangelical organization aligned with a sympathetic male head into a national, female-led organization. With Waller Barrett at the helm, the NCFM attracted more female workers and volunteers and coincided with the national maternalist movement of primarily middle-class women who became increasingly active in the public sphere. She embodied the politics of the maternalist movement that helped push the state into areas concerning aid for women and children. She tapped into a vast turn-of-the-century network of women to push a religiously based, women-and-child-centric political position. In this way, Barrett and the early NFCM exemplify the associational elements of the early American welfare state, which did not appear as a monolith in the twentieth century but formed through fits and starts and often had a decidedly Protestant Christian component.

CHAPTER 7

-◦◦◦✑✸◦◦-

Sister Arise

RACIAL UPLIFT AND THE
ASSOCIATIVE STATE

*Now is the time for our women to begin to try to lift up their heads
and plant the roots of progress under the hearthstone.*[1]

In 1892 Frances E. W. Harper published the sentimental novel *Iola Leroy: Or, Shadows Uplifted*, a story about a young woman of mixed-race heritage who survives the violence of slavery then dedicates her life to racial uplift after emancipation. The novel weaves the tale of Iola Leroy and her younger brother Henry, the children of a Mississippi plantation owner and a mixed-race enslaved woman whom Iola's father frees and marries. Iola and her brother are raised unaware of their mother's former enslavement and mixed-race heritage until the premature death of their father prompts an inquiry into his vast estate and his family's past. Iola's racial heritage is discovered, and she is kidnapped and sold into slavery. After the Civil War and emancipation, Iola sets out to find her lost family members, intent on embracing her Blackness and her quest to work for racial uplift.[2]

Frances E. W. Harper uses Iola's mixed-race heritage as a vehicle for exploring the creation of turn-of-the-century middle-class Black identity. Iola chooses racial pride over comfort when she rejects a marriage proposal from the white Dr. Gresham, who wants her to pass as white when they are married. Her refusal of, "No, Doctor, I don't think that I could best serve my race by forsaking them and marrying you," supports her decision to overtly identify as Black, affirming loyalty to her race.[3] Her decision not to pass is a literary metaphor that exemplifies the development of Black middle-class racial pride and uplift in turn-of-the-century America. As white society increasingly pathologized Blackness, Black middle-class reformers built a movement based on networks of overt racial identity, becoming "race" women and men. In this way, racial pride and racial uplift were ways Black Americans hoped to build communities and gain access to the fruits of the booming American economy.

Harper's novel dramatized Black reform work by exemplifying how many middle-class Black women defined themselves in a post-emancipation America through sentimental representations of respectability, Blackness, Christianity, and temperance. The novel's underlying themes of "proper" morality lay bare internal struggles within the Black community and what scholar Andreá Williams terms the "fear of misclassification," or an anxiety of not being recognized by one's self-identified social class.[4] Black fiction writers like Harper characterized the precarious relationship between racial uplift and class differences in Black communities through sentimental storytelling and, in Harper's case, additional activism. She is most famously known for the 1892 bestseller *Iola Leroy*, but her activism was not relegated to the printed page.

Harper moved to Philadelphia as a young woman to assist on the Underground Railroad. She delivered her first public antislavery speech to the American Anti-Slavery Society, titled "Education and the Elevation of the Colored Race," in 1854. She traveled throughout the northern United States and Canada during the 1850s and 1860s, delivering abolitionist speeches and reading her poetry. Her 1854 work, *Poems on Miscellaneous Subjects*, which included themes exploring the horrors of slavery, was widely acclaimed and by 1874 was on its twentieth printing. She traveled throughout the South after the Civil War, lecturing to both white and Black crowds and, according to abolitionist William Still, "going on the plantations and amongst the lowly, as well as to the cities and towns, addressing schools, Churches, meetings in Court Houses, Legislative Halls, &c., and, sometimes, under the most trying and hazardous circumstances."[5] Her experiences in the Reconstruction South influenced her 1872 volume of poems, *Sketches of Southern Life*, which chronicled her observations amongst freedmen and women. She published numerous books and articles throughout the latter half of the nineteenth century in addition to civil rights activism and race work.

Harper's advocacy centered on racial and gender uplift, living out the culture of sentimentality so integral to white and Black middle-class women's understanding of collective action. She became the only Black woman on the Woman's Christian Temperance Union's (WCTU) executive committee, working as the national superintendent for "Work Among the Colored People of the North" from

1883 to 1890. She combined her real-world advocacy with sentimental fiction by upholding temperance as one of the pillars of racial uplift throughout the pages of *Iola Leroy*. Additionally, Harper was a cofounder and vice president of the National Association of Colored Women (later the National Association of Colored Women's Clubs) from 1896 to the year of her death in 1911.[6]

Harper and her protagonist exemplified the ideal of Black womanhood at the turn of the twentieth century for which middle-class values were of extreme importance.[7] As a countermeasure to racism and white violence, Black middle-class women conformed to "the politics of respectability," which entailed "reform of individual behavior as a goal in itself and as a strategy for reform."[8] The politics of respectability was crucial to racial uplift, a middle-class movement designed to encourage working-class Black people to eschew "immoral" behaviors and convince white Americans that Black Americans were deserving of their respect. "Before character, education and wealth," wrote Mary Talbert, noted reformer and cofounder of the Niagara Movement, "all barriers will melt, and these are necessary to develop the growth of the race."[9] Middle-class Black reformers asserted that their class and gender made them especially qualified to uplift the race by guiding and reforming the actions of the Black working class.[10]

For race women like Harper and the fictional Iola, Black women must be educated, refined, sexually unavailable, and temperate—all traits found in Iola's character and expressed through sentimental fiction as a model for turn-of-the-century race women. These upstanding women were believed to be the best future mothers for the race, creating deeply gendered implications as the uplift of the race weighed heavily on the sexuality of the Black female body. The sentimental bond between mother and child not only functioned as the central point of true womanhood but also the central tenet to building a strong, Black race as a whole.

Through social welfare, middle-class women would guide the race toward uplift and respectability. Black women reformers founded social welfare organizations, such as settlement houses, kindergartens, and rescue homes, to build their communities while imposing a moral ideological framework centered on middle-class values. Through a look at some of these women-run Black organizations it is possible to see why and how middle-class Black reformers operated within the confines of Victorian morality and white supremacy while developing aspects of the associational welfare state. Addressing issues of Black sexuality by prescribing a strict moral code and assisting or policing when that code was broken was an attempt to improve the social standing of the race by intertwining the control of Black women's bodies with the building of Black institutions for social welfare. Contrary to some findings, my research shows that Black women did have a strong impact on welfare formation at the local level and built many private institutions and organizations for the public good. Primarily, these organizations attempted to uplift the race by addressing issues tied to women's sexuality and motherhood.[11]

The Colored Florence Crittenton Home in Topeka, Kansas, is an example of a Black woman-run organization that tied racial uplift with female sexuality, and which received considerable monetary assistance from the state government. The "colored" Topeka Home was one of the few homes in the National Florence Crittenton Mission (NFCM) network that served primarily Black women and girls. The home's founder, Sarah Malone, worked tirelessly for young Black women and girls with the Crittenton organization for over twenty years, beginning with her work in Kansas and later as an NFCM organizer.[12] At the same time, a Crittenton home for Black women and girls exemplified the uneasiness surrounding working-class Black women's sexuality and the importance of Black mothers and strong nuclear families to the uplift of the race.

The role of Black women as the creators of the future of the race, both through their biological reproductive capabilities and their capacity to mold the outcome of future generations, was central to uplift.[13] Frederick Douglass's daughter, Rosetta Douglass Sprague, summed up how important mothers and the home were to uplift in 1902: "The home life of the Negro has taken on a new significance during the past thirty or more years, and the zeal required to show the parents to-day their duties in the rearing of their children should be untiring."[14] Therefore, the "colored" Crittenton Home in Topeka served two aspirations: the social welfare of young, unmarried mothers and the institutionalization of middle-class sexual values in the pursuit of superior future Black generations.[15] Even though young women at the Crittenton homes had fallen, or at the very least were heading down a wayward path, the home nevertheless intended to make "respectable" women out of them.

Sarah Malone originally founded the "colored" Florence Crittenton Home in 1904 as The Rescue Home Society "for service to negro girls" with the purpose to give "help by private boarding" to women who were homeless and vulnerable to prostitution. Malone was known as an ardent race woman in the Topeka community and was praised for doing "rescue work among her own people."[16] Malone and board members voted to affiliate with the NFCM in 1907, and in so doing joined the largest network of rescue and maternity homes in the nation, complete with funding from the NFCM home office.[17] In her first official report to the NFCM, Malone proclaimed that, "We have succeeded in getting some of the best people of my race interested in this much needed work" and asked the white leadership and readership of the NFCM's magazine for "prayers and continued interest of the friends of my race."[18] *The Topeka State Journal*, a white publication, touted the colored Florence Crittenton Home as the only home of its kind for Black women and girls. In reality, many rescue and maternity homes for Black women operated in cities like New York City; Saint Louis; Los Angeles; Kansas City; and Indianapolis at the time. Additionally, many NFCM homes in northern cities operated integrated homes.[19]

However, Kansas presented a unique locale for Black women's reform work as thousands of Exodusters, formerly enslaved families from southern states, migrated to Kansas during the late nineteenth century.

Foreshadowing the Great Migration mass exodus of Black Americans from the South during the interwar years, the Exodusters were the first African Americans to leave the South in large numbers after the Civil War. Sarah Malone and her husband Balie were part of this migration. Sarah was born in 1859 in Tennessee, and sometime between 1874 and 1880 she married Balie T. Malone, who was three years her senior. They migrated to Kansas in the early 1880s, shortly after the summer of "Kansas Fever," when six thousand Exodusters migrated to Kansas. Many Exodusters settled in the larger towns of eastern Kansas, namely Topeka, Lawrence, and Kansas City.[20] However, migration to Kansas started much earlier, as approximately 9,500 formerly enslaved people from Tennessee and Kentucky migrated beginning in the 1860s and continued throughout the 1870s.[21] Migration to Kansas was fueled by a variety of hardships, most notably the violence and danger Black people faced in the South after Reconstruction and from white supremacist "Redeemers" who wielded control over many areas. Other pressing reasons included severe crop failures.[22]

The Tennessee-born Malones were in good company, as the largest number of Exodusters came from Tennessee, Mississippi, Missouri, and Kentucky. In 1879 the *New West Monthly*, a paper printed in Atchison, Kansas, promised Black immigrants to the state "a school for every child; -a field to labor. -respect that sees in every man a neighbor; the richest soil a farmer ever saw/ and equal rights to all before the law."[23] Black migrants to Kansas, swept up by such rhetoric, encountered a better reality than what they experienced in the deep South, but they still faced hardships.

The rapid demographic changes caused by the influx of so many Exodusters created a white backlash in the state, particularly in cities like Topeka where many formerly enslaved migrants and their families settled. The Republican mayor of Topeka, Michael C. Case, did not believe his city had a moral duty to aid the migrants and went so far as to suggest that the southern "Redeemers'" violence was a fair consequence for those Black people "who were always talking politics."[24] Absent strong municipal support from white city leaders, cities like Topeka presented unique locales in need of social welfare services for Black migrants.

The first Black women's organizations in Kansas were aid societies to help newly arrived Exoduster migrants. One of the earliest such organizations was the Lawrence Aid Club, founded in 1870, which helped with clothing, food, and housing for new arrivals.[25] Even after the initial Exoduster movement waned, there maintained a steady flow of migrants into the state and women's organizations continued to care for the newly arrived.[26] The Colored Women's Suffrage Association, formed in Topeka in 1887, advocated for women's right to vote but also for social reforms such as temperance and social purity for the protection of Black women lured into prostitution. The Women's Benevolent Society, Lodge No. 3, formed in 1889 and had over five hundred members who organized social welfare through church and private donations.[27] Not all migrants to Kansas were poor; many Black professionals moved to Kansas throughout the 1880s. Over time, a thriving Black community developed in Topeka, and the middle class set up social service organizations that filled a need that city and state officials did not address.[28]

The formation of these Black, women-run social welfare organizations in Kansas mirrored larger trends throughout the United States. Black women's clubs, created in response to both racial and patriarchal oppression, proliferated and built an infrastructure of civic involvement and social welfare organizations that functioned by both public and private means.[29] For example, the largest Black women's organization, the National Association of Colored Women's Clubs (NACWC), had a membership of forty-five thousand women by 1911, and boasted in its leadership some of the most influential Black women in the nation, including Frances E. W. Harper, Mary Church Terrell, Ida B. Wells, and Mary McLeod Bethune.[30] Their politics and activism rested upon a shared identity as Black women, based on a sentimental understanding of the need for welfare for women and children in defense of the race.

Racial segregation was piecemeal in Kansas and by no means universal. Some top hotels and restaurants in Topeka operated on an integrated basis, others did not. There were integrated and segregated schools in Kansas as well as both integrated and segregated public facilities. Many Black Kansans applying for public sector employment found work in professional municipal jobs. In 1889, there were thirteen Black policemen and nine Black firemen in integrated departments across the state. Additionally, Black voters in Kansas voted in high numbers and made up an important proportion of voters in the state. Their votes were courted by all political parties.[31]

Kansas was unique, as the state legislature apportioned funds to white and Black welfare institutions in fairly equal amounts. Kansas state charitable institutions like the State Insane Asylum and the School for the Blind were integrated. The private Kansas Home for the Friendless in Leavenworth was also integrated.[32] The Colored Florence Crittenton Home was opened with funds raised by local community reformers, like Malone, funds from the NFCM, and $407 in state funds for the home's initial operations. Nevertheless, Topeka had both a white Crittenton home and a home for Black women, mirroring many other national reform organizations like the Young Women's Christian Association YWCA and the WCTU.[33]

Like other Crittenton homes, the focus of the "colored" Topeka home was to offer unwed mothers or fallen girls a way to support themselves and their children. However, it was also a rescue home and provided lodging and training to young women caught up in the Topeka court system. The home housed girls and young women ranging in age from twelve to twenty-two and was located at the corner of 24th Street and Jefferson. It consisted of five rooms, two of which occupied the half-story attic. The property included eleven empty lots surrounding the home, which held "thirty-two bearing fruit trees and other improvements."[34] Crittenton-paid matrons as well as volunteers taught young women skills that could be put to use in their own homes or in the homes of others by working as domestics. Residents were "carefully trained and taught different branches of industries," which included cooking, decorating, and catering. Additionally, skills were put to use inside the home to economically support the girls themselves. Much of the work in the homes was performed by the girls, including growing fruits and vegetables and keeping chickens. This labor was not unique to the "colored" home but was a component of all Crittenton homes.[35]

In 1909 W. E. B. Du Bois wrote that "sexual immorality among Black Americans is probably the greatest single plague spot among Negro Americans" because, in his opinion, slavery denied enslaved Black people the ability to develop strong ties to the benefits of marriage. He lamented that after emancipation "the disregard of a black woman's virtue and self-respect, both in law court and custom" further degraded the sexual morality of the race.[36] Many middle-class reformers agreed. Anxieties over "proper" sexuality during the Progressive Era marked a time of heightened public concern over juvenile delinquency and its more insidious cousin, the "girl problem," as many reformers and social commentators, both Black and white, had an intense preoccupation with teenage girls' sexuality. However, white supremacist oppression and violence gave the "girl problem" an added element of contention in Black communities. Not only were middle-class Black reformers worried about Black teenage promiscuity but they also understood that Black girls faced a greater risk of sexual exploitation and violence. Although middle-class Black women, like their white counterparts, attempted to shield working-class girls from the dangers of gentlemen seductors, dance halls, saloons, and the street, Black reformers also wanted to shield Black women and girls from the sexual predation of white men.

As Black middle-class matrons fretted over teenage sexuality and racial uplift, African American teenage girls reveled in emerging cultural expressions and styles of street life, music, and fashion. An older African American contingent of social reformers worried about the new amusements that distracted young African American women from the preceding Victorian ideal of self-denial and moral uplift.[37] Many middle-class reformers wished to impose "bourgeois respectability," as historian Victoria Wolcott calls it, by encouraging adherence to "proper" manners of dress and comportment. However, this type of respectability was not embraced by all, either by choice or circumstances, and plenty of working-class youths rejected its strict formula.[38]

On the other hand, many middle-class Black reformers were sympathetic to the perils of temptation and hard lives. A Crittenton matron recorded eighteen-year-old Leann's "cause of fall" as an inability to "resist temptation."[39] However, instead of casting aspersion on the young mother, the matron recorded how Leann's mother had also been a fallen girl, which undoubtedly contributed to her daughter's harsh upbringing. Leann's mother was also a young, unwed mother. She died when Leann was only two years old. Absent her mother's influence, Leann spent her childhood being "shifted from place to place." Thus, the matron concluded, Leann's "hard life" led her to "fall," as her mother's had eighteen years earlier. Leann found her way to the Crittenton home, where she delivered a baby on January 3, 1919.[40]

Many of the young women who came to the "colored" Crittenton home had similar backstories to Leann. Malone lamented that many girls came from broken families and poverty or were homeless before they came. The home provided them and their babies a much-needed opportunity to receive proper medical care and a chance to bond with their babies and convalesce. Additionally, Crittenton workers assisted girls in training and in finding jobs with employers that would allow them to live and work with their babies. Yet, the middle-class ideal of a nuclear family was always of paramount importance. Malone was happy to report that a number of girls, through compassion and help, achieved a modicum of "respectability" through marriage and home ownership after having been saved and trained at the Crittenton home.[41]

The politics of respectability arose in a moment when it became clear to Black communities that they were distinctly vulnerable to accusations of sexual misconduct. White southerners conflated Black men's political and economic advances with sexual predation. Black men were characterized as sexual predators intent on harming "pure" white womanhood. In the 1890s Ida B. Wells documented how white Americans used lynching to intimidate and oppress Black Americans who were seen as economic and political competition to existing white power structures, all under the guise that Black men raped white women. Wells and others continually highlighted how white male dominance was upheld by a sexual double standard that did not punish the rape of Black women by white men and conflated the rape of white women by Black men.[42]

The notion that Black people were hypersexual was used not only as a rationale for the lynching of Black men but for the rape of Black women as well. White male supremacy relied on a claim of access to Black women's bodies. Black women reformers worked with urgency to shape the morals and environments of Black Americans at the turn of the twentieth century, not only for appearances but in the hope to literally save Black people's lives. Black clubwomen took on an image of unassailable propriety in order to protect themselves from sexual attention and to create moral authority. As Wells pointed out, lynching and white sexual hypocrisy were inexplicably tied together.

In 1904 *The Outlook* magazine, with a circulation of over one hundred thousand, published an article by white social commentator Eleanor Tayleur entitled, "The Negro Woman—Social and Moral Decadence," in which she turned her pen to the role of Black women in the so-called "race problem." According to Tayleur, the Black woman "is the pivot on which the great race question turns." Tayleur acknowledged the "few negro women who in intelligence, nobility of character, and refinement would challenge comparison with any women in the world," yet set them aside as she bemoaned the state of "the great dark, helpless, hopeless mass" of Black women as she saw it. Tayleur claimed the Black woman had become "the Frankenstein product of civilization" because Black women, outside the bonds of slavery, no longer had close proximity to white women who guided them in moral living. She avowed that Black women were licentious and would rather earn a living "any way" rather than "working for it," implying Black women were prostitutes. She described Black women as animalistic, a "furious demon who not infrequently kills her rival or the lover that forsakes her." Tayleur's answer to this "problem," therefore, was to rouse in white women a sense of the "God given and appointed task" of teaching the Black woman how to manage her home; a "white burden," so to speak.[43] The difference between Tayleur's white burden and the self-help ideology of Black reform women was stark.

In order to counteract common narratives, like Tayleur's diatribe, Black women reformers developed a reliance on a Victorian sexual morality based on an ideology of sexual control or even denial to counteract the white social construction of "devious" blackness. Members of the Black middle class felt intense pressure to adhere to Victorian sexual respectability, for their own safety against white men, and to control their tenuous grasp on their middle-class economic and social power. Strong Black families with a patriarch head and a loving, protected mother who raised healthy, moral children seemed to be the best reproach to mainstream white discourse that relegated Black women as easy and promiscuous, and Black men as rapists. To counteract this narrative, Black reformers believed they had to be beyond reproach, exhibiting strict morality and creating patriarchal households with women attuned to the needs of their vulnerable Black children.

Therefore, sexual practice took on classed meanings. Du Bois postulated it was a sign of progress that emancipation brought on the advent "of successive classes with higher and higher sexual morals."[44] Many Black reformers subscribed to ideas that the race could improve itself through proper, strategic mating. Historian Michele Mitchell contends that many members of the Black middle class believed they could "subvert racism" through positive eugenic "solutions and sex regulation," as a means of bolstering strong families, healthier babies, and decreasing Black morbidity. Eugenic theory was deleterious in many ways, promoting racist, gendered, and classed interpretations of scientific theory and human propagation.[45] However, to a cohort of Black women reformers, well-born babies would inevitably promote "race betterment."[46]

To accomplish these goals, sexual intercourse was to be in moderation and *only* within a marriage.[47] This is why social welfare organizations like the "colored" Crittenton home were intensely focused on young women and teenage girls. Middle-class Black reformers wanted to curb girlhood sexual indiscretions and unmarried pregnancies in order to strengthen the race through strong babies born into stable Black nuclear homes. Steering teenagers and young women toward the respectable path was an attempt to prevent teenage pregnancy and illegitimacy as illegitimate births did not ideologically create the positive, eugenically made babies that were supposed to further the race. Therefore, prevention was a principal element in controlling young women's sexuality for the endgame of racial uplift. As Black reformer Charlotte Hawkins Brown said, "these 'wayward girls' will be the mothers of tomorrow."[48] The "colored" Crittenton home, and reformers like Malone, offered policing and prevention to "wayward" girls through the Topeka court system and reprieve, healthcare, and job training for single mothers.

From the "colored" home's inception, the Kansas state legislature appropriated an equal amount of funds to both the white and Black Topeka Florence Crittenton Homes. In 1909 both homes received $500 from the state.[49] That is commensurate to the amount the NFCM allotted to the "colored" home in the previous year, so $500 was no small amount (equivalent to roughly $15,000 in 2021). The amounts that both the white and "colored" homes received from the state changed from year to year, ranging from $300 to $500, but the amount given to both homes was always equal between the two.[50] Both white and Black Florence Crittenton homes were listed by the board of control as charity institutions, received state aid, and were exempt from paying taxes.[51]

Although the state of Kansas appropriated equal amounts of funding to both the white and Black Crittenton homes in Topeka, the homes did not operate on equal footing. In 1906, the original (white) Florence Crittenton home occupied a three-story building with ten rooms and a dormitory, appraised at $4,000. It also included a five-room hospital appraised at $1,200. This compared to the one-and-a-half story "colored" home, with no adjoining hospital. Even without an official hospital, the Topeka Crittenton home for Black women and girls provided professional obstetrics, gynecological, and pediatric medical care. Additionally, the home provided an opportunity for Black physicians and nurses to gain internship and practical experience.[52]

Both homes admitted roughly the same number of women and girls each year. In 1919–1920, the white home cared for twenty-five girls and twenty-two babies. They had fifteen births and two deaths (stillborn). They took in $3,945.96 and spent $3,837.17. Compare that to the "colored" home in the same year, which cared for twenty girls (all homes referred to them as girls) and fifteen babies, had nineteen births, four stillborn deaths, and one death of a mother. Their intake was $1,636.98 and their expenses were $1,250.92, less than one-third the operating budget of the white home. This is telling because both houses took care of almost the same number of girls and children yet had a difference of over $2,000 in money they received.[53] One reason for the discrepancy in funding was the amount of donations each home was able to drum up. Women reformers often spent much of their time soliciting funds from the community. Even so, private funds for the white Crittenton home far exceeded those for the Black home.

The white home most likely had more opportunities to tap wealthier benefactors who donated higher amounts. Additionally, women and girls in all Crittenton homes paid for their own boarding and care if they were able. It is likely that more white inmates were able to pay for their room and board than were Black inmates. For example, in 1915 the Black home only collected $400.55 from inhabitants, which totaled 26 percent of the home's total intake for that year.[54] Therefore, Malone had to rely on the fundraising skills of Black clubwomen to keep the home afloat. The "colored" Crittenton home relied on the Kansas Federation of Colored Women's Clubs, which aided the home and used it as one of their service projects.[55] Many such institutions for Black Americans relied on the fundraising acumen and voluntary labor of women's clubs. In fact, a 1909 Atlanta University study showed that in at least three states (Virginia, North Carolina, and Georgia), contributions from private individuals and businesses accounted for more funding of the Black public schools than did public tax revenues.[56]

Even though the "colored" home received moderate operating funds from the state and the NCFM, money was tight. In 1909 Malone worried that a $10 insurance bill and a $15 grocery bill were "some very pressing obligations."[57] In December 1917 the "colored" home was in dire need of money and began asking the public directly for funds, in addition to the clothing and provisions typically asked for. By March 1919 the home needed extensive repairs and was much too small for the number of women and girls using it.[58] Malone worried that the home would close because funds were so tight and lamented in her annual NFCM report of 1918–1919 that it was "a great struggle to keep open." On average, it cost $10 a month to keep a girl in room and board, fed, and with proper medical care. The home charged girls $8 per month if they could afford it. However, most girls in the home had no means to pay for their stay and medical care at the home.[59]

Newspaper reports stated that the "colored" Crittenton home's 1919 fundraising campaign was successful and was supported by prominent white and Black Topekans. The white-run newspaper, *The Topeka State Journal*, said the city had pride that it was the only "colored" Crittenton home in the United States.[60] A white editor wrote, "Every child that is born in the world is to become either an asset or a liability to the country. We desire to help those that are born under unfortunate conditions to at least have a chance to make good in the world."[61] The paper went on to explain that this was the first time a city-wide campaign was successfully launched for the benefit of Black residents.

Even though each Topeka home received identical amounts from the state, they did not operate on equal footing. The "colored" home sometimes received increased scrutiny from white organizations in the city. In 1915 a local parent-teacher organization of white women, the Pierce Parent-Teachers' association, decided to become the self-appointed public commentators on the "colored" home. The parent-teacher organization wrote that the "colored" home only housed one "girl" in November 1915. Their scrutiny was in response to the "colored" home's plea for donations. The white club took it upon themselves to deem if the "colored" Crittenton home was worthy of Topekans' cash. Apparently, no one at the "colored" home was aware of any uninvited inspection, and they publicly questioned if one even took place. In a swift response, Malone made a public statement to the *Topeka State Journal*, stating that if anyone from the Pierce Parent-Teachers' association "has ever been at the home to investigate the number of inmates or for any other purpose, it is unknown to any one in authority" in the home. They welcomed a visit "by any *unprejudiced* person or persons" who would like to come and set the record straight (emphasis added). The board of the "colored" home continued, "We should be pleased to know who the members of the Parent-Teachers' league are. As no names were signed to the article. This to us looks like cowardice."[62] The "colored" Crittenton home provided social welfare to Black women yet had to contend with unwanted white oversight.

Since both integrated and segregated public institutions were common in Kansas, one could beg the question as to why the original (white) Florence Crittenton Home in Topeka, founded in 1900, did not simply operate as an integrated home.[63] There are no records illuminating if this was even discussed. It is possible that the white superintendents and board did not wish to have an integrated home. Each NFCM home made its own rules and bylaws and as long as the homes adhered to the NFCM's rule that mother and child stay together if at all possible, leaders were free to govern their homes as they saw fit.[64] In 1906 the original (white) home requested a state appropriation, arguing that the home "belongs to every citizen of the state, as every citizen of the state is at liberty to avail himself of its benefits." Yet, there is no indication that the home was ever integrated, and therefore it did not actually serve all citizens in the state.[65]

It is highly likely that Malone and others did not wish to participate in an integrated home but wanted to build one in which they would have complete control over their finances, board of directors, volunteers, and the hiring of matrons. Black women garnered more organizational control when they were in charge of their own, segregated organizations. When Black and white clubwomen did meet together, they were not meeting in interracial clubs but as *delegates* of their respective clubs. For example, when the NACW affiliated with the National Council of Women (NCW) in 1900, Mary Talbert went as a *delegate* of the NACW to the

NCW meeting in Columbus, Ohio, in 1900.[66] Mary Church Terrell *represented* the NACW at the International Council of Women in Berlin in 1900, when she delivered her address in French, German, and English.[67] Black women were welcome at these women's meetings but always as representatives of their race, not as representatives of women in general.

Nationwide clubs like the WCTU and the (YWCA) organized "colored work" programs directed by white women. Throughout the 1890s, the WCTU organized multiple "colored" women's groups that were controlled by the local white women's organization with the goal of educating Black people under white guidance. This prompted Black women in North Carolina to organize the WCTU No. 2, which other Black women replicated across the South. The No. 2 organizations answered directly to the national WCTU, apart from local white women's control.[68] In 1907 the YWCA passed a bylaw that resolved there could be only one YWCA organization per city, which in the South guaranteed that the "official" association would be a whites-only association. If Black women organized their own association, the bylaw stated it would operate as a "branch" of the main association. De facto segregation of YWCA associations meant, particularly in the South, that "main" YWCA branches were white and had control over subsidiary "colored" branches. Black reformers like Lugenia Burns Hope and others agitated for autonomous, Black-run YWCAs throughout the 1910s and 1920s.[69] It was not until 1922 that the YWCA directed all associations from the national office, as opposed to local (white) control.[70] In light of these illustrations, Sarah Malone stands out as an example of Black women working within, and having true autonomy over, their "sister" Black organization in a primarily white institution/network.

Work with fallen girls among middle-class rescue workers could have the same negative connotations in the Black community as with white workers. It was not easy work, and some African American members of the middle class feared interacting with women and girls who had stepped outside of the limits of "proper" sexuality. The writer of the Black *Plaindealer* warned the "better classes to place great distance between themselves and the 'vicious classes'; otherwise their own skirts would become 'daubed with the mud of contamination' that would preclude securing 'the recognition they deserve and clamour for.'"[71] Kate Waller Barrett soothed anxieties regarding the status of women rescue workers and their charges in the sentimental overtures so common to Crittenton writings when she said, "Women will not be soiled by trying to help their fallen sisters to rise. They can only be glorified as they realize their responsibility and use their power to protect and elevate their sex."[72] Yet, the fact that Waller Barrett had to speak out about guilt by association suggests that some women reformers worried about their own reputations.

However, rescue work could also be fulfilling to reformers and bring a sense that they were uplifting the race for the greater good. Malone summed up her feelings about her life's demanding work in 1926, insisting, "It is a simple calling and I am not a bit more tired now than I was when I started."[73] Single motherhood at the turn of the century was extremely difficult, yet many Crittenton workers felt their taxing work was the stopgap between out-of-wedlock motherhood and certain shame and possible death. Malone and workers at the Crittenton home risked their own reputations by working with "undesirable" women and girls while also adhering to ideals of racial uplift and Christian sympathy so integral to the Crittenton mission. The Black Topeka home took as its motto, "We as a race must care for our girls, when she falls we must take her by the hand and say, sister arise."[74] But race women at the home were dealing with more than just societal attitudes against premarital sex; they encountered the deep class divisions within the Black community. Malone recounted that one of the girls at the Topeka home told her, "How can I be anything, my mother was nothing, my father was nothing, how can I be anything?"[75] Girls at the home were up against more than just their own reputations; they were up against ideals of class and "proper" womanhood.

Within the Victorian code of sexuality, the appearance of purity or moral sexuality was easier to claim when one labored inside of one's own home. A majority of Black women of all economic statuses worked outside of the home, primarily out of economic necessity. Many Black women saw no moral issues with balancing female paid labor with the obligation to tend to the needs of their family.[76] This should not gloss over class stratifications in the Black community. The nature of work differed among poor, working-class, and middle-class Black women. Impoverished and working-class Black women worked in primarily domestic service positions such as laundresses, nannies, or cooks. Many middle-class Black women worked in education, as social workers, and in racial uplift reform organizations. Middle-class women had the wealth and cultural capital to choose work that benefitted themselves, their families, and the uplift of the race, instead of primarily working for the benefit of white people.[77]

Often, Black-run reformatories and institutions like Florence Crittenton homes offered an alternative to jail for many working-class Black women. Florence Crittenton matrons and volunteers were a common fixture in women's and juvenile courts, wearing ribbons printed with the words, "Florence Crittenton Home, Can I Help You?"[78] As the home became an integral institution in the

Black Topeka community, policing young women's sexuality, not only through moral suasion but also through the court system, became a key component of the home. Malone was appointed by the mayor as a peace officer for "special work among the colored people" in Topeka.[79] This was not unheard of as many NFCM homes had direct relations to police and juvenile court systems. It is however further evidence of the effort to curb the sexual practices of working-class girls through social welfare and police pressure.

This was part of a larger Progressive Era movement for court matrons and policewomen to aid women and girls in the court system. Many Black and white women reformers advocated for more policewomen to become involved in protective and anti-vice work within the police and court system. Chicago became the first city in the country to appoint a Black policewoman. Three Black women took the police examination in 1916 and the first Black policewoman was appointed to the Chicago police force in 1918.[80] This was part of a larger movement to insert women into the court system in order to protect vulnerable women and girls inside.[81] Black women reformers worked to transform the court systems so they would treat juveniles as needing correction and guidance, as opposed to jail time as with adult offenders. The juvenile justice system was a way to limit the exposure of juveniles to the actions and crimes of adult offenders. Unlike adult courts, juvenile courts could exercise greater flexibility in sentencing and theoretically concentrate on rehabilitation rather than punishment.[82] Malone occasionally acted as a case manager and used her position in the Crittenton organization, as an appointed member of the court, to create a type of satellite foster care system within the juvenile legal system. Officers of the court in Topeka lauded Malone for her work in assisting the juvenile court with finding homes with stable families for "colored" children. *The Topeka State Journal* wrote, "Mrs. Malone has been able to assist the juvenile court in providing for children of delinquent parents who have not come directly into the sphere of the Crittenton Mission's activities." The paper went on to chronicle that "eight children were placed the past year [1914]."[83] The key was "worthy" families. Attempts to create strong families though moral suasion, the courts, or foster care were attempts to protect and mold children into uplifted citizens.

Sarah Malone was an integral presence within the NFCM. She participated and spoke at many national Florence Crittenton yearly meetings and personally met Charles Crittenton before his death.[84] Even after stepping down as superintendent of the "colored" Topeka home and becoming an NFCM field organizer, Malone stayed indispensable to the home well into the 1930s, acting as a liaison between the matron and the day-to-day running of the home, board, and circle.[85] One of Malone's neighbors, Bertha Dandridge, took over the role of superintendent. Both the Malones and the Dandridges owned their own homes, as did a majority of their neighbors, further highlighting the importance of community and class in middle-class race work.[86]

The work of the "colored" Topeka Crittenton home shows middle-class Black women performing uplift work while helping form the associative state through the conjuncture of private, female-driven labor and public funding. Women like Malone did race work in their own communities and partnered with predominantly white, women-led organizations like the NCFM when it proved beneficial to their goals. Malone used the NCFM network to build a local home for local needs, tapping into the vast wealth of information, social science, and funding available to her through the NCFM. Race work in this way tapped the associative state as well as much larger coffers of money than local organizing ever could while not threatening white status. Malone said to her fellow NCFM workers in 1919, "when our standard is lifted both races will be benefited."[87] However, the goal was always for the betterment of the "race" through the strengthening of the sentimental mother-child bond and its centrality to building strong Black families and communities. The network of Black, middle-class women and community members were the true drivers of uplift, so vital to the health of "the Race," social control and all.

CHAPTER 8

⊸○⌒∾○⊶

The Neighborhood Union

LOCAL SOLUTIONS TO
NATIONAL ISSUES

What does it matter to me what is going on in the next house on the street to my neighbor that is not my business? . . . But woe woe mother—have care you be so thoughtless—so narrow, so self-centered.[1]

Middle-class Black reformers' focus on the home, and the sexuality of Black women, was more than a preoccupation with appearances or superficial aspirations of status but was borne of a real need to protect Black people in white America. In reality, no matter how "pure" Black women were or how much respect they deserved, Black people from all social classes experienced daily insults and violence. White thinking on race was not relegated to anxieties about Black women's sexuality but was ingrained into all aspects of white society. Atlanta reformer Lugenia Burns Hope recounted the experience of a woman leaving the South because of the racism she experienced. The woman worked as a caregiver for a white household and recounted how the little girl she had cared for, who "had previously put her dear little arms about my neck and kissed me" suddenly "drew back her little hand and gave me a slap on the face, saying: 'You are a n———.'" In Burns Hope's retelling, the woman was deeply hurt by this but not surprised. The little girl's older siblings had all done the same when they became a certain age. The woman said to Burns Hope, "Why was it necessary to teach that beautiful young soul the burden of race prejudice which will probably from now on be a lasting memory? How can such an innocent little girl be blamed if from now on it will seem to her that every dark face should be slapped or ill treated?" In Burns Hope's retelling, the experience exemplified how familial closeness, comportment, or "respectability" could do little to compete with the social and cultural constructions of Blackness in the white mind.[2]

Burns Hope, a middle-class veteran of the settlement house movement, created the Neighborhood Union in 1908, one of the first Black woman-run social welfare organizations in Atlanta. Like the Topeka "colored" Crittenton home, the Neighborhood Union functioned with particular concern for young women and worked with the Atlanta judicial system to help Black women and girls navigate the system safely and guide Black children to proper homes and institutions. However, the Neighborhood Union's focus was broader in scope than the Topeka home and was not associated with the NFCM. Established as "an organization for the Moral, Economic and Social Advancement of Negroes," the Neighborhood Union worked on improving health and housing for Black families in Atlanta, better education and childcare for Black children, and initiatives to improve the health and safety of the Black community. Burns Hope and the Neighborhood Union, like Malone and the Crittenton home, organized a privately funded social welfare organization built for the public good, which relied heavily on sentimental understandings of home and family. Eventually the Neighborhood Union, like many Crittenton homes, was also able to tap into municipal funding outlets to further its reform, health, and education campaigns.[3]

The earliest Atlanta charities focusing primarily on women's needs were the Home for the Friendless, which took in the children of destitute women; the Atlanta Florence Crittenton Home; and The Grady Hospital, which provided gynecological and maternity care for poor women. These were, with rare exception, segregated organizations offering services for white women only in Jim Crow Atlanta.[4] The Neighborhood Union was the first organization to exclusively help needy Black women and girls in the city. In its founding year, the Neighborhood Union enrolled seventy-seven girls and young women between the ages of eight and twenty-two years old in classes and activities held at the Union.[5] They learned sewing and millinery skills, took cooking and dance lessons, and played sports and games in a gymnasium. The purpose was to keep the young women occupied, off the streets, and out of the dance halls and other concerning venues. It was also to exert wholesome, moral influence over impressionable youth. Women of the Neighborhood Union intended to save young girls and women "from evil courses by the touch of sympathetic neighborly hands."[6] Yet sometimes more than sewing and cooking classes were needed to steer girls in the right direction. In some cases, the Neighborhood Union, assisted by "Colored Juvenile Probation Officer" Mr. Moore, was able to put a number of girls and boys into reformatories, orphanages, and placed in better homes. Additionally, many "wayward and abandoned girls" were either sent to programs conducted by the Neighborhood Union settlement home or placed in reformatories.[7] In this view, these wayward girls needed to be protected from the harsh realities of their world, which included sexual and domestic violence and the threat of prostitution. Since they did not have a proper home to shelter them, the Neighborhood Union and the women of the organization stepped into a mothering role, acting as the protectors of the youths and extending their influence on the neighborhood and community.

Private charities and city officials worked together to aid and control impoverished and working-class women when they entered the court system. When white or Black women were arrested or under surveillance in Atlanta, they were flagged to a charity organization or matron associated with charities and the courts who could figure out what to do with the young women. In Atlanta, oftentimes the Associated Charities or the Florence Crittenton homes were alerted to seemingly troublesome or in-need women.[8] The Neighborhood Union worked with the Associated Charities and directly with the municipal relief office to assist Black women. Atlanta police records for this period show that in 1913 police arrested 636 white and Black women, but only 452 of them went to court. The remaining 184 women were dealt with by the police matron who either sent them back to their parents and possibly alerted an organization like the Neighborhood Union to the girls' whereabouts, to the care of a social welfare agency like the Florence Crittenton Home (if the girl was white), or to a public institution or reformatory.[9]

Lugenia Burns Hope was born in Saint Louis, Missouri, in 1871. Throughout her young adulthood, she lived in Chicago, where she attended school at the Chicago Art Institute, the Chicago School of Design, and the Chicago Business College. After college she supported her widowed mother and occasionally her adult brothers by working for social welfare organizations, including King's Daughters and the Silver Cross Club. This work put her in contact with Hull-House and Jane Addams, whose settlement work deeply inspired her and connected her to the larger women's welfare network.[10] Later in her life, Burns Hope said of Jane Addams and of settlement work in general, "for fifty years or more [Addams] has sheltered the homeless, nursed babies, organized clubs for boys and girls and industrial classes for older needs. No curtain of race, color, or creed hang at Hull House." She went on to profess that she pursued social welfare work because it is "the most worth-wile human endeavor" to commit one's life toward.[11]

In 1893, while attending a party at the World's Columbian Exposition in Chicago, Lugenia met John Hope, a professor at Roger Williams University, a coeducational Black college in Nashville, Tennessee. After a prolonged courtship, they married in 1897 and soon thereafter moved to Atlanta, Georgia.[12] In Atlanta, Burns Hope found a Black community in great need of social services and community-organized assistance. Growth of the city was fast. Between 1870 and 1880, the Black population of Atlanta increased 64 percent. Between 1880 and 1890, the population increased 72 percent. This massive movement of Black people to the urban environment happened as the average increase of Black people throughout the population as a whole was only 20 percent.[13] Like the Exoduster movement into Kansas, late nineteenth-century mass Black migration into cities like Atlanta created opportunities as well as increased conflict between old and new arrivals.

Booming postbellum Atlanta was concentrated around a central business district surrounding the intersection of train tracks vital to the city's growing New South economy.[14] Black neighborhoods were largely located outside of this area, consisting of six sections scattered around the periphery of the city center. Water and gas lines extended only to the edge of the central business district, leaving many working-class and Black neighborhoods without access to drinking and bathing water. Many neighborhoods relied on water from nearby fire hydrants and local wells up until World War I. Furthermore, trash removal and proper drainage were absent from these areas, causing the area near Atlanta Baptist College to be used as a city dumping ground. This lack of infrastructure and basic city services exacerbated issues of poor hygiene and disease, particularly influencing rates of infant and child mortality. Higher-than-average death and illness rates in many of Atlanta's Black neighborhoods fueled racialized thinking among whites that Black people were unhealthy due to their moral failings, uncleanliness, and biological propensity for disease, instead of on the outcome of a segregated and subpar built environment.[15]

These issues were not relegated to southern cities like Atlanta either. Infant mortality was rampant in America at the turn of the twentieth century and notably affected Black neighborhoods. Most local governments did not fund public health initiatives like trash removal, sewage drainage, or even running water, resulting in higher instances of contamination and disease.[16] In one regional study of Philadelphia from 1900, 1,467 babies were born to Black mothers. Of those, 25 percent died before the age of one. Additionally, for every five African Americans that died that year, two were children under the age of five.[17] Overall death rates across the country were higher for Black people than white. In 1900 the national Black death rate was twenty-five out of every thousand compared to the white death rate of seventeen out of thousand. Statistics of soaring Black infant mortality, coupled with the reality that premature death was 150 percent higher among Blacks than whites, provided fodder to white prejudices while subsequently pushing Black middle-class reformers to focus on health, sanitation, and the proper care of Black children in order to uplift the race.[18]

The disingenuousness was not lost on contemporaries. Medical doctor H. R. Butler pointed out the hypocrisy of soaring Black death rates: "They [white people] have all the parks where they and their children can go in the hot summer days and breath the pure, cool air, but for fear we might catch a breath of that air and live, they put up large signs, which read thus: 'For white people only.'" He went on, "they live in the cleanest and healthiest parts of the city, while we live in the sickliest and filthiest parts of the city; the streets on which they live are cleaned once and twice a day, the streets on which we live are not cleaned once a month, and some not at all."[19] The disadvantages of municipally neglected communities were apparent. Many adverse health conditions in Black communities were the direct result of civic stinginess. In just one example, social scientists found that between 1900 and 1903, infantile marasmus (extreme malnutrition) and cholera infantum (severe intestinal disturbance) were two of the top five diseases that killed African American babies. Cholera infantum was a catchall term for diarrhea and intestinal maladies more pervasive and deadly in the summer months, which could often be linked to impure drinking water.[20]

As much as respectability, education, temperance, and other "uplifting" values were adhered to, the built environment many Black Americans were forced to live in created obstacles to health and prosperity that no amount of moralizing could overcome. Sentimentalizing the unjustness of racialized America, poet Olivia Ward Bush-Banks wrote:

> The mother of the dusky babe,
> Surveys with aching heart
> Bright prospects, knowing all the while,
> Her off-spring shares no part.[21]

The seventh stanza of her 1904 poem "Heart-Throbs" emotionally portrays the feelings of a mother and the helplessness she could experience in protecting her child in an unjust world.

Absent the power to redirect municipal funds to Black neighborhoods in equal amounts of those to white, Black reformers addressed infant mortality through individual families. One way to combat infant mortality was to focus on the care of children whose mothers worked away from the home. As much as patriarchal families and virtuous mothers were a desire and point of focus for many reformers, many recognized that working-class women had to work outside the home in order to feed their families. "A day nursery is an institution erected for the sole purpose of caring for the children of wage-earning mothers," lectured settlement home reformer and writer Eloise Bibb Thompson. Nurseries were for those women "who cannot possibly remain at home to rear their own children because they must support the family."[22] The needs of many Black mothers, whether married, divorced, single, abandoned, or widowed, to work outside of the home led many reformers to open free kindergartens and day nurseries for preschool-age children.[23]

In 1900 Burns Hope attended "The Welfare of the Negro Child" conference in Atlanta where Gertrude Ware, the kindergarten training instructor at Atlanta University, discussed the need for day nurseries. Ware recounted horror stories of children locked inside of homes, or children wandering the streets while their mothers were away for work. Inspired to action, Burns Hope, Ware, and other middle-class Black women and men formed the Gate City Free Kindergarten Association to establish free daycare for working mothers. Within the year they opened two half-day kindergartens and a third in the following year. A wealthy business owner gifted a large stone building to Gate City, and within a few more years they opened and operated a full day care center.[24] Pleas to the community for monetary support linked the emotionality of the care of children in uplift work to the betterment of the race and spiritual redemption. Supporters of the kindergarten were assured that, "the money expended upon these kindergartens is not merely charity, it is an investment in human life that will be sure to bring returns here and hereafter."[25]

Black women urged municipal governments and private organizations to open day nurseries all over the country. In Chicago, women and parent clubs petitioned the superintendent of Chicago schools to have kindergartens at all elementary schools in the city. They argued that working mothers needed a place to send their children who were not school age. Editorial writers opined that little children need the "refining and useful influences" of the kindergarten, in opposition to the "hurly-burly of the streets."[26] By assisting working mothers in caring for their children, Black reformers like Burns Hope and Bibb Thompson consciously worked to "decrease the infant mortality which has grown alarmingly large all over our country during the past decade."[27] Day nurseries and kindergartens were designed to give mothers a safe place to keep their children while they were away working, as opposed to locked in the house or wandering the streets—alternatives that could produce deadly results.

Additionally, reformers believed that day nurseries were a way to provide young children with an idealized home away from home. Day nurseries were not just to keep kids off the streets but to give them nutritious food and milk, access to baths and clean clothes, and provide a healthy environment. Relying on sentimental understandings of the mother and child bond, middle-class Black reformers asserted that their class and gender made them especially qualified to uplift the race by instilling healthy morals that aligned with the sentimental understandings of family and honest work in working-class children. They postulated that having children in daycares run by respectable women was a straightforward way to have moral influence on children. A day nursery would care for children's "physical, mental and moral natures" and prevent children from growing up "among the weeds of vice and sin, going from bad to worse, until they are a menace to society," said African American reformer Selena Sloan Butler. Sloan Butler went on to state that one-third of Atlanta's Black deaths occurred among children, and a majority of those deaths were of children with working moms. For "a small cost to the mother" a day nursery could actually save her and her child's life.[28] To those advocating for day nurseries, it was literally a matter of life and death.

Often these types of kindergartens and nurseries did not fully serve working-class women. Class bias could shape how working-class mothers and middle-class reformers interacted in spaces where they both shared assumptions about the necessity of children being properly supervised or mothered in the public good, as opposed to locked inside of homes. After praising the successes of nurseries in decreasing infant mortality, Bibb Thompson went on to say how infant mortality was "due wholly to the poverty, ignorance and neglect on the part of the mothers of the working class."[29] In her worldview, all working-class women needed was training in childcare. She believed that if working-class women *knew* that their children needed clean milk or fresh air, then health problems would go away. This could verge on victim blaming, while organizing pragmatic services alongside sentimental moralizing.

Bibb Thompson described the ideal nursery as sunny and open aired. It was equipped with small and large beds for proper nap times and a "bath room" with both hot and cold water. Additionally, it should have a wardrobe filled with clothing of all sizes for the "little inmates." As children arrived, they should be changed into the clean playclothes, as the children were said to be "meanly and underclothed," then stripped at the end of the day and put back into the clothing they came in.[30] *The Crisis* magazine described this type of day nursery in detail. The Washington, D.C., "N" Street Day Nursery began in 1904 and charged mothers five cents a day to care for their children. The nursery provided clean milk, but mothers had to bring breakfast, lunch, and snacks for their children. When at the nursery, children were changed out of the clothes they came in and put into clothes owned by the nursery.[31] The Gate City Free Kindergarten Association in Atlanta functioned in much the same way and continuously operated a full day care center available for Black working-class mothers well into the mid-twentieth century. The organization grew rapidly and added four additional kindergarten locations in quick succession.

Meanwhile, Lugenia and John Hope were building their family and professional lives. In 1906 John Hope became president of Atlanta University. A few months later a deadly riot consumed the city. In September of that year the city erupted in one of the most violent and destructive riots and massacres in its history. In the months leading up to the riots, Atlanta newspapers published dozens of salacious articles alleging that Black men had sexually assaulted white women, while relegating crimes by white men to the back pages. Many allegations were exaggerations in a city where even a glance from a Black man was taken as evidence of malevolent intent. The 1906 gubernatorial campaign only heightened the racial unease in the city while the white press fueled the fires. Democratic candidates Hoke Smith and Clark Howell advocated for the disenfranchisement of all Black voters in their respective newspapers. Additionally, the white press ran a series of stories about four alleged sexual assaults of white women supposedly committed by Black men. On September 22, 1906, a mob of approximately ten thousand white men surged through Black neighborhoods. The mob destroyed businesses and homes and assaulted hundreds of Black men and women in the process, prompting Black men to organize in self-defense.[32] John Hope and other men from the surrounding Black colleges patrolled the area with guns as white rioters threatened to burn down all the "Negro colleges." Eventually, Atlanta city officials sent the state militia to regain control of the city. Although the violence was largely contained, white groups continued to attack Black neighborhoods for days and weeks after the initial uprising. In all, approximately forty people lost their lives to the white violence. Slowly, some semblance of order fell over the city, but not without leaving a deep scar on future race relations.[33]

Burns Hope, writing about the 1906 Atlanta race riot in her later years, summed up the disillusionment many middle-class Black people experienced when they realized that respectability would not protect them from white racial hatred. She wrote, "Negroes were quite unsuspecting that their white friends had planned to destroy them.... The Negro will never forget or forgive the shock of realizing that their white friends had betrayed them."[34] It was within this charged environment that Lugenia Burns Hope founded the Neighborhood Union in 1908. Although founded only two years after the most devastating race riots in Atlanta's history, Burns Hope focused her attention on building the Black community from within. She summed up her reform work in one concise statement: "People living in slums do not have to die in slums, nor do slums have to continue to be slums."[35] Burns Hope envisioned a community-wide organization that built a sense of cooperation among respectable Black families. The sentimental and maternalist outlook of the organization meant that motherhood was more than caring for one's own family, but also the community at large. Accepting the fact that most families, particularly mothers, worked for wages meant that it was the responsibility of the Neighborhood Union to mother the children of the community.[36] This "mothering" relied on the unquestioned acceptance of the gendered division of labor and women's unpaid, voluntary work as caretakers of the home and family. Overall, men's voluntary organizations rarely if ever organized around health and family issues, as that was considered the domain of women.[37]

It was Burns Hope's intention to unite the Black community and build networks of social welfare while also policing the community to act within a middle-class standard of living. Burns Hope explained the way the Neighborhood Union was organized: "our method of relief in the neighborhood is to have each neighbor feel the responsibility of his next-door neighbor. So, when families are in need, the director passes the word [along] and the present need is supplied."[38] Access to Black families flowed through women and Black mothers and did not question the legitimacy of "women's' work" as the caretakers of the home and the bodies within. The networks of women in the Neighborhood Union crossed class lines, and by the nature of its system, the Union incorporated working-class women into the structure of the organization.

Black neighborhoods in Atlanta were divided into sixteen zones throughout the city. One woman, who was aided by ten supervisors, was appointed to oversee a zone or section. Each supervisor would in turn appoint ten other women within her zone to assist her, resulting in 111 female volunteers per city zone. These women went door-to-door to visit each home, told people about the Neighborhood Union plan, and requested their cooperation. Once on board, each participating family paid dues of ten cents a month if they could. According to Neighborhood Union records, this strategy proved quite successful. Overall, a total of 1,700 women participated as volunteers in the organization. Each neighborhood leader would meet with the families in her section and report back to the larger monthly meetings.[39]

The Neighborhood Union utilized the social work acumen of Burns Hope and faculty members at Atlanta University and the neighboring Morehouse College. The work and organization of the Union included the science of making "surveys of small communities showing the operations of factors and forces at work therein; and, at intervals, to take a census of the neighborhoods in Atlanta showing the status of each family and individual therein as well as to prepare maps of the sections inhabited by Negroes."[40] Within the first year of existence, the Neighborhood Union made an Investigation Commission of seven women whose duty it was "to investigate, and report to the N.U. every thing [sic] that seems to be a menace to our neighborhood."[41] This meant patrolling the homes and private lives of families and women in the neighborhood. In October of 1909, the Investigation Commission "reported a house of questionable character on Roach [Street]. Mrs. Brice one of the residents of that street was present and told of the many horrible things done there. The Union then decited [sic] to present a petition to the City Council for the removal of this house."[42] In another example, in February of 1911, a commission member "succeeded in getting two families out of her district who indulged in doing things that were immoral, such as breaking the Sabbath and gambling."[43] Race and class intersected with space in these instances. In analyzing the Union's neighborhood surveillance, historian Elsa Barkley Brown highlights how "the struggle to present Black women and the Black community as 'respectable' eventually led to repression."[44] The Neighborhood Union was there to help and to connect the community, but it was also a force used to expel undesirable elements in the name of social hygiene.

The Union operated within bourgeois respectability by working to "abolish slums and houses of immorality; to investigate dance halls, pool rooms, and vaudeville shows; and generally to co-operate with city officials in suppressing vice and crime."[45] It was the real-life enactment of the "proper" Black experience that Harper wrote about in *Iola Leroy* and championed in real life. These Black reformers' Victorian comportment and sentimentality demanded the eschewing of alcohol and activities outside of a commitment to home and thrift. Burns Hope inspired other reformers when she asked:

> The question arises "Am I my brother's keeper?" What does it matter to me what is going on in the next house on the street to my neighbor that is not my business. I am to look after my own home, pay my debts, and carefully rear my own chil-

dren, and that is all the time I have. I certainly have no time to look after those street and alley children. Furthermore I don't want my children to mix with them either. But woe woe mother—have care you be so thoughtless—so narrow so self centered.[46]

However, this concentration on the home and homelife to help with racial uplift and respectability came with a hefty amount of public oversight. The Neighborhood Union constitution held numerous examples of the imposition of middle-class values to uplift the race. One section proposed "to establish lecture courses that shall instruct and help the mothers of the neighborhood in the proper care of themselves and their infants," which addressed the health measures that could be taken to curb infant mortality prevalent in the hot summer months.[47]

Without direct access to money and power, one of the easiest ways to address healthcare concerns and high mortality rates was on a house-by-house basis through individual organization and moral suasion. Some of the earliest Neighborhood Union outreach reached inside Black homes by engaging Black mothers with education on cleanliness and hygiene. Trained Black nurses would give demonstrations and talks on the latest sanitation science, and then Union organizers could go out and share that information with women in their neighborhood sectors.[48] As much as these measures were intended to help, they also shifted the collective healthcare of a community onto the shoulders of individual women.[49]

One of the earliest projects the Neighborhood Union took on was the establishment of a health clinic. The first Neighborhood Union health clinic was held in 1908, which became part of a nationwide, grassroots movement to bring health professionals into working-class neighborhoods. Community members could get quality medical care from doctors, nurses, and dentists. The Neighborhood Union even created a mobile medical clinic that traveled around the city in 1917, giving health services to Black people.[50] In 1919 the Union organized health clinics with seventeen volunteer doctors and twenty-three nurses.[51] By 1924 they had thirty-three physicians and many more nurses, and by 1930 the Neighborhood Union assisted over four thousand Black Atlanta residents.[52] In addition, they opened free health clinics with doctors, nurses, and dentists.[53]

In 1915 the Neighborhood Union began organizing National Negro Health Week campaigns. The health initiative was launched by Booker T. Washington from Tuskegee Institute in Alabama as a means to uplift the race through Black health education. However, it was middle-class and working-class women across the country who carried out the organizing and labor that made Negro

Health Weeks successful well into the twentieth century.[54] In Atlanta, the Neigh-borhood Union used its impressive voluntary organization to successfully pro-mote and gain the participation of a large contingent of Atlanta's Black popula-tion in Health Week activities. In addition to providing lectures in schools and churches and distributing health information door-to-door, the Union also over-saw cleanup plans under the Health Week slogan, "Burn, Bury, and Beautify." Ad-ditionally, women of the Union highlighted unsanitary conditions of businesses owned by white merchants in Black neighborhoods and led school-age children in the cleanup of vacant lots.[55]

Black health initiatives gained the support of white businesses and munici-palities because "germs know no color line." White people recognized the hazards of an unhealthy Black workforce, as the majority of middle-class white house-holds relied on the domestic labor of Black working-class women. One white newspaper warned that "negro nurses would still emerge from diseased homes, to come into our homes and hold our children in their arms; negro cooks would still bring bacilli from the segregated district into the homes of the poor and the rich white Atlantan."[56] Tuberculosis was one of the most feared diseases, and as early as 1909 the white-run Anti-Tuberculosis Association (ATA) reasoned that "any movement directed toward the ultimate elimination of the disease in any Southern city must, of necessity, include the negro population."[57] This racialized fear presented opportunities to organizations like the Neighborhood Union to petition white financiers for increased funding and health resources in Black neighborhoods.

Black reform women recognized that they could use the realities of white su-premacy to tap the power of the state. They joined the white-led (ATA) as a way to lobby city government for better sanitation services without fear of retribu-tion.[58] The Neighborhood Union Women's Civic and Social Improvement Com-mittee, headed by Burns Hope, initially formed to investigate racism and segre-gation in Atlanta schools but soon turned its attention to health conditions in Atlanta homes and neighborhoods. The group spearheaded a partnership with the ATA and formed the Black-run "Negro Committee." The Committee set out "to investigate and report on the housing and home conditions among Negroes," which resulted in five hundred households in Atlanta "colored districts" being in-vestigated for signs and potential threats of tuberculosis.[59] That data was imme-diately used to petition city officials for access to clean water, working sewers, trash pickup, and recreation areas for Black children.[60]

The Neighborhood Union was an example of Black women working for social welfare services through the associative state. Women in the Union who organized into the Social Improvement Committee advocated for the "Negro public schools" in Atlanta.[61] Petitioners to the Atlanta board of education framed the "deplorable" condition of public schools for Black children as a danger to their own community and to Atlanta at large: "A very large number of the children of school age in South Atlanta are running the streets and are liable to become acquainted, at a very early age, with vice and crime of all kinds."[62] Women of the committee were able to secure small pay raises for the teachers at the "Negro" schools as well as a "make-shift" school for the excess children enrolled in overcrowded South Atlanta schools. They were also able to skirt funding shortages by running three of their own summer school programs, staffed by Neighborhood Union members but held in public schools. In essence, they accessed the state, used it to their advantage, but did not actually get direct money from the state.[63] They recognized the importance of working Black women's contribution to their families and the community by opening day nurseries for working women's children.[64] Nevertheless, they also expected a certain level of decorum, especially of young women.

Burns Hope succeeded in building a legacy of Black social work in Atlanta that would thrive for years to come. She established training classes in social work offered through the Neighborhood Union, and in 1918, the Union developed a Social Service Institution at Morehouse College that consisted of workshops and lectures on the prevention of maternal and infant mortality, juvenile delinquency, and health services. This endeavor developed into the Atlanta School of Social Work, which became affiliated with Atlanta University in 1920. She was also an integral organizer in the YWCA movement and acted as the organization's special war work secretary during World War I.[65]

"I belong to this race, and when it is down I belong to a down race; when it is up I belong to a risen race."[66] Frances E. W. Harper wrote these words in 1871, aptly describing the work and burdens of Black women reformers intent on the uplift of the race. Black reformers like Sarah Malone and Lugenia Burns Hope did work that filled a void in the social services for Black women and families. The organizations they founded accessed networks of reform-minded women, worked to build their communities, and imposed a moral ideological framework on the people in their communities, all while developing ties to public funding and support, which formed the associative state. These examples show how the welfare state began on the local level, often developed by women reformers to create social services for women in need. In the Black community, this resulted in workarounds that allowed Black people to access social services. Although Black people may not have had direct access to welfare programs, they were still able to tap public monies, infrastructure, and resources in small and piecemeal ways. This was done through the ideology of upbuilding, which came with the exertion of power over working-class women and young women's sexuality.

CHAPTER 9

───────⊸०৫৶৩०⊶───────

The Women's Welfare Network

REFORM ON A FEDERAL LEVEL

*The prevention of a large degree of infant mortality
requires the cooperative efforts of many public and private
agencies, and of individual and collective action.*[1]

A cadre of female reformers built a network of women focused on child welfare
in the later part of the nineteenth century. This movement had deep roots in the
settlement movement, particularly Chicago's Hull-House and New York's Henry
Street Settlement. These two settlement houses were part of a vast network of
settlements generally situated in burgeoning industrial cities. However, these two
important organizations were not the only ones, as hundreds of women reformers created settlement houses throughout the United States, like Atlanta's Neighborhood Union discussed in the previous chapter. Educated middle-class women
managed most settlement homes with the intention of alleviating the plight of
the poor and immigrants, not only through charity and alms but also through direct action and organizing. It is fascinating to see how many of the prominent female reformers during the Progressive Era had some connection to one another,
through the women's welfare network and to Hull-House and its luminary Jane
Addams.[2]

Addams, founder of Chicago's Hull-House, created an environment where educated middle-class women could develop a sense of self and meaning while addressing poverty and injustice in the urban landscape. Addams was part of a new
generation of college-educated women that sought to put their educations to use

in a world that did not value female professionalism and expertise. The settlement route allowed educated women, and a handful of men, to develop a professional and helpful career path. After a trip to London's Toynbee Hall, which provided social services to the city's East End, Addams and Ellen Gates Starr decided to model Toynbee's example in Chicago, Illinois. Through her tutelage and mentoring, Addams brought a number of exceptional women into her fold who developed a strong activist network capable of shaping and controlling elements of the burgeoning women's welfare network.[3]

An emphasis on community support required that settlement workers physically live and work in the neighborhoods that they sought to aid. Women in Hull-House, the Neighborhood Union, the Henry Street Settlement, and other settlements spent their time and energy physically moving throughout the built environment of urban cities, giving them first-hand knowledge of the spatial injustices experienced by the poor living in inadequate conditions with no access to healthcare, job or market security, or organized public assistance. These lived experiences transformed middle-class reformers as they gained new understandings of urban poverty while their aid efforts simultaneously transformed the neighborhoods in which they lived and worked. Injustices affecting the urban poor often coincided with higher-than-average rates of infant mortality. Because these settlement workers and other reformers across the country experienced infant mortality firsthand or through the communities they served, the welfare of children became of paramount importance.[4]

Florence Kelley was an elemental member of the women's welfare network. She worked closely with Addams and was integral to running Hull-House and New York's Henry Street Settlement, founded by activist and professional nurse Lillian Wald. By the time Kelley began working at Hull-House in 1891, she was already well versed in political and social activism. The daughter of a long-serving radical Republican congressman, she became literate in politics at an early age. However, it may have been her family's experience with child and infant mortality that shaped her activist work. As a child, Kelley watched helplessly as five of her eight siblings died—all under the age of six—and her mother slipped further and further into debilitating depression. After graduating from Cornell University, Kelley went to Zurich, Switzerland, for graduate school, where she became an active member of the socialist party. Friedrich Engels became a friend and mentor, and Kelley translated his *The Condition of the Working Class in England* for American audiences in 1844. She joined the women of Hull-House after the dissolution of her marriage to a Russian doctor, with whom she had three children.[5]

Kelley's activism on behalf of children focused on labor organizing and measures to enforce child labor legislation. Her earliest professional government post came in 1892 when she was hired by the Illinois Bureau of Labor Statistics to study the sweatshop system and working conditions of Chicago's immigrant neighborhoods. This "sweating" system of contingent labor relied on the underpaid labor of many women and children. One of Kelley's co-inspectors described the typical sweatshop as "a basement with an entrance so dark we had to find our way in by the light of matches. There were no windows in the hallway and only two windows in the workroom . . . [the] stench of filth and refuse made this the most horrible hole."[6] Kelley's experience walking through the environment of exploitative labor and tenement dwellings further propelled her activism on behalf of women and children. As early as 1900, Kelley proposed in a series of lectures, eventually published in *Some Ethical Gains through Legislation*, the creation of a government commission comprised of social workers and healthcare providers that could analyze data and disseminate information relating to child health. She would see that vision realized twelve years later with the formation of the U.S. Children's Bureau.[7]

Julia Lathrop was another early resident of Hull-House who formed and shaped the women's welfare network. A graduate of Vassar College, she moved to Chicago in 1890 and, during the depression of 1893–1894, volunteered to help the county welfare department with interviewing neighborhood families who applied for public relief. Later, the governor appointed Lathrop to the Illinois Board of Charities, where she investigated all of the counties' institutions, including poorhouses and asylums for the insane and disabled. Her articles, annual reports, and speeches detailing the appalling inadequacy of these Illinois institutions elevated her as a vocal opponent of political patronage jobs for charitable institutions. She argued that various dependent people in the state, including the blind and the mentally disabled, needed different types of institutions as opposed to being housed under one roof, as they were in many counties. She published *Suggestions for Visitors to County Poorhouses and to Other Public Charitable Institutions*, where she recommended the segregation of patients based on sex, age, and disability and advocated for care that was more humane. In 1903, Lathrop helped form the Chicago School of Civics and Philanthropy. She served on its board until the school became part of the University of Chicago in 1920. Lathrop was also deeply involved in the juvenile court movement. She became the chief of the federal Children's Bureau at the suggestion of Jane Addams.[8]

Hull-House residents, including Kelley, Agnes Holbrook, and Lathrop, created

Hull-House Maps and Papers, a collection of essays and systematic surveys of "each house, tenement, and room" in the Nineteenth Ward of Chicago. These maps created a geographical survey of health, sanitation, income, and nationality in the Nineteenth Ward by color coding public health information onto each block. These maps exemplified what settlement reformers and other charity workers were doing to publicize the threat of poverty, ill health, and exploitative labor practices, particularly in regard to children's welfare. Women reformers, like Kelley, and other maternalist women in voluntary organizations disseminated what they learned via public lectures, magazines, and newspaper articles. Through publications like the *Hull-House Maps and Papers* and public speaking events, these reformers reached other women and expanded the network of reform-minded women. By bringing awareness to the plight of the poor and exerting their expertise in the burgeoning field of social science, the women of Hull-House and those connected to its orbit developed what Robyn Muncy calls a female dominion over child welfare policy in the male-dominated sphere of politics and government bureaucracy.[9]

Many women organized around infant and maternal mortality and the deeply gendered aspects of this problem. Because birth registration was not uniform across the county, only estimates of the nation's infant mortality rate could be made. The 1911 census report on mortality statistics set the infant mortality rate at an estimated 124 per 1,000 live births. A cursory look at a study commissioned by the Charity Organization Department of the Russell Sage Foundation in 1910 of 985 widows and their families showed that almost half of the mothers surveyed experienced the death of a child. The death of children, especially infants, was a visceral reality for many American women. Yet because the United States did not have a system in place to adequately register births, the numbers were never exact. In fact, the chief statistician of the government Board of Vital Statistics deplored the inadequate birth registration efforts of the United States. Numerous industrialized countries had already enacted programs to document and prevent infant and maternal mortality, and there were pockets in America, like New York City, that were working toward more accurate birth records, but the majority of states had no systematic programs to gather the data, and rural areas were the least accounted for.[10]

Lilian Wald, director of the Henry Street Settlement in New York City, led the campaign to establish the New York City Bureau of Child Hygiene. In 1903 Wald and Kelley—who had since moved to the Henry Street Settlement—proposed the formation of a federal agency that would collect and disseminate information regarding the welfare of children. Now that Kelley tied Hull-House to the

Henry Street Settlement, and voluntary women's organizations across the country were involving themselves in the women's welfare network, there seemed a real opportunity for national child welfare reform. Wald and Kelley enlisted the aid of Edward T. Devine, a social welfare advocate, editor of *Charities* magazine, and longtime political associate of President Theodore Roosevelt, to introduce the idea of a federal children's bureau to the president. Roosevelt famously replied, "Bully, come down and tell me about it." Wald, Devine, Addams, and Mary McDowell, another Hull-House resident, met with the president, who supported the idea.[11]

Agitation for a federal response to the plight of mothers and infants from settlements and other reformers resulted in the first White House Conference on the Care of Dependent Children in 1909. This meeting drew national charity organizations and social reformers together for a meeting at the White House to discuss child welfare issues. Two-hundred and fifteen delegates from various charity and religious organizations attended the conference. Of those, only thirty were women, including Jane Addams, Florence Kelley, Julia Lathrop, Lillian Wald, Kate Waller Barrett, and Hannah Kent Schoff—president of the National Congress of Mothers. No Black women reformers were invited to attend.

President Roosevelt opened the conference with a call to address the issue of more than seventy-five thousand children living in orphanages and asylums across the country. Many of the children living in these institutions were placed there because their families were poor and could not afford to raise them at home. Roosevelt considered the fate of these children, coupled with the needs of families grappling with poverty, to be "of high importance to the well-being of the nation." He warned that "these children [represented] a potential addition to the productive capacity and the enlightened citizenship of the nation, or if allowed to suffer from neglect, a potential addition to the destructive forces of the community." Underlying these fears and assumptions was a Protestant middle-class ideology of the proper housing and upbringing of children. Roosevelt warned of the underclass of "criminals and other enemies of society" potentially lurking within a pool of dependent children, "bereft of their natural homes and left without sufficient care."[12] Roosevelt echoed the sentiment of many attendees at the conference when he insisted the best plan of action was to keep the mother and child together in their own home, as opposed to institutions. In addition to calls for a federal children's bureau, the idea of cash payments to mothers in the form of "mothers' pensions" took hold. Already initiated by juvenile court judges on a small scale since 1906, the idea of a "wage" for mothers' services gained traction.[13]

The motive to keep families together, as opposed to institutionalizing dependent children because parents and caregivers were too poor to care for them at home, was admirable in its desire to protect familial bonds. It was also entirely based on the long history of sentiment around child and maternal bonds. However, this ultimately increased the burden of women's responsibility for childcare and their dependence on a wage-earning husband. Jane Addams presented a strong voice emphasizing the underlying causes of poverty that resulted in the need for institutional types of remedies. Addams questioned why America "was so slow" in adopting policies to protect families and workers. She asked why "are we, at best . . . suggesting foster families rather than schemes to protect the father, the mother, and the little children living together as they were meant to live?" She gave examples of other industrialized countries such as Switzerland and Germany that already created state-sponsored policies that promoted the education of children over industrial work and compensated the family for the loss of a wage earner due to disease or industrial accident. She held up England's Employer Liability Act that compensated workers and families for the loss of life and limb. Addams asked why it was that America, which purported to be the most advanced country in the world, did not protect the people who created its wealth along with their dependent children. While other conference attendees, mostly male, voiced concerns over orphanages and foster care, Addams pragmatically targeted the cause of the problem, not superficial remedies that ignored the roots of poverty. However, as valiant as it was, her insistence on family compensation did more to support the family wage system than it did to help single mothers.[14]

Many Conference attendees wanted to press Congress to fund a national child welfare bureau, like the one Wald, Kelley, and Divine proposed that would report on all aspects of child life in America. Numerous charity organizations across the country were involved in programs to alleviate infant mortality, child labor, and family poverty, but there was no central agency to bind their efforts together. The states and private organizations were not capable of enacting real changes on their own; they needed a central organizing authority backed by federal dollars to organize child welfare efforts. The primary purpose of a federal bureau would center on data collection and tabulation

> and shall especially investigate the questions of infant mortality, the birth rate, physical degeneracy, orphanage, juvenile delinquency and juvenile courts, desertion and illegitimacy, dangerous occupations, accidents and diseases of children of the working classes, employment, legislation affecting children in the several

States and Territories, and such other facts as have a bearing upon the health, efficiency, character, and training of children.[15]

Conference attendees favored a central bureau to collect data on child life in the United States but were divided as to how the bureau would be organized. All three of the female reformers who spoke in favor of the bureau wanted a federal board to direct data collection and then distribute its findings. Mary Wilcox Glenn, former secretary of the Charity Organization Society of Baltimore and a pioneer in the field of social work, praised the scientific benefits of a federal board, stating, "We need to be prepared to make the communication direct, to make it scientific." Her plea in the name of science called for the collection of "accurate data" that would be correlated and analyzed.[16] Moreover, Wald espoused the power that a government bureau would yield as only the federal government had the power to collect investigative material on such a large basis. In turn, those that needed that information could "hold the Government responsible" for giving them access to that data. Advocates argued that a children's bureau would be a clearinghouse where disparate studies and programs could be analyzed, organized, and acted upon under one roof.[17]

Although in favor of a centralized board to collect and analyze data regarding children, some conference attendees felt that the government had no authority to distribute persuasive data, or propaganda, in regard to child welfare. Homer Folks, secretary of the State Charities Aid Association of New York and the elected vice-chairman of the conference, believed that it would be a mistake for the "federal children's bureau to take on many of the things that would be extremely proper and extremely desirable for a voluntary association to undertake."[18] James E. West, secretary of the National Child Rescue League, argued, "It is not the function of a government body to do promotional work."[19] They wanted to see the bureau organized voluntarily, arguably so that the board would be free to focus on data collection and distribution that their own private charities organized and controlled. Members of the women's welfare network, however, saw federal action as the only means of systematically collecting and distributing the data to those unable to obtain such information. They argued that individual states and scattered charity organizations had thus far been unsuccessful in collecting usable data for national purposes. Therefore, a centralized federal bureau was the only option that the women reformers and a few male proponents like Devine viewed as a workable solution.

Hannah Kent Schoff, president of the National Congress of Mothers, spoke in favor of the federal bureau and referenced the wide web of voluntary organizations and laypeople who were in favor of such government action. In referencing her own organization of women across the country, she pronounced, "I represent an organization that for ten years has had for one of its objects the extension of propaganda for the care of dependent children." She stressed how average citizens needed the information that a federal bureau could provide, saying, "We have to reach these people. If such a committee had headquarters here in Washington and a press bureau that was continually sending out information all over the country, to every little ... town in this country, telling of the needs of these dependent and neglected children, we would arouse a sentiment."[20] Kent Schoff and others believed that if only middle-class citizens knew the plight of the urban poor, they would be morally obligated to act and, in turn, grow the women's welfare network. Like nineteenth-century sentimental writers, the National Congress of Mothers wanted to center the private, domestic suffering of children as a cause worthy of public, political action.

Furthermore, Wald referenced public support for a federal children's bureau:

> The national organizations of women's clubs, the consumers' leagues throughout the country, college and school alumnae associations, societies for the promotion of special interests of children, the various state child labor committees, representing in their members and executive committees education, labor, law, medicine and business, have officially given endorsement.[21]

It seemed almost a foregone conclusion to many conference attendees that a clearinghouse type of organization was needed. So much so that many of the conference attendees discussed how the proposed children's bureau would work with and further connect the network of voluntary, private, and state organizations already in place. Waller Barrett's long support for state oversight of private charities and the large number of times the NFCM was mentioned attest to how important the Crittenton missions were to this network of reformers and to the framework that would become the maternalist welfare state. In fact, Lucy M. Sickles, superintendent of the Michigan State Industrial Home for Girls, agreed that the cooperation between her institution and the local Florence Crittenton Mission was of vital importance to allowing her institution to help single mothers keep their babies. A federal bureau would certainly aid in connecting disparate services to the wider social welfare network.[22]

Eleven bills calling for the formation of the Children's Bureau appeared from 1906 to 1911; eight were proposed in the House and three in the Senate. Opponents of the formation of the bureau, citing fears of government bureaucracy, large salaries, and infringement on states' rights, editorialized in the *New York*

Times about the "dangerous" formation of a children's bureau. They feared the bureau would "invade rights . . . entrusted to the individual states." They further feared that "the enforcement of the law and the meeting of practical conditions seem to have been sacrificed for the sake of philosophical studies and the glamour of the limelight."[23] Wald followed up the editorial with a cool rebuff, writing, "even a cursory reading of the bill will convince one of the inaccuracy of this statement." She went on to describe how "the bureau would be a clearing house . . . and report upon the questions . . . now nowhere answered in complete or unified form." Drawing on the power that many women reformers felt was the only way to enact protective legislation, she reiterated that only the federal government had the resources to support and aid measures enacted by the individual states.[24]

The women's welfare network worked to push for more federal oversight and funding of the social service work they promoted. Women like Waller Barrett, who was a member of numerous organizations, including the Daughters of the American Revolution (DAR) and the National Council of Women (NCW), encouraged club members to write their representatives in support of the proposed bureau. Jane Addams tapped her vast network in Chicago and beyond. Florence Kelley rallied the support of the National Consumers League, Charles Devine mobilized the attention of the readers of *Charities*, and all aroused support from the National Conference of Charities and Correction, the National Child Labor Committee, and the national web of women's voluntary organizations, including the General Federation of Women's Clubs (GFWC), National Congress of Mothers, and the American Federation of Labor, among many others. This vast letter-writing campaign and social activism on the part of everyday American women created enough momentum to move bills in the House and Senate to passage.[25]

Despite opposition, the Federal Children's Bureau bill passed the House and Senate, and President Taft signed the bill into law on April 9, 1912, establishing the U.S. Children's Bureau within the Department of Commerce and Labor with the stated mission to "investigate and report . . . upon all matters pertaining to the welfare of children and child life among all classes of our people." The bureau was transferred to the newly created Department of Labor in 1913.

An article in the *New York Times* praised the formation of the Children's Bureau and the development of a unified front aimed at children's welfare, which until that moment was "split up into bits, and has therefore, been insoluble." Black reformers were also keenly interested in the Children's Bureau, running articles in support of its formation.[26] Days after President Taft signed the bill into law, Addams wired Wald and Taft asserting that her network supported the nomination of Julia Lathrop to head the division. The Senate approved Lathrop's nomination on April 17, 1912, and she became the first woman to lead a federal bureau. From its inception, the Children's Bureau was home to a female dominion of professional women reformers.[27]

The first major effort undertaken by the Children's Bureau was a focus on curbing infant mortality, which relied on accurate birth and death records. The Census Bureau counted the population every ten years but did not implement protocols for registering every infant birth or death between censuses. The vital statistician of the Census Bureau, Dr. Cressy L. Wilber, estimated that approximately 300,000 babies died yearly in the United States before reaching the age of one. Yet without accurate numbers, "There are no complete records for the United States as a whole which show how many babies are born and how many babies die year by year," Lathrop lamented.[28]

The Children's Bureau enlisted the aid of women's clubs in a birth registration campaign so that the true nature of American infant mortality could be determined. These birth registration efforts were meant to make data collection easier and public health more efficient, as there were no federal laws to enforce registrations and only a handful of states and municipalities established laws to systematically register births. When birth registration numbers were correct, health officials could monitor infant mortality rates using an accurate baseline and quickly act when epidemics struck.[29] Women's voluntary clubs were extremely helpful in gathering birth registration data. Lathrop explained how women's organizations took "small areas in which they have an acquaintance and, selecting the names of a certain number of babies born . . . learn by inquiry" whether the babies are registered.[30] Thousands of women connected with the network of voluntary women's organizations took on public federal government-sponsored work as birth registration volunteers for the Bureau. Under Lathrop's leadership, the Bureau enacted the first door-to-door campaign, aside from the census, sponsored by the federal government. Employees and volunteers for the Bureau not only registered births, but they also inquired about health and hygiene, milk supply, economic conditions, and sanitary conditions concerning children under one year of age within designated areas of study.[31]

Women from the National Congress of Mothers, the GFWC, DAR, and other such organizations sent committees to knock on doors with copies of standardized birth certificates. The GFWC even requested a pamphlet explaining the birth registration process to aid their registration efforts, resulting in the publication, *Birth Registration: An Aid in Protecting the Lives and Rights of Children*. This was the first of many publications created by the Children's Bureau to coordinate efforts between the federal government and private citizens.[32] Committees of volunteer clubwomen received copies of the standardized birth certificates that they filled out for all children in their neighborhood under the age of one. Then, they compared their records with those in the local registrar's office. Once checked for accuracy and duplication, they sent the certificates to the Children's Bureau for analysis and tabulation.[33]

Over three thousand clubwomen participated in the registration effort in 1915 alone. Clubwomen physically went neighborhood-to-neighborhood and door-to-door to gather data. As they spoke with women in their communities about the importance of birth registration, they helped spread consciousness of infant mortality, something that so many women had previously faced alone or within their insulated families.[34] The registration effort designated ten states and the District of Columbia as "birth registration areas" where there was at least a 90 percent accuracy rate for birth and death records of all babies born. By 1920, fifteen states were compliant, and by 1933 all states were registering 90 percent of babies born.[35]

Infant mortality was not the only social ill the women's welfare network wanted to combat; they also wanted to curb maternal mortality. Dr. Grace L. Meigs, the director of the Children's Bureau Hygiene Division, compiled available data on maternal mortality that revealed childbirth in 1913 accounted for more deaths among women aged fifteen to forty-four than any other disease except tuberculosis. Her data also showed that the maternal death rate from 1900 to 1913 had not fallen, even as improvements in combating other preventable diseases, like typhoid and diphtheria, marked the period. Moreover, Meigs's report showed that death from childbirth was twice as high among Black women as among native-born and immigrant white women. Many infant deaths occurred during the first few days of life; therefore better postpartum maternal care ultimately decreased infant mortality rates. Meigs concluded that "the sickness or death of the mother inevitably lessens the chances of the baby for life and health." When the mother's health was stable, she was better able to care for the health of her baby. Ultimately, this was no surprise to the thousands of women who suffered postpartum injuries or the death of an infant.[36]

To make lawmakers listen and act, large numbers of American women agitated en masse for their demands through the women's welfare network. Subsequently, almost every issue of the Mother's Congress *Child Welfare* magazine in 1916–1917 encouraged readers to insist on better obstetrical care from their doctors and support from their elected representatives. Dr. Mary Sherwood, director of the Mother's Congress Department of Obstetrics, implored members to demand that elected leaders enforce mandatory birth and death registration in their states. If they refused, Sherwood told her readers those lawmakers should be "regarded as enemies of progress and enemies of your homes and that their defeat is brought about at the next election."[37] Moreover, Lathrop reported that "improvement will come about only through a general realization of the necessity for better care at childbirth. If women demand better care, physicians will provide it, medical colleges will furnish better training in obstetrics, and communities will realize the vital importance of community measures to insure good care for all classes of women."[38] Change relied on public sentiment and public action. The majority of maternal deaths resulted from complications due to infections from unhygienic childbirth. Compounding this was the inaccessibility of skilled care in large swaths of rural America and within crowded enclaves of industrial cities. These inequalities would never be addressed without public pressure.

State health agencies used the birth registration information that clubwomen gathered to lobby for vital statistics laws. For example, lawmakers in Florida used local birth registration results gathered by women volunteers to pass legislation for a statewide vital statistics law. Women reformers in West Virginia lobbied for a state law that would make registration mandatory. In Louisiana, the State Board of Health specifically asked women's clubs to compile lists of all babies born in the state, in order to check their records against the state registrar's records. Average people also appreciated the drive for proper birth registration. One man living in a rural area proclaimed that he was pleased with the registration efforts because, previously, everyone he knew just "guessed at their ages." Throughout the 1910s and 1920s, the Children's Bureau continued to advocate for accurate birth records across the nation, fueled by women's voluntary labor.[39]

In its initial years, the U.S. Children's Bureau conducted two major infant mortality studies. One in Montclair, New Jersey, and one in Johnstown, Pennsylvania. These early studies, coupled with birth registration efforts, occupied the majority of the Children's Bureau's small staff of fifteen for the first two years of its existence. The Bureau conducted the first investigation in Montclair with significant assistance from the Montclair public health office. Bureau employee Sophia A. Vogt gathered field data from local public health nurses who used standardized birth registration schedules provided by the Children's Bureau. After public health officials collected the information, the Children's Bureau tabulated the raw data into usable reports.

The Montclair study showed how poverty correlated to infant mortality. The region was a fairly well-off suburban community, and findings showed that in

1915 the overall death rate of children under one year old was 84.6 per 1,000, whereas the national rate was estimated at 124 per 1,000 live births. But on closer inspection, however, the Fourth Ward neighborhood, which housed the most tenement houses and low-income families, had an infant mortality rate of 134 per 1,000 live births. The report concluded that low income often negated good mothering skills as, "a low income frequently must involve undesirable housing accommodations, an overworked mother, insufficient nourishment for mother and child, and lack of competent medical advice." The area with the most tenement houses and congested living, as well as the ward with "more complaints against nuisances, including complaints of poor plumbing, than from any other ward in the city," corresponded with higher infant mortality. Therefore, the report did not link infant mortality to a lack of medical care, per se, but to the unequal access to the resources necessary for raising healthy offspring. Even though Montclair had an overall lower than average infant mortality rate, the study showed that in areas where the environment was lacking, infant mortality was higher.[40]

The Children's Bureau conducted its second study in Johnstown, Pennsylvania, a steel-manufacturing and coal-mining city whose industry employed almost all able-bodied men, while the majority of middle-aged women "remain[ed] at home." Again, the Bureau worked closely with local public health officials and women's voluntary organizations to collect sensitive information from Johnstown families. Townspeople were asked questions intended to flesh out the "social, civic, and industrial conditions of the family studied," while a detailed record of the first year of life was collected from families with young children, paying particular attention to infant feeding methods. Because the intimate questions tracked breastfeeding, "only women agents were . . . employed in securing the replies." The Bureau was sensitive to detractors' arguments that this was an intrusion by the government into the privacy of the family, so participants were encouraged to participate in the study "to safeguard the lives of babies," not help the government with data collection. Like the Montclair study, the Johnstown investigation occupied significant Children's Bureau resources. A team of four Bureau employees worked solely on the Johnstown study for over a year. One male Bureau employee's time was spent copying birth and death certificates and tracing families that moved away from the region. Three other female agents, one a "qualified linguist," worked with local health officials to visit families in their homes.[41]

Similar to the Montclair findings, the Johnstown study also found a correlation between poverty and infant mortality. The city's overall infant mortality rate was quite low, averaging 50 per 1,000 births. However, in the Eleventh Ward, where many low wage immigrant workers resided, the infant mortality rate was 271 per 1,000 births. Bureau agents concluded that the Johnstown study proved a correlation between "underpaid fathers, overworked and ignorant mothers," and subpar living conditions with the highest infant mortality rates in the city.[42]

Regular reports in the Johnstown newspapers sustained public interest in the Children's Bureau report, which prompted locals to engage in public health activism. In response to the negative findings in the Eleventh Ward, the chamber of commerce created an infant mortality committee with the purpose of "agitating for improved conditions . . . It will constantly solicit the support of the churches, schools, parent-teacher associations, and organizations doing civic and charitable work in the gospel of sanitation." Lathrop concluded that this civic engagement "confirms the theory on which the bureau was created, namely, that if the Government can investigate and report, the conscience and power of local communities can be depended upon for local action." The study thus further enabled communities to build the associational state built upon the women's welfare network.[43]

Sentimentalism, child death, and romanticized motherhood were still very real issues in women's everyday lives. This is one reason the Children's Bureau studies had extremely high rates of participation among all demographics in the cities in which they worked. Most notably, the volunteer work of local women in conjunction with local public health nurses that assisted Children's Bureau professionals with the studies were stepping into women's homes, still steeped in the vestiges of the culture of sentiment. In Montclair, the local baby health clinic, which was supported by a mixture of state and private funds, assisted the Bureau in its study, resulting in only eight mothers out of the 402 polled who refused to participate. Out of 1,551 reports conducted in Johnstown, only two mothers refused to participate.[44] The Children's Bureau conducted eight intensive studies, with many more cities requesting similar studies, in cities ranging from 24,000 to half a million people between 1912 and 1918. The Bureau usually accessed the expertise of local public health nurses and clubwomen from each area, in turn extending the Bureau's web of influence among local health officials, community voluntary organizations, and reform-minded women, which encouraged other cities to seek assistance from the Children's Bureau so that they could conduct similar studies in their own municipalities.

Intertwined with these studies of infant mortality were questions concerning working mothers. As much as adequate data on infant mortality was needed, many of the Children's Bureau studies reinforced Victorian ideals of proper gender roles. The Children's Bureau conducted a study of infant mortality based on fathers' income in 1917. Not surprisingly, the data showed that higher father's incomes corresponded to lower infant mortality rates, further entrenching the tenet of an adequate family wage for breadwinners. The 1917 study found that in Manchester, New Hampshire, a high proportion of married mothers worked outside of the home for wages in correlation to a husband's earnings. The Children's Bureau surmised that these women "do *not* go out to work—leaving babies at home to die at more than twice the rate of more fortunate children—from sheer wayward preference for industrial life but for economic reasons, since the proportion of women gainfully employed reduces itself from 73.3 percent when the father earns under $450 to 9.6 percent if he earns $1,050 or more" (emphasis original) Lathrop and Children's Bureau social scientists concluded that a father's income was "sine qua non of safety for babies." The data convinced them that mothers with young children only worked when a father's income was too small to support a family. These findings supported arguments for a family, or "breadwinner" wage, which argued that men should make a large enough income to support a family.[45] Absent a male wage earner, supporters reasoned that single mothers—most commonly widows—should receive financial assistance in the form of mothers' pensions from the state instead of laboring outside the home to support their families.

Longstanding women's voluntary organizations, coupled with the long history of grief and sentimentalism surrounding child and maternal death, wove the threads that knitted the associational state to the realm of reform and volunteerism. Sentimental understandings about romanticized motherhood and the fear and grief of infant mortality were tools that the women's welfare network utilized to build a grassroots movement intent on creating policies and organizations to assist in child and maternal support. The resulting new policies, like mothers' pensions, were rooted in Progressive Era social science while depending on nineteenth-century understandings of the sentimental family.

CHAPTER 10

⎯⎯⎯⎯⎯⎯⎯⎯⎯⎯⎯⎯⎯⎯

Doing the Work

THE PROFESSIONALIZATION
OF CHILD WELFARE

Without question the greatest asset in the life of children is a good mother.[1]

Debate and passage of mothers' pensions coincided with the early years of the Children's Bureau as sixteen states passed mothers' pension laws in 1912–1913.[2] Many women's clubs advocated for mothers' pensions, particularly the National Congress of Mothers. Kent Schoff insisted that pensions were given to women while "performing her duties as a mother . . . when through extreme poverty or widowhood or other causes she would otherwise be compelled to go out to be the bread winner or break up the home and scatter the children in homes of various kinds." Kent Schoff did not insist that mothers conform to certain cultural values, like being legally married before receiving a pension. She believed the work of motherhood alone made mothers deserving of pensions. However, pensions were not distributed to mothers in such a nondiscerning way.[3]

Mothers' pensions were commonly called widows' pensions, framing a mother not as an individual capable of reproduction but as an extension of a married unit. Some states offered pensions only to widows as a way to keep costs down. Mothers' or widows' pensions effectively erased a woman's sexuality as they often deemed single, nonwidowed mothers as ineligible for funds. Many states only allocated money for children, with no funds provided for the maintenance of the mother herself, essentially erasing the mother altogether. When states gave widows' or mothers' pensions to single mothers, funds were often grossly inadequate to cover all household expenses.[4]

Not all embraced such a narrow-minded view of motherhood. Social scientist and reformer Sophonisba Breckinridge exposed the "needless humiliation" many women suffered at the hands of arbitrary pension laws.[5] She highlighted the plight of Dorothea Lange, whose common-law husband of twelve years was also the father of her four children. "Mrs." Lange applied for a pension when her husband died, but the Illinois Mothers' Aid Department of the juvenile court decided that she was not eligible for funds because the mothers' pension Law applied only to "wives" and "widows." The decision was based on an Illinois law enacted in 1909 that stipulated "all marriages commonly known as 'common law marriages'... are null and void unless after the contracting and entering into of any such common law marriage a license to marry be first obtained by such parties." Therefore, authorities deemed Lange's common-law marriage illegal, making her ineligible for a mothers' pension. The Mothers' Aid Department sent Lange to a city welfare agency where her case file revealed numerous intrusive check-ins by caseworkers.[6]

Indicative of the lacework structure of the early associate state, where some organizations worked together tightly while others formed loose associations with plenty of room for individuals to fall through the holes, numerous volunteer charity organizations assisted the city welfare office in distributing social benefits. The interconnection of various public and private organizations was visible in Lange's case, where city caseworkers asked the voluntary women's club Sorosis to either pay her rent of $16 a month or cover the cost of milk at $9 a month (approximately two quarts of milk a day) for Lange and her children. Lange's experience demonstrated the ad hoc nature of state welfare agencies, laws that governed mothers' pensions, and the interconnectedness of the associational state.[7]

States often administered mothers' pensions in a chaotic manner, making it difficult for mothers to maneuver through the loose, but interconnected, web of organizations they must navigate in order to get funds. Each state that adopted mothers' pensions set up different ways to administer the funds; pensions for needy mothers could even be distributed differently county to county. For example, Idaho administered mothers' pensions through probate courts, while in Pennsylvania the governor elected six or seven women in each county to serve, unpaid, on an advisory board that issued funds.[8] Pension administration in New York was similar to Pennsylvania but was expressly for widows only. Many states relied on unpaid female labor to administer pensions, under the cultural assumptions that it was "properly woman's work to look after other women."[9]

A limited view of motherhood and dependency meant that many mothers were not eligible for benefits under the laws passed. Only those mothers who demonstrated that they could uphold middle-class values, including having a legal marriage certificate, were deemed worthy of mothers' pension aid. Social workers held the power to disqualify applicants based on their sexual practices, cleaning and eating habits, temperance, and other social and cultural elements. Race and ethnicity held huge sway over the mainly white, middle-class professional social workers in what they deemed proper or not, with many white caseworkers deeming Black women ineligible for pensions purely on the bases of race and the ideology that Black women were incapable of moral motherhood. What this perpetuated was the connection of nonwidowed single mothers with stingy means-tested programs and the connection of widowed single mothers to a heteronormative family ideal and a male breadwinner, or state support to those women who lost their legally married breadwinner through death. This subjected mothers, either widowed or single, to a means-tested welfare program where their domestic lives were subject to scrutiny by caseworkers.[10]

Mothers requesting pension funds opened themselves up to intense scrutiny, as investigators determined if their marital status was precarious enough to be worthy of a pension. Women whose husbands no longer supported the family had to prove they were "deserted" with no hope of the husband coming back to support them. If a woman's husband was deemed "insane," there had to be "practically no hope of the husband's recovery" in order for her to get a pension. Strict oversight by middle-class investigators and state stinginess meant that out of 1,358 Pennsylvania applicants in 1915, only 128 received mothers' pension funds.[11] Since states were in control over how mothers' pension funds were distributed, the National Congress of Mothers adopted the standard that, "state aid should be given to women who are competent to serve the state successfully as its agents in the charge of young families ... in the absence of a natural breadwinner." This attitude, codified in many mothers' pension state laws, entrenched middle-class oversight of the funds as "worthiness" became a deciding factor in many pension cases.[12] The sentimental trope of the downtrodden but hardworking woman with child, husbandless because of forces out of her control, dominated understandings of proper mothering and worthiness for assistance.

Once a needy mother determined how to apply for funds by finding the right state agency, the oversight she invited into her home could be overwhelming. In Oregon, when a mother submitted her application, "the investigator calls at the applicant's home, and among the neighbors to get a true report of her condition." Once a mother was determined to be "fit" enough to receive funds, her case went in front of the court-appointed Case Committee for Widows' Pensions. In 1914, four hundred Oregonian women applied for pensions, and only 128 were paid. Investigators visited mothers who received a pension in their homes at least once a month. In some cases, mothers requesting funds were surveilled once a week, and a caseworker was "continually after her to keep the home and children in the proper condition." Additionally, mothers needing funds had to check in with their caseworker once a month, in which their "investigator has another opportunity to have a personal talk with each and every one." Pension recipients had to keep detailed records of all their household expenses. The state provided receipt forms where the mothers filled out their cost of living and provided receipts for each expense, which they sent to the juvenile court each month for review. Investigators made sure mothers spent funds solely on the children's care. If an investigator determined that a mother was not buying the proper foods, "the investigator calls to advise the mother to be more economical and what foods to order." If a mother was still not spending the money the way investigators thought she should, the pension was given to a "friendly visitor" and a supervisor to more closely monitor the way a mother's funds were spent.[13]

Supporters promoted mothers' pensions as remedies to child crime and prison. The pension administrator in Cook County, Illinois, reported that in a period before the Illinois pension law went into effect, 280 children out of 2,000 whose mothers were poor and widowed were charged with crimes in the Chicago juvenile court. However, after mothers' pensions were distributed to poor widows, only eight out of the 2,000 children whose widowed mothers received pensions were charged with crimes in the juvenile court.[14] Reformers touted mothers' pensions as a way to decrease institution populations, particularly in New York City, where historian Maureen Fitzgerald shows how Protestant bias against Catholic institutions led to anti-institutionalization campaigns. After mothers' pensions were approved in New York, administrators in New York City removed approximately two thousand children from private institutions and returned them to their mothers, who received financial assistance and home oversight.[15]

Pensions were not without their detractors, which contributed to their paltry size, ensuring that they were never successful or widespread enough to make systematic social change. Supporters constantly had to defend the pension system and women reformers relied on the data and expertise from the Children's Bureau to push back against their detractors. Clubwomen often wrote to the Children's Bureau asking for advice regarding the effectiveness of pensions. In one instance, the vice president of the Wisconsin Consumer's League wrote to the Children's Bureau to gather data she could use to counter detractors in Wisconsin who were against mothers' pensions in that state.[16]

Supporters also promoted mothers' pensions as a way to curb child labor. President Wilson signed the Child Labor Act on September 1, 1916, with language supplied by the Children's Bureau. The law stipulated that no goods could be shipped or sold that were produced in places where children under the age of sixteen were permitted to work. Congress appropriated $150,000 for the enforcement of the law, and Grace Abbott, director of the Child Labor Division of the Children's Bureau, was appointed the director and charged with overseeing all the field officers.[17] Additionally, the Children's Bureau Industrial Division prepared a series of comparative analytical tables covering U.S. child labor laws, further carrying out their "clearinghouse" function.[18]

The federal Child Labor Law gave new emphasis to the need for accurate birth registration records. To determine the new labor law's effectiveness and application, all child labor laws rested on accurate proof of age. Lathrop stressed that registration efforts must continue so that children would not be "defrauded" of their school years. The image of children as workers was not the sentimental image that reformers promoted, and children's right to a nurturing education helped increase interest in curbing child labor. Yet by 1916, only ten states had birth records accurate enough to be official birth registration areas. The majority of the labor collecting that information was still performed by voluntary women's organizations.[19] The first ten years of the Children's Bureau's existence focused on the collection of accurate birth records, led by women's organizations as part of the women's welfare network. Many women's organizations used their own funds to have birth certificates and parent notifications printed and sent out to state residents.[20]

In addition to the need for accurate birth records to determine the number of children eligible for child labor law protection, the Children's Bureau advocated for studies to determine the number of American families relying on child labor to make ends meet. Estimates of how many children under the age of sixteen who worked for wages, or worked to support their families, were entirely speculative, but evidence supported a rate of employment for children of single mothers to be roughly two to three times higher than for children living with two parents.[21]

The lack of accurate data, as well as common misconceptions of the true nature of childhood poverty, increased the Children's Bureau's need for more scientific study of poverty as well as the need for increased scientific charity. For example, the well-meaning but ignorant assumption that childhood poverty was caused by the death of both parents resulted in gross underutilization of funds in a Philadelphia charity organization. Two wealthy benefactors left enormous sums of money in their wills to help orphaned girls. The executors of these estates joined forces to combine the money. However, both wills stipulated that the money should only go to white orphaned girls between the ages of six and ten. The girls had to be "healthy," meaning they could not be mentally or physically disabled or labeled "feebleminded" in any way. By stipulating that all the benefactors of this money should be "true" orphans, white, and healthy, the executors determined that there were only two hundred to three hundred girls eligible for aid due to the restrictions the benefactors' wills placed on the funds. However, there was enough money in the charitable account to support close to a thousand girls. Both the executors of the charity fund and the Children's Bureau used this as an example of the ignorance and Dickensian views of the public who imagined orphans with no father or mother, when in fact most "orphans" had at least one living parent.[22]

Even the estimate of 200–300 girls was a gross exaggeration, as there were just not that many white "full" orphans in the city. In 1915 alone, the children's bureau of Philadelphia received applications involving plans for 3,751 children. Of those 3,751, there were only twenty-six full orphans requiring charitable support; and of these twenty-six children, eight were Black. Of the remaining eighteen white children, ten were boys and only eight were girls. Of the eight white girls, only four were between the ages of six and ten years. Therefore, out of 3,751 children living in poverty whose caretakers applied for financial assistance, only four were eligible for aid from this particular charity. Lathrop used this example as evidence that the public was unaware of the true nature of dependency and poverty, and she argued that if only the public were made more aware of the realities, better social policy would be enacted.[23]

Many Progressives, including Lathrop and leaders of the Children's Bureau, believed that if only the public knew specific facts, they would be motivated to push for effective action. Lathrop reasoned that "a fruitful fact needs no compulsory legislation nor military sanction; nothing but a chance to be used."[24] Largely this was true, as women's organizations spent a large amount of time in reading groups and seminars educating themselves on the social ills of the day. In turn, groups like the GFWC, DAR, and the National Congress of Mothers were at the forefront of demanding change. Lathrop utilized the power of the popular press to disseminate information and was adept at managing professional public relations and press releases, something new in this era. The Bureau developed an excellent relationship with the press, and in addition to sending press releases to newspapers, which were picked up for wide circulation, popular magazines requested information from the Bureau on a regular basis so that they may share the latest Bureau news with their readers. Publications as varied as *Woman's World*, which had a readership of two million rural subscribers, to Chicago's *Defender*, to the Baptist Sunday School Board requested and printed information from the Children's Bureau.[25] This, is turn, helped grow the associative state and the women's welfare network.

Americans read about the work of the Children's Bureau in magazines and their local newspapers. Many Bureau press releases included an address where readers could write in and request information and advice, and American men and women took advantage of the opportunity. Thousands of letters written to the Children's Bureau from mothers requesting the pamphlets or asking clarifying questions regarding the pamphlets proved their popularity. These letters show that mothers of every class, race, and education level were reading the pamphlets and engaging in the dissemination of government-sponsored scientific literature. The Bureau sent 110,000 copies of *Prenatal Care* and 63,000 copies of *Infant Care* to those that requested them in 1914–1915. They sent 330,737 copies of Bureau publications free of charge to those that requested them in fiscal year 1916, and 430,489 in fiscal year 1917. The sheer number of requests overwhelmed the Bureau, often causing them to deny requests from doctors, nurses, and welfare workers when they asked for greater volumes to distribute in their communities. Roughly 1,500,000 copies of *Prenatal Care* and *Infant Care* were distributed widely between 1914 and 1921. Even so, Lathrop reported, "While the editions were issued by thousands, requests for them ran far into the millions." Many communities and women's organizations requested permission to reprint the pamphlets for distribution at their own expense.[26]

Thousands of letters poured into the Children's Bureau chronicling women's fears over the proper care of their children. Thousands more wrote in describing their grief and pain over the loss of a child or the poor gynecological health they lived with because of inadequate pre- and postnatal care. Some letters written to the Bureau asked very specific medical questions, often because the writer did not have any other way of acquiring medical advice. One woman wrote, "My babys [sic] eyes have been sore but no one worried but myself, and I did only because I had read of the danger of blindness in your books. . . . No one here ever saw a Dr. do any thing [sic] for a newborn baby's eyes."[27] Through reading and sharing Children's Bureau pamphlets, many women circumvented a physical landscape that might be devoid of physicians or openly hostile to modern scientific ideas on child rearing. The ability of professional women at the Bureau to reach ordinary women through its publication exponentially spread consciousness to women across America that maternal and infant health was important and worthy of state protection. The Department of Health, Education, and Welfare estimated that the government distributed one copy of *Infant Care* for every three babies born between 1913 and 1965 and accounted for the vast reach of the Children's Bureau into individual homes.

As birth registration efforts collected more information and as the Children's Bureau studies reached more readers, the Bureau showed in stark numerical detail that infant and maternal mortality in America was appallingly high. For a country that prided itself on its wealth and high standard of living, a soaring infant mortality rate was unacceptable, as it reflected a general lack of care for the poor, women, and children in general. Most of these infant and maternal deaths were suffered in the absence of preventative medical procedures, particularly modern sterilization techniques. Yet the Children's Bureau never set out to approach infant or maternal death as a medical question but instead looked at causal factors, like poverty, associated with high rates of mortality.[28]

As Children's Bureau reports showed, poverty had a direct correlation to infant mortality, but it was not the sole determining factor. Middle- and upper-class women also suffered from infant death or poor maternal health after delivery. A well-off woman from Boston wrote about the death of her baby son and the inadequate medical advice she received:

> My baby was sacrificed through mere ignorance. This happened in the capital of Illinois and money or efforts were not spared to save him. I soon found that not only mothers of large families knew nothing about the scientific care of babies, but the best Doctors in the city knew less. I could not nurse my baby, and he just faded away, never gaining, or rather losing weight all the time on the many foods which the different Doctors tried.[29]

This grieving mother, along with thousands of others, mobilized as a result of their own experiences and those of their friends and acquaintances. They bemoaned the lack of trustworthy medical advice regarding pre- and post-natal care even from their own doctors. They were looking for a way to exert some political authority over the care and management of children and maternal health in the United States.

Letters written to the Children's Bureau show how anxious and sometimes desperate women and men were for gaining information about sex, reproduction, and pregnancy. One woman read a Children's Bureau press release in *The Modern Priscilla* magazine, a publication dedicated to needlecraft fancywork, which prompted her to write to the Bureau for information. Her impending wedding worried her because her parents were very strict, thus she was "quite in the dark" regarding sex and reproduction. Although the snippet in *Priscilla* promoted the pamphlet *Prenatal Care*, she wrote hoping that the Bureau could share information about sexual intercourse and reproduction.[30] This request was not unique to the Children's Bureau. The *Chicago Defender* published an article, "1,000 Things Mothers Should Know," and was "surprised to be flooded with letters asking all kinds of questions about childbirth and pregnancy," further highlighting the desperate need many women and families had for sex education.[31] Organizations like the WCTU had advocated for female sex education—or sex hygiene as it was termed—since the late nineteenth century, but many women were still "in the dark" regarding elements of human sexuality and reproduction. The Children's Bureau gave many women and families a resource to get information they could not seem to find elsewhere.[32]

With that being said, the Children's Bureau did not disperse specific information on sex hygiene or birth control but did refer letter writers to alternative sources. A married woman wrote to the Bureau asking for information on birth control with the simple request, "I need to know so badly." Lathrop replied that although the Bureau did not give information about birth control, the questioner should write to the National Birth Control League for information. Lathrop even supplied the address.[33] Lathrop was a supporter of birth control but avoided publicly supporting it or having the Bureau engage in meaningful discussions about birth control for obvious political reasons. However, the Bureau did publish a report after World War I suggesting that the nation's issue with soldiers infected at high rates with venereal disease could have been largely avoided had sex hygiene been taught in schools.[34]

Many letters written to the Bureau conveyed a sense of agony and fear. One woman desperately wanted information as to how she could obtain an abortion because her husband claimed the baby she was carrying was not his. She wrote that she had done "all I know to do" to self-induce but to no avail. She requested that the Children's Bureau "send me the stuff that will make me lose this baby." Lathrop wrote back in no uncertain terms that the Bureau would provide no such information or "stuff," and that anyone who did would be committing a crime. Lathrop's further assistance was lacking as she suggested that the woman enlist a good friend or confidant to help reconcile her and her husband.[35]

Letters continued to pour into the Bureau, covering appeals for information regarding "child labor, juvenile courts, child-welfare exhibits, mothers' pensions, children's health contests, diet lists for children of all ages, the care of infants, recreation for young people, institutions for exceptional children, etc."[36] Many of the letters contained basic health questions. One husband wrote the Bureau that his wife wanted information on how to "keep the skin clear" and "how to keep the liver and kidneys in good condition."[37] One of the marvels of the early nineteenth century was the rise of printed material and the spread of home health manuals. However, letters written to the Children's Bureau showed that Americans still needed information on basic health care. Even though the domestic health manuals were common, people from all backgrounds still expressly wanted information from the government because they trusted it would be accurate and scientific. If a question arose that Bureau officials could not answer, either because it was outside the scope of their charge or they did not know, they would also recommend other books, publications, or local women's welfare network offices to the writers.[38]

Requests for information threatened to overwhelm the Bureau. Over 113,000 letters were received and duly answered in 1915–1916. Communities from across the country requested educational materials from the Children's Bureau, including lantern slides, posters, and slide reels for presentations. Often, requests for educational materials had to be turned down because the demand outpaced the Bureau's resources.[39] Local organizations held their own health clinics and used the Bureau materials when they were available. Better baby contests were a staple at most local and state fairs, where babies were judged on their supposed "fitness" in an attempt to encourage families to better care for their children. Unsurprisingly, not all women reformers saw these contests as good for the health of babies. One welfare worker wrote, "Our welfare station has departed almost entirely from the idea of competitive contests, because by that means only the healthier class of children are brought. If a mother knows that her child is not to be put into competition with other children she will be more apt to bring the frail, puny baby which needs a doctor's advice."[40] Bureau visual aids helped reformers within the women's welfare network spread health information with or without gimmicky contests.

The Children's Bureau presented a child welfare exhibit at the Panama-Pacific International Exposition in 1915, consisting of informational panels and slides displaying the needs of children at various ages and information on proprietary medicines safe for children. The most dramatic element of the exhibit was a miniature replica of the state of North Carolina, lit up by electric bulbs in one hundred tiny villages scattered across the state. Periodically, the lights would dim and shut off in proportion to the numbers of children that died under the age of one each month. The exhibit also included an operational health clinic held inside a glass-walled room, where fairgoers could watch baby exams while seated outside the window. Examinations of older children were done behind a screened partition. Parents booked appointments for their children to visit the clinic months before the fair opened. The entire Children's Bureau display proved to be so popular that it won the grand prize for exhibits.[41]

The women's welfare network and the associative state acted reciprocally as the Children's Bureau often built upon the ideas and programs of local organizations. In 1916 the Bureau launched a nationwide "Baby Week," largely modeled on Chicago's baby week of 1914 and New York's baby week of 1915. The Bureau cooperated extensively with the GFWC to publicize the public health campaign and carry out its goals. National Baby Week launched in March of 1916 throughout the nation, buoyed extensively by a national advertising campaign that encouraged breastfeeding and warned against "Poverty, Ignorance and Bad Surroundings" as baby's worst foes. The Bureau also used connections with other governmental departments to spread the word.[42]

Although highly successful in garnering attention for the plight of American children, the Bureau operated on a shoestring budget. The original operating budget of $25,640 was only enough to support a staff of fifteen when the House appropriations committee denied Lathrop's request of an increase of $139,000.[43] In response, she reached out to the women's welfare network, and soon letters from members of the GFWC, the Consumer's League, the National Federation of Settlements, and others bombarded legislators demanding that appropriations for the Children's Bureau be increased. The publicity and pressure worked, and the House approved the increase in spending. The Children's Bureau began the third year of its operations with an appropriation increased from $25,640 to $164,640, allowing the Bureau to increase its staff by sixty-one members. The total of seventy-six Bureau employees included child experts, field agents, research and statistical clerks, and stenographers. Two major hires included Dr. Grace Meigs as head of the hygiene division and Emma O. Lundberg as head of the division of social service.[44]

It soon became apparent that the Bureau was still short-staffed and underfunded. The Bureau's need for capable statisticians was high, as they were expected to act as a "clearinghouse" to compile available data as well as new information coming in from Bureau field studies. Soon Bureau employees found that the volume of data was more than the staff could efficiently handle, prompting Lathrop to request an increase of fifty-seven additional staff members and the authority to hire temporary staff members as needed. This time Congress responded with an additional appropriation of $109,120, which brought the total to $273,760 for the fiscal year 1917–1918. Yet the amount of work and low salaries still meant that the Children's Bureau could not keep a highly educated staff up to the standards that it needed. Lathrop lamented that the Bureau suffered a "serious administrative embarrassment" due to an influx of calls and letters during National Baby Week. The Bureau suspended all normal operations to handle the additional work. Lathrop reminded the appropriations committee that they expected the same challenges in the following year. Nevertheless, the Bureau continued its charge to "investigate and report . . . upon all matters pertaining to the welfare of children and child life" by compiling data and educating the American citizenry.[45]

Despite a small budget, the Bureau was able to accomplish so much because of the support of the women's welfare network. Although women's clubs and organizations had various causes at the base of their missions, a majority of the larger, national organizations kept women's and children's welfare at the fore of their efforts. In 1916, under the guidance of President Waller Barrett, the National Council of Women (NCW) invited organizations like the National Congress of Mothers and Parent-Teacher Associations, DAR, and the GFWC to join under the NCW umbrella, which they readily accepted. National clubs like the National Association of Colored Women's Clubs were already longtime associates of the NCW, and the International Council of Women comprised women's groups from twenty-six other countries. This interconnected group of women welfare reformers worked together often for common goals, as evidenced by the 1918 NCW meeting where Waller Barrett, Lathrop, Addams, and Dr. Anna Howard Shaw all brought their expertise and the power of their respective organizations to advocate for social policies to benefit women and children.[46] The interplay of private women's clubs and the public Children's Bureau resulted in many mutually beneficial exchanges between the respective parties.

The government relied on the groundwork that local organizations laid while local organizations benefited by having their causes supported and taken seriously by the government. For example, the NFCM was integral to how the Children's Bureau understood dependency and illegitimacy. Bureau workers realized that the issue of illegitimacy as it concerned children overlapped many topics studied by the Bureau and other welfare organizations, particularly in regard to infant mortality. The Bureau, under the supervision of Director of Social Service Emma O. Lundberg, began a study of illegitimacy by gathering statistics from a defined area in Massachusetts, including Boston, in order to present a preliminary study on illegitimacy and its relation to dependency and health. They collected data from various public and private volunteer organizations, most notably the Boston Florence Crittenton home and the larger NFCM. Then, they spread their study to a wider area by developing "illegitimacy schedules." The Bureau sent the schedules to various welfare agencies to fill out in order to create a uniform data set tracking children born to single mothers through their first year of life.[47] Many of those working with unmarried mothers welcomed the systematic collection of records. One director at a maternity home in New York City remarked that she was glad to use the illegitimacy schedules provided by the Children's Bureau, as "record keeping at the Home is very poor." The NFCM and Kate Waller Barrett had long encouraged Crittenton satellites to cooperate with any organizations that studied unmarried mothers and illegitimate children in order to keep the NFCM on the cutting edge of social scientific reform work. Partnering with the Children's Bureau achieved that goal.[48]

Social workers within the women's welfare network and the Children's Bureau supported much of the Crittenton agenda. The NFCM and Waller Barrett were integral in creating a government understanding of illegitimacy. Julia Lathrop told delegates at the annual Florence Crittenton meeting that "there can be nothing better than for a mother and child to stay together if it is at all possible ... the fundamental need of childhood is maternal care, no less for children of illegitimate birth than for others."[49] Other social welfare workers agreed, and many charity and public maternity homes and hospitals strove to keep babies with their unwed mothers, if only for the sake of the nursing infant's health.[50]

In 1920 the Bureau printed the findings of Emma O. Lundberg and Katharine F. Lenroot's study on illegitimacy in America, titled, *Illegitimacy as a Child-Welfare Problem*. Using records from the NFCM as well as bibliographic sources from Kate Waller Barrett and other welfare workers, the study showed that children born out of wedlock were three times more likely to die than children born to a married couple. The report affirmed what the NFCM had been saying for decades, that maternity homes like the Crittenton Missions were in "the most strategic positions since a large number of mothers come to them first for assistance." Furthermore, the report concluded that the domestic job training and health services Crittenton homes provided were the most advantageous for helping both mother and baby survive and thrive.[51]

The Children's Bureau, working with other interested organizations like the NFCM, advocated for more uniform laws to protect the health of illegitimate children and their mothers, such as mothers' pensions becoming more widely available or adequate municipal baby clinics in every state. Bureau staff analyzed laws in different states that dealt with illegitimate children and single mothers, noting that many states had outdated laws that did more to protect individual jurisdictions from financial responsibility than they did for "the adequate protection and care of the mother and child." Lundberg and Bureau staff found that many state laws had not been revised in years and did more to increase stigma on the unwed mother than they did for protecting future citizens. In New York, "bastardy" laws were carried over from eighteenth-century law. For example, New York Law Criminal Law 839 found single mothers who could not support themselves to be subject to the "provisions of the poor law." The poor law provided that "such mother and her child shall, in all respects, be deemed poor persons." Additionally, the law stated that magistrates could compel a single mother to disclose the name of the father, and if she refused, she could be jailed. Bureau professionals determined that state laws must be revised to avoid the "stigma" attached to laws such as these. Like Waller Barrett and the NFCM, the Bureau advocated for laws that were less punitive to single mothers.[52]

Unmarried mothers had a vastly different take on their maternity than did many of the reformers and social workers running welfare programs. Many mothers did not feel the shame and stigma that middle-class reformers felt they should feel. Helen Welsh, supervisor of the Minneapolis Maternity Hospital worried about the loss of "regret" that many single mothers exhibited in her hospital. In correspondence with Lathrop, Welsh decided that a "problem" occurred when young women, upon entering the maternity hospital, realized they were not the only girl who had "done what they should not." Walsh determined that this realization made the young women lose their shame, so to speak. She believed the "girls" came to this conclusion because of their naiveté and immaturity. However, Welsh expressed a desire to not be perceived as someone "who wishes a girl to suffer 'the torture of the damned' for her offense." Yet, as much as she wanted to paint herself as a "friendly" reformer type, her words belied her true intent; she wanted to see that the girls were sorry for what they had done and they recognized that what they had done was outside of the bounds of "proper" society.[53]

Rhetorically, if not always in fact, welfare reformers did not want single mothers to be shamed by society and punitive laws. Many progressive maternalists wanted to create a social construction of motherhood that allowed single women the opportunity to thrive in a world in which "nameless" babies had the same opportunities as babies born in wedlock. On the other hand, single mothers were expected to be properly ashamed; they must not be happy or proud of their motherhood. Instead, they must learn to be respectable, to *harness the power of motherhood* through hard work, religious faith, and some semblance of repentance. As reformers in the women's welfare network waxed poetic about the special needs of single mothers and their illegitimate children, benefits like mothers' pensions—paltry as they were—were not extended to the majority of single mothers.

Unmarried mothers also needed different support than perhaps some middle-class reformers were willing to provide. Many reformers in the women's welfare network created day nurseries for use by working mothers (as discussed in the previous chapter), but many were unwilling to care for children "whose legitimacy could not be proven."[54] In addition, many native-born white women reformers began to question the beneficial impacts of day nurseries. Jane Addams, whose Hull-House provided childcare for working mothers in Chicago, feared as early as 1905 that reliable childcare was a double-edged sword. She worried that unqualified caretakers and nursery environments were detrimental to impressionable children. Moreover, she worried that accessible childcare would convince mothers that they could do "the impossible" act of working and raising children. Maternalists feared that low wages and exhaustion were not a good trade for quality childcare. They instead felt that mothers' pensions were a better way to take care of young families.[55]

Yet, mothers' pensions were never a widespread solution for working mothers because of their meager sums, and the rules governing them meant that few women were actually eligible to receive them. Thus, childcare was always a pressing issue for working-class women, many of whom turned to boarding their babies while they performed wage labor. These types of boarding houses were dubbed "baby farms," a derogatory term used to describe homes in which single and working mothers boarded their babies for days, weeks, or months at a time. During the 1870s there was a "panic" over alleged "baby farms." In some iterations, baby farms were a place where a single mother could abandon her baby; in other iterations they were makeshift childcare for working-class women. Most "baby farms" were homes where one working-class woman cared for a number of babies in her home, allowing their mothers to work for wages. Most often it was a poor woman who served the working-class women in her neighborhood by running the so-called baby farms.[56]

Although by the late 1910s the baby farm "panic" had largely subsided, historian Leslie Reagan found that peaks in 1914–1917 of abortionist arrests and newspaper coverage of abortion coincided with local and state investigations of baby farms because all were seen as ways for women to get rid of unwanted children.[57] Places of all types could fall under the designation of "baby farm." A 1917 survey by the Chicago Juvenile Protective Association found that of 129 alleged "farms," six of them were day nurseries, six were adoption placement agencies, and seventy-four were boarding homes for children. The report stated that 50 percent of children left in the "farms" died, many of them suffering malnutrition, unhygienic living conditions, lack of medical care, and abuse. In one case, investigators found a baby farm where the caretaker's syphilitic husband infected many of the children living with her.[58] An investigation by Bureau staff found a "farm" where an uncovered jar on the porch was the only toilet and a child was found tied to the bed.[59] However, these were the worst of the worst and came to investigators' attention because people in the community were policing themselves and calling in instances of abuse.

Commentators overwhelmingly deemed women who ran "baby farms" as "immoral," or at least "dirty" or "untidy" in their personal appearance. Additionally, the blurring of color lines, even in northern cities, troubled social workers. Investigators were disturbed when they found three "'farms' operated by Black women who cared for white babies. They were most alarmed by a farm where "one colored woman and two white children slept together." At its core, baby farming was a way for working-class women to use informal neighborhood networks for childcare resources. Reformers saw this need for adequate childcare as a reason to regulate childcare establishments and a reason to increase mothers' pensions so that childcare was not needed. It also further buoyed support for maternity homes like the NFCM, which were working to keep mothers from having to board their babies while they worked.[60]

Baby farms sometimes operated as ad hoc adoption agencies and served as a means for single mothers to relieve themselves of unwanted babies. Welfare workers worried about the unregulated nature of adoptions that happened outside of the court system for fear not only that children could be abandoned or abused but also to protect potential adoptive parents. One child welfare worker argued in favor of legislation that would mandate a court-appointed investigation before adoption as both "a safeguard not only to the infant, but to those who plan to adopt it." He justified his eugenic stance with an anecdote about a recent adoption, saying, "Although an infant lately advertised was to all appearances a fine specimen, its mother, when traced, was found to be of loose character, with a scandalous medical history." So-called "baby farm" adoptions were not part of a hidden network, as readers could easily find advertisements in newspapers for both boarding situations (baby farms) and children available for adoption in the classified section of the local newspaper. Baby farms, adoption, and maternity care were often conflated.[61]

Childcare became a larger concern during World War I. America entered

World War I in April of 1917, but in the lead up to the war, Congress created the Council of National Defense in 1916 with the Woman's Committee as part of the Council. Suffragist Anna Howard Shaw headed the committee and managed a team of ten divisional directors, with state chairpersons under them. In June 1917 the Woman's Committee, the Children's Bureau, and other associational organizations concerned with maternal and child welfare developed a child-welfare policy for the war period. These resolutions requested gynecologists and obstetricians not be pulled away from the care of mothers and babies in order to deploy their services in the war effort. They also requested public health nursing be part of wartime "service" so as not to pull those resources from where they were needed domestically, and for the council to officially recommend that provisions be made to keep single mothers and nursing infants together and in the home, cared for by mothers' pensions or otherwise. The group recommended that childcare should be state supervised and meet the requirements set forth by the National Federation of Day Nurseries. The larger body of the Council of National Defense approved these resolutions.[62]

The war years proved to be a boon to the Children's Bureau as the nation's attention turned toward the battlefront and the loss of life. Infant mortality and child health became a greater concern as America needed to focus on repopulating the citizenry through investment in America's children. Lathrop was quoted as saying in a speech at the end of World War I, "we cannot help the world toward democracy if we despise democracy at home; and it is despised when mother or child die needlessly."[63] Additionally, draft data showed American men had high rates of illiteracy, poor health, and mental deficiencies, prompting a "discovery of 'feeble-mindedness' across the nation." R. M. Yerkes, a primatologist and psychologist, conducted tests on draftees and determined his tests showed "low intelligence" among non-native-born whites in the military. According to his data, Italian immigrants had on average a mental age of 11.01 years, Blacks 10.41 years, and Polish immigrants 10.74 years. However, where eugenicists read the military draft results as proof of cultural and racial traits, many in the women's welfare network viewed these results as reasons to bolster the health and well-being of children.[64] Dr. S. Josephine Baker, director of the Child Hygiene division in the New York City Department of Health, argued that the draft data allowed the American people to see how important it was to bolster government funding of child welfare. Mothers were the conduit to this goal, as the nation's future soldiers became tied to the future of American democracy.[65]

As part of this initiative to care for the nation's babies and mothers during wartime, the Woman's Committee and the Children's Bureau jointly launched

Children's Year in April 1918. The Bureau issued a chart that listed the number of children each state should save based on the population of the state with the goal of saving 100,000 babies by the end of the year.[66] The women's welfare network sprang into action, with local reform committees asking the Bureau for help in furthering child welfare in their communities. The Bureau provided the Woman's Committee of the Council of National Defense roughly 6.5 million record cards. They distributed the cards to volunteers and health clinics in order to record the height and weight of children aged zero to sixteen. Mothers were informed that it was their "patriotic duty" to take their children to the nearest weighing stations because they contributed to the strength of the nation, and a future stock of healthy soldiers, by making sure their children were receiving the minimum of healthcare.[67]

Efforts by the Children's Bureau during World War I to make a lasting impact on welfare for mothers and children were marginally successful. Before the Children's Year campaign of 1918, only eight states had functioning child welfare divisions. By 1920, thirty-five states established child welfare divisions. In some cases, states took the lead and created infant-welfare clinics. When the war ended and the zeal for government spending dwindled, these newly formed clinics lost funding. However, instead of disappearing, many were picked up, supported by local volunteer organizations and physicians' professional organizations, and placed under the supervision of state public health associations and obstetrical and gynecological societies. Essentially, private and public organizations stepped in to cover the lack of state appropriations, allowing newly created welfare clinics to stay open when public funds were lacking. These are examples of citizens wanting state and federal interventions. When the state faltered, they picked up the slack.[68]

The war created new anxieties because industries were actively recruiting women laborers to work in their factories, drawing a large number of young or single (at least in the sense that their husbands were away) women to industrial areas. Women's groups were concerned with what would happen to all of those young women who traveled to industrial centers to take jobs and were subsequently let go after the war.[69] Additionally, welfare workers feared that increased wages during wartime would entice mothers of young children to enter the workforce. The 1917 Conference on Infant and Maternal Welfare in War Time, sponsored by the American Association for the Study and Prevention of Infant Mortality and the medical section of the Council of National Defense, made the formal recommendation that employers should provide adequate childcare for mothers working in industry. Dr. Grace Meigs, director of the Children's Bureau

Child Hygiene Division and a member of the executive committee responsible for constructing the group's final report, objected to the recommendation "that adequately supervised care [for children of working mothers] be furnished at the place of employment." Meigs believed mothers' pensions and family allowances should be the only recommendations. In the end, she acquiesced and insisted the report include that "the employment of women with young children may be avoided by local patriotic effort."[70] Nevertheless, the number of women working in industry increased during the war, both because husbands left for war and because there was just more opportunity for women to work.

In response, the Children's Bureau conducted a brief survey of day nurseries in several American cities. The report concluded that city and state oversight of childcare facilities would help ease the burden of childcare. Investigators criticized the lack of municipal oversight of day nurseries, finding many acceptable nurseries but also many that were extremely subpar. In calling for more state and local oversight, the report fell back on the primacy of the mother and child bond by suggesting that local defense councils do everything they could to discourage mothers from working in their factories. As a last resort, "special provision at school or in day nurseries is made for young school children when necessary." Some factories did create temporary childcare facilities, but most did not. The federal government never sponsored a full-fledged effort for childcare, even when many reformers advocated for it.[71]

The influx of women into the paid labor force increased anxieties about young women's sexuality, children's illegitimacy, and wayward youth. The Bureau received many letters expressing anxiety that young women in towns near cantonment camps were having babies out of wedlock with soldiers stationed locally. Rumors that a wave of young women were getting pregnant by encamped soldiers led to an increase of letters to the Bureau requesting that they look into the matter. After examination, the Bureau found the rumors to be untrue.[72] Additionally, news that European countries were experiencing an increase in illegitimate births during wartime also proved false. Lundberg found that illegitimate births had not increased in European countries. In fact, the number of illegitimate births in England and Wales actually decreased between 1913 and 1916.[73]

In 1920, at the request of the Inter-City Conference on Illegitimacy, the Children's Bureau organized two conferences to discuss single mothers and their children. The conferences resulted in a number of resolutions, aimed at codifying uniform standards for children born out of wedlock. Conference attendees agreed upon a number of resolutions, including provisions to impart legal status and rights of inheritance for illegitimate children. The Bureau, in collaboration with the National Conference of Commissioners on Uniform State Laws, combined conference resolutions into the Uniform Illegitimacy Act of 1921, which the Bureau urged each state to adopt. At a 1922 follow-up meeting, the conference attendees agreed to drop support for full inheritance rights and agreed that parents owed a child "maintenance, education, and support." Additionally, they decided that the father was responsible for the mother's medical expenses related to her pregnancy and confinement.[74]

A big takeaway from these meetings was that mothers' pensions were still woefully inadequate and should be available to a wider number of women. By 1921, forty states had some kind of mothers' pensions in effect, but administrative laws were still vastly different. The Bureau complained that the pension amounts in many areas were completely deficient to keep mother and child well fed and housed. They also criticized the conditional nature of many pensions that rendered some mothers' pension laws "practically inoperative."[75] Without specifically saying the public welfare funds should support single mothers and illegitimate children, the Bureau and delegates of the Inter-City Conference on Illegitimacy leaned heavily in that direction. They argued that if mothers' pensions would not support mothers and their children, child labor laws were pointless.

Thus, the need for an associational welfare state continued. Private organizations that tapped public funds, like the Gate City Free Kindergarten in Atlanta or the NFCM, would continue to provide social services to members of local communities on an ad hoc basis. Even as significant Children's Bureau energy and resources were devoted to addressing illegitimacy, it seems the primacy of the mother and child bond on the federal level could only be protected within the ideal of a nuclear family, not in fully funded mothers' pensions or federally funded childcare facilities that would allow women to work and support their children adequately.

CONCLUSION

Networks and Spheres
SENTIMENT COMES FULL CIRCLE

Why does Congress continue to wish to have mothers and babies die?[1]

After the success of the U.S. Children's Bureau in formalizing child welfare work as a program deemed worthy of federal oversight, women further entrenched themselves into the fabric of the emerging welfare state. Additionally, the reliance on local organizations to carry out the Children's Bureau mission continued to build the associational state as members of the women's welfare network across the country advocated for policies that would protect the health and wellbeing of women and children. Taking a cue from the health activism that many in the women's welfare network were doing at the grassroots level, Lathrop proposed an idea that would move beyond the Children's Bureau data "clearinghouse" and helper role and take on a more ambitious plan to establish medical programs for mothers and infants. Lathrop's 1917 federal report for the Children's Bureau called for a nationwide, federally funded program that would include public health nurses, pre and post-natal care for mothers and babies, and accessible healthcare for babies and children. Women's organizations across the country immediately took up the campaign for such a program. Jeannette Rankin, a Democrat from Montana, sponsored the first bill in 1918 proposing Lathrop's plan. Other manifestations of the bill were subsequently introduced. Lathrop's proposed program finally converged in the "Sheppard-Towner" version with co-sponsorship from Morris Sheppard, a Texas Democrat, and Horace Mann Towner, an Iowa Republican.

The bill moved slowly, prompting over twenty-one national women's organizations to take up a strenuous letter-writing drive to their House and Senate representatives in order to pass the Maternity and Infancy Act. The newly formed Women's Joint Congressional Committee, a coalition of lobbyists and major women's organizations, including the WCTU, National Congress of Mothers, the National Women's Trade Union League, The Young Women's Christian Association, the National Consumers' League, and the National Council of Jewish Women, mounted an intense lobbying campaign directed at members of Congress. Major women's magazines, including *Good Housekeeping, Woman's Home Companion, McCall's,* and *Ladies Home Journal,* also publicized the bill and promoted a letter-writing campaign among their readers. One *Ladies Home Journal* article described the pressure some congressional representatives felt from women's reform efforts. "He [the congressman] knows that all these organizations with their differing activities . . . have one uniform, fundamental purpose—human welfare—and that, when emergency requires it, they have the perfect machinery for mobilizing all their forces."[2] The millions of women who were active in voluntary organizations or who were private readers of women's journals and were engaging in politics and demanding more government involvement in their lives were a real worry to some conservative lawmakers, particularly as more and more states granted full women's suffrage and as the Nineteenth Amendment snaked its way through Congress.

Mary Stewart, of the Women's National Republican Executive Committee, stated, "there is a new politics abroad in the land . . . women are the cause of it. . . . bringing women into politics have brought new ideas of Governmental responsibility."[3] Elected officials were unsure of how newly enfranchised women would vote, prompting them to listen to women's demands more than they had in the past. Women bombarded their elected officials with letters supporting the Sheppard-Towner Act. One senate staffer joked, "I think every woman in my state has written to the Senator."[4] Even in hearings conducted on the Infancy and Maternity bill, the specter of a women's voting bloc was presented as a very real threat to those who failed to work for women and children's welfare as "a great many women . . . are going to be voting for the first time" in the fall.[5] Feeling pressure from their constituents and without knowing how women were going to act with their newly won vote, representatives allowed the bill to pass to the House floor for discussion.

The House Committee of Labor held the first hearing conducted publicly on the Sheppard-Towner bill. Jeanette Rankin began the hearing with a brief and detailed description of what the measure proposed to do. She alluded to the women's welfare network that supported federal government expansion of maternity and infant social services in her remarks regarding the "many communities throughout the United States" that had been influenced by the work and pamphlets of the Children's Bureau and were "eager" for the development of more direct action to curb infant and maternal death.[6] Dr. Anna E. Rude, the new director of the Division of Hygiene in the Children's Bureau, also referenced the vast network of women who were interested in and affected by the work of the Bureau. She explained how American women were forcing the issue through the thousands of letters that they wrote to the Bureau.[7]

The sentimental specter of child death still drove the movement, even when couched in the social science of the Progressive Era. Dr. Dorothy Reed Mendenhall of the Children's Bureau gave expert testimony to the committee by detailing her experience addressing infant and maternity care in rural Wisconsin. She recalled a woman who had given birth to a child with a "harelip," and was tragically instructed by a rural doctor to let the baby die, as it would never be able to properly feed. The woman, once limited by the inevitable death of her child, was instead able to attend a child health clinic held in her rural village through agriculture extension work offered through funds from the Smith-Lever Act. There, Dr. Mendenhall was able to show the woman how "she could pump her own milk and feed it to the baby, and also advised her where she could go later for the necessary operation." On a visit to the village two years later, Dr. Mendenhall happily found the child to be living and perfectly healthy. She was able to testify how basic, humane medical knowledge helped rural women avoid the once inevitable deaths of their children. Mendenhall showed how an expansion of government-sponsored healthcare could aid mothers and babies in every locality.[8]

Florence Kelley, speaking as the secretary of the Consumers' League, discussed her travels and activism among the urban poor and the rural South, Northeast, and New England. In Maine, she found "Uncle Sam, caring most solicitously for the young lobsters . . . but the American mothers there must depend for assistance on their rural neighbors."[9] Supporters of the Maternity and Infancy Act bill often used federal government expenditures on agriculture as a talking point, showing how the federal government spent millions on crops and livestock but very little on the nation's yield of future citizens. Kelley's knowledge of the plight of poor women and children, her position of authority among women reformers, and her straightforward and sometimes confrontational demeanor positioned her as an expert speaker who commanded respect within and without the female dominion of social reform.

In contrast, Addie Daniels of the National Democratic Committee began her testimony within the context of her embodiment as a mother of six children. Hers was an impassioned speech that did not rely on the command of scientific investigation but on justice and sentimental empathy for American mothers. Daniels stated, "Mr. Chairman, I come to you to say that the women of America offer their bodies and their blood for the children whom they bring into the world, and they pray you will do all that you can to see that every aid is given these mothers and their babies."[10] Daniels and other women at the hearing positioned themselves as mothers but also soldiers in the service of the nation—and therefore as experts in demanding federal welfare reforms. Other statements highlighted this theme of mothers sacrificing their bodies for the nation. Loss of life in the war had been tremendous during World War I, as stressed by Anne Martin of the National Women's Party when she stated, "other countries have taken steps toward compensating the populations of their countries for their great war losses.... We have a means right here of compensating in this country for that loss by preventing the great loss of mother and infant life in this country."[11] Motherhood in service of the nation was a strong discourse throughout calls for federal infant and maternity provisions, situating mothers at the crux of citizenship and public virtue.

There was, however, major opposition to the bill. The American Medical Association (AMA) denounced the bill in their trade journal *JAMA*. Describing the women of the Children's Bureau and other leading female reformers as a band of childless "spinsters" at the head of a "radical, socialistic, and Bolshevistic" plot, the AMA and conservative congressmen rallied hostility to the bill. Opposition arguments purported that Sheppard-Towner violated states' rights, threatened private medicine, was socialistic and represented a power grab by feminist zealots intent on expanding government control over the family and private medicine. Doctors from Massachusetts framed the bill as "paternalism, socialism, communism, and all the other isms of the kind condensed into one."[12] Opponents of the bill questioned the accuracy of the Children's Bureau statistics, as House member Alice M. Robertson argued to the *New York Times* "that without complete statistics which 'are not to be had'...the 'sob-stuff' claim which she said had been made by Mrs. Florence Kelley ... that '600 babies die every day' was absurd on the face of it."[13] Representative Robertson's comment alluded to the sentimental strain of "sob stuff" prevalent throughout the women's welfare network but gave no indication of why she questioned the statistical records gathered by the Children's Bureau.

Florence Kelley, exasperated with the slow passage of the Maternity and Infancy Act, made her frustrations known in a statement before the Senate Committee on Public Health in 1920. In the midst of heated debates, Kelley earnestly asked, "Why does Congress wish to have mothers and babies die?" One can imagine her voice ringing through the committee room. She angrily went on, explaining that "the case as to the number of deaths was perfectly clear two years ago," at the first hearing on the bill. She explained that since that time the hogs, the ticks, and the boll weevil had gotten more federal attention than the deaths of children. Interrupting, the chairman asked, "Perhaps we are destructionists and not constructionists, since we are destroying the ticks and boll weevil?" Without a pause she replied, "Actions speak louder than words, and inaction shrieks to Heaven at the present time." She threatened, "I think it is going to be one of the most interesting questions from now until New Year's if this bill isn't passed; it will be one of the most interesting questions that will go on in the press, because our organization will see to it that it goes on." She then asked again, "Why does Congress continue to wish to have mothers and babies die?" Interjecting, Senator Joseph Ransdell of Louisiana alluded to the small number of senators at the hearing. "They are all very busy with a variety of things . . . they do not realize the importance of this bill. They are so absorbed with other things, perhaps with hogs and cattle, and the boll weevil taking their time, since the agricultural appropriation bill is now in conference." He emphasized, "I speak in all seriousness." Kelley replied, "Oh Senator, so am I."[14]

This contentious exchange between the senators and Kelley resulted from the culmination of vigorous campaigning by women across the country who networked with other politically minded women with the hope of protecting their domestic sphere through the power of the government. Kelley was a tireless Progressive reformer and her exasperation with the political process was evident in her statement before the Senate. However, it was also apparent that sentimentalism was still a useful tool for enacting change. Asking congressmen why it's apparently acceptable to let mothers and babies die on a daily basis was surely meant to tug at the heartstrings. Perhaps as a way to lighten the tense mood, or perhaps to bring home the imperativeness for the passage of the bill, Frances Parkinson Keyes, author and wife of New Hampshire Senator Henry W. Keyes interjected, "Might I call your recollection to Napoleon's remark that if anything is possible it can be done; but if it is impossible it must be done? [Laughter]."[15]

And it was done. The Sheppard-Towner Act was signed into law on November 23, 1921. After a heavy campaign of lobbying efforts by women across the country and what the *Ladies Home Journal* dubbed the "clearinghouse" of the Women's Joint Congressional Committee (WJCC), women's lobbying efforts and the threat of a new bloc of angry female voters had paid off. Although, as one senator stated, "If the members of Congress could have voted on the measure in their cloak rooms, it would have been killed as emphatically as it was finally passed in the open."[16] The Promotion of the Welfare and Hygiene of Maternity and Infancy Act, the act's full name, provided matching funds to states that developed educational programs in maternity and infancy health and hygiene. Funds were only to be used for resources like public health nursing, consultation centers, medical and nursing care for mothers and infants at home or at a hospital, and general community outreach. States were barred from using Sheppard-Towner funds for "stipends" like mothers' pensions or for the erection and maintenance of buildings. The act gave an annual appropriation of $1,240,000 per year, $50,000 of which was appropriated to the Children's Bureau for administrative expenses. The remaining balance was to be divided between states, based on population, that developed infancy and maternity health programs eligible for matching funds. The Act stated that the work "should originate in the state and be carried out by the state." The Act created a Federal Board of Maternity and Infant Hygiene that oversaw state-originated plans for the use of federal matching funds. The board consisted of the U.S. surgeon general, the commissioner of education, and the chief of the Children's Bureau, Grace Abbot, who replaced Lathrop after her retirement in 1921. Staff in the Children's Bureau administered funds and worked in consultation with states as they developed programs eligible for federal funds. Sheppard-Towner funds became available to states in April of 1922.[17]

What was different about the Sheppard-Towner Act was that benefits were not means tested. Mothers did not have to engage with case workers that would scrutinize their married state and domestic conditions for assistance from the program. That meant, theoretically, that every mother and child could avail themselves of the health clinics, milk stations, and nursing care available through state-sponsored programs funded by the Sheppard-Towner Act; the Act was for all children, even illegitimate ones. The Act was also designed to aid children only. Mothers received no benefits from the program besides the peace of mind that their children were receiving medical care. The omission of mothers meant that women's sexuality was invisible in the exchange, something that potentially excluded mothers and their children from other means-tested programs like mothers' pensions.

Maternalists in the women's welfare network held a tenuous grasp on professional and political power. Undoubtedly, they were professionals because of their expert knowledge and their connections to the broader network of reformers pushing for child and human welfare. Yet the time it took for such an important bill to pass, and vociferous opposition from conservative groups, congressmen, and the AMA, showed that newly politicized reform-minded women across the country had a steep hill to climb. Maternalist reformers had extended their field of influence into the male-centered domain of politics. By 1922, forty-two states had accepted the terms of the Sheppard-Towner Act. Additionally, Puerto Rico and Hawaii expressed their desire to participate in the program.[18] Between 1922 and 1929 Sheppard-Towner health workers distributed twenty-two million pamphlets, organized 2,600 rural child-health centers, convened 183,000 health conferences, and visited three million homes. Less than three years after the program began, more than 162,000 women in forty-three states had attended Sheppard-Towner mothers' classes, 75,000 women had attended prenatal conferences, and 600,000 young children and infants had been examined by Sheppard-Towner nurses. In its last four years, the program reached 700,000 women and four million babies.[19] The Sheppard-Towner Act allowed the Children's Bureau to spread its influence even further into communities nationwide, but not forever. Sheppard-Towner was repealed in 1927 amid a strong and forceful conservative backlash spearheaded by the physician lobby of the AMA. The benefits in the Act expired in 1929.

Concurrently, as the Sheppard-Towner Act was extending healthcare to American children, private insurance companies were funneling healthcare to working men through welfare capitalism, the channeling of social benefits through private employment. In an effort to curb labor militancy and retain loyal (male) employees, companies began offering benefits and pensions to some employees. In the 1920s insurance companies aggressively insisted that group insurance plans would benefit American employers by allowing industry to meet social welfare needs, eschewing a more active federal government that may impose regulations on business and labor management practices. Thus, the two-channel welfare state began to take hold. One channel funneled white industrial workers through welfare capitalism and privatized security while the second channel funneled single and widowed mothers with young children through mothers' pensions, piecemeal programs with matching funds like Sheppard-Towner, or strictly charity care. Historian Jennifer Klein contends that insurers laid "a foundation for the proliferation of private security programs" that shaped the New Deal and the subsequent American welfare state. Private insurers embraced elements of the New Deal because it allowed them to create supplemental benefits, most importantly health insurance, that would usurp the need for a more socially active government by funneling the majority of social insurance through private employers. This channel of the associational welfare state linked many stable and non-means-tested social benefits to private employment and left many women and children to depend on benefits through a male breadwinner or through means-tested avenues, particularly after the Sheppard-Towner Act was overturned.[20]

Six years after Sheppard-Towner benefits expired, the Social Security Act of 1935 codified gendered and racialized disparities into the American welfare state. The Social Security Act was crafted through compromises with southern Democrats to exclude domestic and agricultural laborers from the Act's benefits, which disallowed most Black women who disproportionately worked in domestic positions to reap the benefits of Social Security. This was the same for Black men and ethnic Mexican women and men who worked in agriculture on a large scale. Thus, Social Security overwhelmingly served white men and their dependents.

Section V of the Social Security Act restored some of the Children's Bureau infancy and maternity health work that expired with the Sheppard-Towner Act. Additionally, the New Deal Aid to Dependent Children (ADC) program was designed to match federal funds with state funds for the financial assistance of dependent children. Children's Bureau employees and alumni Grace Abbot, Katharine Lenroot, and Dr. Martha May Eliot designed the ADC program by modeling it after mothers' pensions. Much to their consternation however, the Social Security Board was chosen to administer the ADC program, not the Children's Bureau. As Social Security expanded and allowed widowed women and their dependents onto the Social Security rolls, single mothers and their dependents became the primary recipients of ADC funds, tainting the program with the specter of poverty and immoral sexuality, which kept funds low and only covered the care of children, not caretakers. Additionally, like mothers' pensions, ADC grants were administered locally and suffered from the same means-tested and biased administration of funds.[21]

Historian Robyn Muncy maintains that the Sheppard-Towner Act, "with its emphasis of federal-state cooperation and its demotion of private agencies in the provision of social services, provided a model for subsequent social programs that formed the U.S. welfare state in the 1930s."[22] However, I have shown throughout this book that there was never a delineated line between private agencies and federal-state cooperation. The work of women reformers dating back to the early nineteenth century ensured that private social welfare endeavors were never entirely separate from state power, through either policing or funding. Entities like the Children's Bureau could not have come into existence without earlier organizations like the NFCM or the bombardment of club-women and letter writers demanding that their elected representatives pass legislation creating the agency. Once in existence, women volunteers became agents of the federal government as they went door-to-door collecting birth registration information for the Children's Bureau. When rural health clinics were run by the Children's Bureau, women volunteers often organized communities in preparation of the clinics. They recruited people with cars to drive children back and forth to the clinic and asked their local doctors and dentists to volunteer at the clinics. Women volunteers made government programs like these possible.[23] These kinds of activities continued with the implementation of the Sheppard-Towner Act. Furthermore, the 1930s did not prove to be the moment when federal and state governments usurped associational partnerships with private organizations. A cursory look at elements of the welfare state today shows this is not the case. Medicaid benefits do not run directly through the government but through third-party, for-profit insurance companies. Food and nutrition benefits in Women, Infants, and Children (WIC) are not administered through the federal or state government alone but often through private charity organizations, for example, Catholic Charities in New York state.[24]

A diverse cadre of women took it upon themselves to address societal needs during the Gilded Age and Progressive Era. "The state," in this case meaning local, state, or national government, never footed the full price of any welfare programs because much of the internal work and organizing was performed freely by women, their labors overshadowed by the sentimental elements of motherhood, childhood, grief, and love that were not, and are not, valued as worthy of true compensation or accolades. Women-run benevolent societies dating as far back as the antebellum period greatly relieved the government of much responsibility for the poor and or needy.[25] That trajectory had not changed by the twentieth century, nor has it changed in the twenty-first. Ultimately, the state and taxpayers benefited from, and still benefit from, the voluntary or underpaid work of women. For example, today public schools are underfunded, and teachers are underpaid across the country while 76 percent of public school teachers are women.[26] The field of social work is a profession made up of almost 90 percent women, and the average pay in this profession hovers around $47,000 per year, only $5,000 more than the average high school graduate makes per year. Yet social workers must obtain a postgraduate degree to practice their profession—a profession that overwhelmingly serves families with dependent children.[27] If we use gender as a lens of analysis, we can see that policies, resources, and careers focused on or around women and children are chronically undervalued or derided.

Regardless, state expenditures (however paltry) on formerly "private" matters fueled the growing public preoccupation with how taxpayer money is spent.[28] Concerns over taxpayer money helping the "unworthy" are nothing new and can be traced back to the poor laws of the colonial era. During the hearings discussing the Sheppard-Towner Act, Frances Keyes relayed a popular argument against the bill that asked, "Won't this bill if it is passed help mothers who are unworthy as well as mothers who are worthy?" Her answer to the assembled committee was, "It certainly will. I am very glad it will. . . . no matter how bad a woman may be, certainly her baby has got a perfectly good right for a fighting chance."[29] Thus, the interconnection of infant death and sexual immorality continually wove through arguments over the growing welfare state. As was true in the past, some mothers are still seen as deserving and others not, leading to polices that punish sexual immorality, such as abstinence-only health education, or assumed immorality inherent in abortion bans. Gender and sexuality are still at the center of debates regarding the American welfare state and social policies. Arguments against universal healthcare say that men and non-child-making people should not have to pay for pregnancies, while two-thirds of maternal deaths are considered easily avoidable through simple preventative care. Women and people who are capable of giving birth constantly test the limits of "The State," as concerns over taxes collide with sentiments of "deserving" and "unworthy."

Furthermore, sentimentalism is still an important element in public discourse surrounding children, sexuality, and welfare. Abortion and birth control opponents refer to sentimental pictures and descriptions of chubby, six-month-old babies and equate them with preterm fetuses. Longform commercials touting the benefits of scientific discoveries in battling childhood leukemia are choreographed with slow motion hugs and tinkling piano music. Sentimentalism as a driving force of social welfare has not gone away; it is an integral part of twenty-first century discourse.

The piecemeal, associational welfare state that we have today has of course aided in lowering child mortality in the United States, but the country is in no way at the vanguard of safeguarding infant and maternal health. Healthy outcomes for American women and their children are drastically determined by race and ethnicity, with African American women experiencing infant loss and miscarriage more than twice as often as white women and are three times more likely to die during childbirth than white women. Overall, the United States has the highest maternal mortality rate among developed countries.[30] The United States does not guarantee paid leave or healthcare to support parents and their newborn children, thus continuing the lack of parental support that pushed so many reformers to advocate for mothers' pensions in the early twentieth century. American children and families face many of the same issues and lack of support that they did over one hundred years ago.

Too Late

I hear their little footsteps—
The children that I bore;
Their eyes are big with weeping
And they haunt me evermore.[31]

This poem wasn't written in 1830 but in 1914, nestled between articles on the evolution of mothers' pensions and calls for women to join the National Council of Women. Overemotional sentimentalism marched right alongside women's step into the public sphere of political action. The concerns over infant mortality and the "fall" of young women interconnected with sentimentalism to elicit public action in the formation of the American welfare state. Elements of the associational state were built by the voluntary and paid work of female reformers working in the late nineteenth and early twentieth century. Women saw a need, filled it, and cobbled together a network of voluntary organizations that tapped state funding and support when available. Their work provided safeguards for women and children and created a network of female-oriented programs that policed and aided fertile-age women at the turn of the twentieth century.

The limited supports of the current welfare state have their roots in the powerful networks of women who marshalled both sentiment and social science to advance women's presumed shared interests. They created policies that provided for—and policed—women and infants in need. As imperfect as supports for American families currently are, none would exist without the collective action of thousands of everyday women at the turn of the century who were motivated by sentimentalism based in real-world experiences to work for government policies that would aid more than their immediate families. It is in this collective action that perhaps we can find hope and power in the emotion, dare I say, the *sentimentalism* that creates support for policies that promote the welfare of all.

NOTES

INTRODUCTION

1. Lillian D. Wald, "The Federal Children's Bureau A Symposium," *The Annals of the American Academy of Political and Social Science*, Vol. 33 (Mar. 1909): 23–48.

2. Wald, "Federal Children's Bureau A Symposium," 23.

3. This engagement in what Paula Baker terms "political domesticity" reflected a distinct nineteenth-century women's political culture. Baker, "Domestication of Politics," 621–632. For women acting in machine and party politics during the nineteenth century see Edwards, *Angels in the Machinery*.

4. U.S. Children's Bureau, Department of Commerce and Labor, *Establishment of the Children's Bureau*.

5. Scholars who argue that sentimentalism shaped everyday culture include Lehuu, "Sentimental Figures" in *Culture of Sentiment*, ed. Samuels, 74. Scholars who argue it also affected the twentieth century include Kunzel, *Fallen Women, Problem Girls*, 44; Williamson, *Twentieth-Century Sentimentalism*, 2, 18. "Sentimental power" is a term coined by Jane Tompkins.

6. Ryan, *Cradle of the Middle Class*, 116–120.

7. Ufford, "Possible Improvements in the Care of Dependent Children," 125.

8. See Koven and Michel, "Introduction: 'Mother Worlds,'" in *Mothers of the New World*; Wilkinson, "The Selfless and the Helpless"; Skocpol, *Protecting Soldiers and Mothers*, Part 3; Freedman, "Separatism as Strategy."

9. Glenda Gilmore argues that some politically organized Black women reformers circumvented some mechanisms of white supremacy in the South by acting as "diplomats" to the white community because, as Gilmore argues, they were less threatening than Black men. Their gender allowed them to lobby in public for new Progressive Era benefits and reforms. Gilmore, *Gender and Jim Crow*.

10. Higginbotham, *Righteous Discontent*, 1.

11. Qtd. in Gilmore, *Gender and Jim Crow*, 14; Culp, *Twentieth Century Negro Literature*, 184–185.

12. Higginbotham, *Righteous Discontent*, 187. Also see Giddings, *When and Where I Enter*; White, *Too Heavy a Load*; Gatewood, *Aristocrats of Color*; Gaines, *Uplifting the Race*; Mitchell, *Righteous Propagation*; Wolcott, "'Bible, Bath, and Broom.'"

13. Mitchell, *Righteous Propagation*. See also Hickey, *Hope and Danger in the New South City*; Wolcott, *Remaking Respectability*.

14. Black women's reform operations worked in ways similar and different to white women's reform work and sometimes intersected. Linda Gordon finds Black female reformers working toward maternalist goals such as support of dependent mothers and children. What Gordon found to be different, however, was the prevalence of Black female reformers focused more on the "betterment of the race" as a whole instead of concerning themselves with controlling other groups of people. Gordon, "Black and White Visions of Welfare Activism," 578.

15. Cahn, *Sexual Reckonings*, 27.

16. "The Story of the Gate City Press Kindergarten Association," NU—Neighborhood Union Papers (hereafter NU), Box 12, Folder 25.

17. Ladd-Taylor, *Mother-Work*, 45.

18. Dr. H. V. Davis, "Mothers and the Flag of Our Country," *Child Welfare Magazine*, Vol. 11, No. 11 (July 1917): 332–334. Women could vote in many local elections. Also, by 1912, 10 percent of the nation's women were already casting votes for president in many western states. Black women could vote in some of these states, like Colorado, although their numbers were marginal.

19. Historians disagree as to how the WCTU movement played out in the larger growth of American feminism and women's rights. Scholars such as Barbara Epstein argue that movements like the WCTU acted as a stepping stone for women to engage and champion women's suffrage and women's rights. Elaine Frantz Parsons sees the women of the WCTU embodying a radical conservatism that championed women's rights and suffrage, not as a way toward gender equality but as a way to return to protected and safe domesticity, free of the danger that drunk and violent men could pose to the domestic sphere. Epstein, *Politics of Domesticity*, chap. 5; Parsons, *Manhood Lost*, 10; DuBois, *Woman Suffrage and Women's Rights*, 38–39. Regarding race, see Gilmore, *Gender and Jim Crow*, 32.

20. Tomes, *Gospel of Germs*, 135; Kathleen Brown, *Foul Bodies*, 367.

21. Muncy, *Creating a Female Dominion in American Reform*; Skocpol, *Protecting Soldiers and Mothers*; Gordon, ed., *Women, the State, and Welfare*; Gordon, *Pitied But Not Entitled*; Mink, *Wages of Motherhood*.

22. Ladd-Taylor, ed., *Raising a Baby the Government Way*. On the social aspect of death in nineteenth and twentieth century America, see Rothman, *Living in the Shadow of Death*; Jalland, *Death in the Victorian Family*.

23. Wexler, *Tender Violence*.

24. Theda Skocpol's analysis of maternalism argues that mothers of all classes and races shared a civic value of mothering, and in the absence of a universal social welfare apparatus, maternalist reformers created a maternalist welfare state that focused on the needs of mothers and children. Skocpol, *Protecting Soldiers and Mothers*, 33. Linda Gordon argues the absence of critical examinations of race, class, and gender creates a "mystification of power" in a purely political analysis of maternalism. Gordon, "Gender, State and Society: A Debate with Theda Skocpol," 134, 141. For a political history of maternalism, see Muncy, *Creating a Female Dominion in American Reform*; Skocpol, *Protecting Soldiers and Mothers*.

25. On the "girl problem," see Odem's *Delinquent Daughters*; for health initiatives, see Ladd-Taylor's *Raising a Baby the Government Way*; for politics, see Skocpol's *Protecting Soldiers and Mothers*.

26. On maternalism as a form of social control see Mink, *Wages of Motherhood*; Rembis, *Defining Deviance*; Gordon, *Women, the State, and Welfare*; Gordon, *Pitied but Not Entitled*; Fitzgerald, *Habits of Compassion*; Gordon, *Great Arizona Orphan Abduction*; Cahn, *Sexual Reckonings*.

27. Nelson, "Origins of the Two-Channel Welfare State," in *Women, the State, and Welfare*, ed. Gordon, 125–151; see also Kessler-Harris, "Designing Women and Old Fools," in *U.S. History as Women's History*, ed. Kerber, 87–106. For an analysis of how this affected welfare later in the twentieth century, see Quadagno, *Color of Welfare*. Arguably this two-channel approach can be altered to include three channels. Disability historians have chronicled the third channel reserved for those with disabilities or somehow not included in the first two categories: Ladd-Taylor, "The 'Sociological Advantages' of Sterilization," in *Mental Retardation in America*, ed. Noll and Trent, 281–299; Ben-Moshe, Chapman, and Carey, eds., *Disability Incarcerated*; Ferguson, *Abandoned to Their Fate*; Grob, *From Asylum to Community*; Goffman, *Asylums*; Rembis, *Defining Deviance*. For an analysis of who is accepted as being a part of the state, see Welke, *Law and the Borders of Belonging in the Long Nineteenth Century United States*; DeWolf, *Gendered Citizenship*.

28. Novak, "Myth of the 'Weak' American State"; Novak, *New Democracy*, 260–263; Patterson, *America's Struggle Against Poverty in the Twentieth Century*; Katz, *Undeserving Poor*; Leuchtenburg, *Franklin D. Roosevelt and the New Deal*; Katznelson, *Fear Itself*; Brinkley, *End of Reform*; Balogh, *A Government Out of Sight*.

29. Hawley, "Herbert Hoover, the Commerce Secretariat, and the Vision of an 'Associative State,' 1921–1928."

30. For a discussion of the "associational synthesis" of state building, see Balogh, *Associational State*.

31. Historian Mary Ryan chronicled the rise of "the era of association" during the early nineteenth century by showing how the wives of merchants, who were freed from the duties of family production, founded charitable societies and maternal associations in their new leisure time in *Cradle of the Middle Class*.

32. Hemphill, *Bawdy City*, 19–20.

CHAPTER 1. TAKE THE SORROWS OF OTHERS TO YOUR HEART

1. Stowe, "Mourning Veil," 63–70.

2. Stowe, "Mourning Veil," 69.

3. Matthews, *Rise of the Public Woman*, 76.

4. Rust, *Prodigal Daughters*, 64–65.

5. Rowson, *Charlotte Temple*, 29.

6. Davidson, *Revolution and the Word*, 186.

7. Rust, *Prodigal Daughters*, 48–49.

8. Samuels, *Sentimentalism and Domestic Fiction*; Ross, *Sentimental Novel in America*, 176.

9. Boydston, "Woman Who Wasn't There"; Stanley, "Histories of Capitalism and Sex Difference"; Hart, "Work, Family and the Eighteenth-Century History of a Middle Class in the American South," 573.

10. Boydston, "Woman Who Wasn't There," 199.

11. Cott, *Bonds of Womanhood*. On Republican Motherhood, see Kerber, *Women of the Republic*.

12. Beecher, *A Treatise on Domestic Economy*, 37.

13. *Mothers' Monthly Journal* (Feb. 1833), 22–26, qtd. in Ryan, *Cradle of the Middle Class*, 159.

14. Welter, "Cult of True Womanhood"; Lerner, *Majority Finds Its Past*, 26; Giddings, *When and Where I Enter*, 43.

15. Jones-Rogers, *They Were Her Property*, 1–2.

16. Zaeske, *Signatures of Citizenship*, 28; Mintz, *Moralists and Modernizers*, 127.

17. American Tract Society, *Child's Anti-slavery Book*.

18. Sánchez-Eppler, *Touching Liberty*, 26–27.

19. Nora Doyle, *Maternal Bodies*, 177.

20. Jacobs, *Incidents in the Life of a Slave Girl*.

21. Laura Doyle, "The Folk, the Nobles, and the Novel," 174; Yellin, introduction in *Incidents in the Life of a Slave Girl*, by Harriot Jacobs; Andrews and Kachum, "Editor's Introduction," in *Curse of Caste*, ed. Collins, xxxvi.

22. Douglas, "Introduction," in *Uncle Tom's Cabin*, by Stowe, 19.

23. Stowe, *Uncle Tom's Cabin*, 387.

24. Sánchez-Eppler, *Dependent States*, 101.

25. Stowe, *Uncle Tom's Cabin*, 113.

26. Studies of the death of Little Eva include Douglas, *Feminization of American Culture*, 3–12; and Tompkins, *Sensational Designs*, 122–146.

27. Noble, *Masochistic Pleasures of Sentimental Literature*, 66; Doane, *Desire to Desire*, 73.

28. Truth, *Narrative of Sojourner Truth*, 134. This recounting of Truth's speech was written twelve years after it was given and is questionable in its literal translation, particularly because the writer, Frances D. Gage, writes Truth's speech with an attempt to imitate southern dialect. Truth, however, was born in New York and spoke only Dutch until the age of nine and would not have spoken with a southern accent. Regardless, contemporary reports of her speech testify to its power and intensity. See Balkansky, "Sojourner Truth's Most Famous Speech."

29. Gillian Brown, *Domestic Individualism*, 33.

30. Stowe, *Uncle Tom's Cabin*, 521; Patton, *Women in Chains*, 36–37.

31. Andrews and Kachun, "Editors' Introduction," in Collins, *The Curse of Caste*, ed. Collins, xi–liii.

32. Andrews and Kachum, "Editors' Introduction," in *Curse of Caste*, by Collins, xv; Day, *Consumptive Chic*, 53.

33. Andrews and Kachum, "Editors' Introduction," xviii.

34. Carby, *Reconstructing Womanhood*, 87–94.

35. Stowe, "Mourning Veil," 69.

36. Phelps, *Chapters from a Life*, 96.

37. Faust, *This Republic of Suffering*, 185; Frank Luther Mott lists *The Gates Ajar* as a "better-seller" as opposed to a bestseller, Mott, *Golden Multitudes*, 321.

38. Phelps, *Gates Ajar*; Phelps *Three Spiritualist Novels*; Robert S. Cox, *Body and Soul*.

39. Gardener, *Is This Your Son, My Lord?*

40. Powell et.al., "The Shame of America," 194.

41. Gardener, *Pray You, Sir, Whose Daughter?*

42. Powell, et.al., "The Shame of America" the United States: A Symposium," *The Arena*, Vol. 11 (1895): 196–215; Hamlin, *Free Thinker*, 136–137.

43. Sánchez-Eppler, *Dependent States*, 146; Samuels, ed., "Introduction," *Culture of Sentiment*, 14. Ann Douglas argued that the "sentimental heresy" of middle-class female writing in the 1850s undermined the "toughness" and "intellectual rigor" of the dominant northeastern Calvinist philosophy. Douglas's *Feminization of American Culture* dismissed much female-written Victorian literature as shallow, apolitical, and in support of the status quo. The "feminization" that Douglas found was not "feminist," but instead an intellectually bankrupt means of supporting materialism and consumerism. She found sentimental literature embarrassing, reasoning that because sentimental women writers concerned themselves with the domestic sphere, their writings were not a part of the masculine "solutions" for the trials of the world. In rebuttal, Jane Tompkins claimed sentimentalism was a formidable cultural phenomenon that was powerful because of the skill and adeptness that sentimental writers wielded. Tompkins lamented that "twentieth-century critics have taught generations of students to equate popularity with debasement, emotionality with ineffectiveness, religiosity with fakery, domesticity with triviality, and all of these, implicitly, with womanly inferiority." Tompkins argued the mundane nature of sentimental novels made them powerful because women writers worked within an accepted mode of cultural understanding. By doing so, sentimental writers were able to create a fictional domestic sphere that many readers could relate to and then, within that sphere, push against its boundaries just enough to question the status quo. Authors influenced their readers through the dependence on a conservative belief system and family structure. Then, by appealing to their readers emotions, sentimental writers could push against those boundaries and provide a means for cultural or political growth. The Douglas-Tompkins debate is still useful in thinking through sentimentalism and its influence on middle-class culture in the nineteenth century. The debate is also a cultural event itself, framing how second-wave feminism grappled with questions about the validity of separate spheres, domesticity, and motherhood. The debate made sentimentalism so integral to historical inquiry that any study into the period has to consider it. Douglas, *Feminization of American Culture*, 11, 18; Hendler, Sánchez, and Travis, "Twentieth-Anniversary Reflections on The Culture of Sentiment," 122–128; Tompkins, *Sensational Designs*, 122–146.

44. Stowe, "Mourning Veil," 68.

CHAPTER 2. OUR LITTLE CHILDREN LEAVE US

1. H. E. B., "After the Funeral," *Mother's Journal and Family Visitant*, Vol. 37 (Lange, Little, & Hillman, 1872), 106.

2. L. B., "The Dead Infant: Or, the Agonizing Mother," *The New-York Weekly Magazine: Or, Miscellaneous Repository*, Vol. 2, No. 53 (July 6, 1796): 3.

3. Seeman, *Speaking with the Dead in Early America*, 131; Ryan, *Empire of the Mother*, 70.

4. Laderman, *Sacred Remains*, 60–61; Cross, *Burned-over District*, 38; Mintz, *Moralists and Modernizers*, 27–28.

5. Memoirs of Miss Huldah Ann Baldwin, by Rev. Amos Glover Baldwin, of Trinity Church, Utica (Utica: Seward & Williams, 1814), qtd. in Ryan, *Cradle of the Middle Class*, 87.

6. Braude, *Radical Spirits*, 53.

7. Ryan, *Cradle of the Middle Class*, 220. See also Braude, *Radical Spirits*, 53; Joseph and Tucker, "Passing On," 110–124.

8. Samuels, ed., *Culture of Sentiment*, 6.

9. "19th Century Mourning," permanent exhibit, National Museum of Funeral History, Houston, Tex. See also Faust, *This Republic of Suffering*, 147–148.

10. Letter to Queen Victoria of England from Mary Todd Lincoln, May 21, 1865, Mary Todd Lincoln Papers 1861–1930, Library of Congress, qtd. in Gleeson, "Feminizing Grief," 1.

11. Stowe, "Mourning Veil," 68.

12. Bender, "Rural Cemetery Movement," 204; Laderman, *Sacred Remains*, 40; Seeman, *Speaking with the Dead*, 219.

13. Laderman, *Sacred Remains*, 53; Stannard, *Puritan Way of Death*, 119; Wells, *Facing the 'King of Terrors,'* 66.

14. Seeman, *Speaking with the Dead*, 15–18; Cothran and Danylchak, *Grave Landscapes*, chapter 3.

15. Linden-Ward, *Silent City on a Hill*, 49.

16. H. E. B., "After the Funeral," 106.

17. Tompkins, *Sensational Designs*, 137.

18. Ruby, *Secure the Shadow*, 29–30, 37–38.

19. Tagg, *The Burden of Representation*, 43; On mortuary photography, see Burns, *Sleeping Beauty III*; and Ruby, *Secure the Shadow*. Historian Laura Wexler points out that photography was not the "democratic" medium that many scholars celebrate it to be, as accessibility and the cost were prohibitive for almost any person enslaved in the South. Wexler, *Tender Violence*, 1.

20. Sánchez-Eppler, *Dependent States*, 137; Ruby, *Secure the Shadow*, 6.

21. Barthes, *Camera Lucida*, 88–89, qtd. in Tagg, *The Burden of Representation*, 1.

22. Barthes, *Camera Lucida*, 21, 16; in Noble, *Masochistic Pleasures*, 77; Sánchez-Eppler, *Dependent States*, 109.

23. Willis, *Reflections in Black*, 66.

24. Homemaker, "Tired," *The Woman's Journal: Boston* (Saturday, Sept. 7, 1901): 286.

25. Mary Clemmer Ames, *Eirene: Or, A Woman's Right* (New York: G. P. Putnam, 1871), 193, qtd. in Ryan, *Cradle of the Middle Class*, 220–221.

26. Sánchez-Eppler, *Dependent States*, 145; Ryan, *Cradle of the Middle Class*, 219–221.

27. Caroline Leslie, "Self-Folded," in *A Mother's Scrap-Book Only* (Cincinnati: Hitchcock & Walden, 1878), 166–177, qtd. in Sánchez-Eppler, *Dependent States*, 145.

28. Sánchez-Eppler, *Dependent States*, 146.

29. D'Emilio and Freedman, *Intimate Matters*, 140–141; Pivar, *Purity Crusade*, 67–69, 78–195; Wagner, "Virtue Against Vice," 26; Gilfoyle, *City of Eros*, 185; Gordon, *Moral Property of Women*, 72–75; Mintz, *Moralists and Modernizers*, 69.

30. Gordon, *Moral Property of Women*, 72–75, 80; Mintz, *Moralists and Modernizers*, 69.

31. Stowe, "Mourning Veil," 69.

CHAPTER 3. PAPA'S BABY

1. Crittenton, *Brother of Girls*, 69.

2. On child-angels as a sentimental tool, see Tompkins, *Sensational Designs*, 137. Although not a household name today, Florence Crittenton was synonymous with women's welfare work at the turn of the twentieth century and continued to be well-known into the mid-twentieth century, even having a World War II "liberty" ship named the *Flor-*

ence Crittenton. See Greg Williams, *Liberty Ships of World War II*, 88, ship number 207. Ricki Solinger's *Wake Up Little Susie* examines the National Florence Crittenton Mission during the latter part of the twentieth century. However, changes in social work and ideas about child wellbeing made the Crittenton Mission in the later part of the twentieth century look vastly different than its first fifty years.

3. Frances E. Willard, "Arousing the Public Conscience," *The Arena*, Vol. 11 (1895): 200, 201.

4. Anna Rice Powell, "American Purity Alliance," in Powell, *National Purity Congress*, 134.

5. Sellers, *Market Revolution*, 243–244; Gilfoyle, *City of Eros*, 23; Clare Lyons argues that commercial sex was not relegated to areas around the wharf in eighteenth-century Philadelphia in Lyons, *Sex Among the Rabble*, 110.

6. Crittenton, *Brother of Girls*, 30; Gilfoyle, *City of Eros*, 120.

7. Crittenton, *Brother of Girls*, 30.

8. Gilfoyle, City of Eros, 117.

9. Walt Whitman, *The Uncollected Poetry and Prose of Walt Whitman*, edited by Emory Halloway. Garden City, N.J.: Double Day, 1921, 6.

10. Gilfoyle, *City of Eros*, 119. For the prevalence of commodified sex, see Rosen, *Lost Sisterhood*; Wood, *Freedom of the Streets*; Blair, *I've Got to Make My Livin'*; Anne M. Butler, *Daughters of Joy, Sisters of Misery*; MacKell and Noel, *Red Light Women of the Rocky Mountains*.

11. For a map of the theaters and brothels in the vicinity where Crittenton lived, see Gilfoyle, *City of Eros*, 121.

12. Gilfoyle, *City of Eros*, 119–123; Pivar, *Purity Crusade*, 235. See also Chauncy, *Gay New York*, chapter 1; Werble, *Lust on Trial*, chapter 3.

13. Gilfoyle, *City of Eros*, 99–105; Chauncy, *Gay New York*, chapter 1; Werble, *Lust on Trial*, 164.

14. Gilfoyle, *City of Eros*, 99; Gordon, *Moral Property of Women*, 66.

15. Whitman, *Uncollected Poetry and Prose*, 6.

16. Crittenton, *Brother of Girls*, 36.

17. Quote in Gilfoyle, *City of Eros*, 112.

18. Crittenton, *Brother of Girls*, 39.

19. *The Pharmaceutical Era*, vol. 16. (New York: D. O. Haynes & Company, 1896), 493.

20. Crittenton, *Brother of Girls*, 53.

21. Crittenton, *Brother of Girls*, 53–55.

22. Crittenton, *Brother of Girls*, 48; "Charles Nelson Crittenton," memo, n.d., SWHA—Social Welfare History Archives Florence Crittenton Collection (hereafter SWHA), Box 1, Folder 5.

23. Crittenton, *Brother of Girls*, 62.

24. Crittenton, *Brother of Girls*, 64–65.

25. Alan R. Katz and David M. Morensm, "Severe Streptococcal Infections in Historical Perspective," *Clinical Infectious Diseases*, Vol. 14, No. 1 (Jan. 1992): 300.

26. Crittenton, *Brother of Girls*, 66–67.

27. Crittenton, *Brother of Girls*, 67.

28. "Charles Nelson Crittenton," memo, n.d., SWHA, Box 1, Folder 5; Crittenton, *Brother of Girls*, 70. In regard to the child-angel, see Tompkins, *Sensational Designs*, 137

29. Crittenton, *Brother of Girls*, 71.

30. Crittenton, *Brother of Girls*, 69, 65.

31. Campbell and Knox, *Darkness and Daylight*, 210; Frances Kellor, qtd. in Gilfoyle, *City of Eros*, 176; Crittenton, *Brother of Girls*, 74; Rosen, *Lost Sisterhood*, 44, 142–143.

32. "National Florence Crittenton Mission Records," SWHA, Box 1, Folder 5; Crittenton, *Brother of Girls*, 85.

33. Crittenton, *Brother of Girls*, 85.

34. Crittenton, *Brother of Girls*, 86.

35. Crittenton, *Brother of Girls*, 86–88.

36. Hobson, *Uneasy Virtue*, 11–49; Stansell, *City of Women*, 69; Gilfoyle, *City of Eros*, 182.

37. Pivar, *Purity Crusade*, 67–69, 78–195; Gilfoyle, *City of Eros*, 185; Gordon, *Moral Property of Women*, 74.

38. Sanger, *History of Prostitution*, 18, 20.

39. Sanger, *History of Prostitution*, 606; Pivar, *Purity Crusade*, 16.

40. Sanger, *History of Prostitution*, 643–46; Gilfoyle, *City of Eros*, 185.

41. Earls, "Locked Up and Poxxed"; Philippa Levine notes that while these acts targeted women, the Acts were specifically geared to protect the health of military men. Levine, "Venereal Disease, Prostitution, and the Politics of Empire."

42. Walkowitz, *Prostitution and Victorian Society*, 116; Mathers, *Patron Saint of Prostitutes*, 45–46.

43. Pivar, *Purity Crusade*, 18; D'Emilio and Freedman, *Intimate Matters*, 149.

44. Gibbons, *Life of Abby Hopper Gibbons*, 251.

45. Powell et al., "The Shame of America," 192.

46. Samuel Blackwell, "The Lesson of Geneva," *Woman's Journal* (Aug. 22, 1896), 268.

47. KWB—Kate Waller Barrett Papers (hereafter KWB), "State Regulation of the Social Evil," 1896, Box 3, Folder: Prostitution.

48. Society for the Suppression of Vice 1873 charter, qtd. in Gilfoyle, *City of Eros*, 187–188.

49. Werble, *Lust on Trial*; Gilfoyle, *City of Eros*, 187–188, 162; Sante, *Low Life*, 107.

50. Committee of Fifteen, *The Social Evils*, 155–159; Samuel Blackwell, "Responsibility of the Remonstrants," *Woman's Journal*, Vol. 27, No. 24 (June 13, 1896): 186; Gilfoyle, *City of Eros*, 166; Pivar, *Purity Crusade*, 206.

51. Crapsey and Loewy, *The Nether Side of New York*, 13; Gilfoyle, *City of Eros*, 251.

52. "Rescue or Arrest," *Florence Crittenton Magazine*, Vol. 1, No. 9 (1899): 212.

53. Washburn, *The Underworld Sewer*, 28–31, 42; Anne M. Butler, *Daughters of Joy, Sisters of Misery*, 55. For a look at how the word of sex workers was not trusted in the American court system, see Patricia Cline Cohen, *The Murder of Helen Jewett*, 360.

54. Wood, *Freedom of the Streets*, 123–24; Gilfoyle, *City of Eros*, chaps. 6, 12; Gilfoyle, *Pickpocket's Tale*, 100–101; Freedman, *Their Sisters' Keepers*, 10–21, 60, 112; Anne M. Butler, *Daughters of Joy, Sisters of Misery*, chaps. 3, 4.

55. Frances E. Williard and Mary A. Lathbury, "Mrs. J. K. Barney of Providence, R.I.," *Woman and Temperance: Or, The Work and Workers of the Woman's Christian Temperance Union.* (Hartford, Conn.: James Betts & Co., 1883), 586–587.

56. Freedman, *Their Sisters' Keepers*, 60; Wood, *Freedom of the Streets*, 104; Pivar, *Purity Crusade*, 100–103.

57. Rosen, *Lost Sisterhood*, 148; Pivar, *Purity Crusade*, 105–106. On informal economies, see Wolcott, "Culture of the Informal Economy."

58. Goldman, qtd. in Gilfoyle, *City of Eros*, 247; Hemphill, *Bawdy City*, 77–78. See also "The 'Raines Law Hotel' and the Social Evil," in Committee of Fifteen, *The Social Evil*, 135–142.

1. Mary Frazier Gaddis, "Opportunity," *Florence Crittenton Magazine*, Vol. 4, No. 11 (Jan. 1903): 344–347.

2. Gilfoyle, *City of Eros*, 177.

3. Campbell and Knox, *Darkness and Daylight*, 212.

4. Crittenton, *Brother of Girls*, 99.

5. Crittenton, *Brother of Girls*, 98–99.

6. Campbell and Knox, *Darkness and Daylight*, 217–221; Mintz, *Moralists and Modernizers*, 115; Crittenton, *Brother of Girls*, 86.

7. Crittenton, *Brother of Girls*, 87.

8. Kate Waller Barret, "History of the Florence Crittenton Movement," *Florence Crittenton Magazine*, Vol. 2, No. 3 (1901): 56.

9. Campbell and Knox, *Darkness and Daylight*, 228; Crittenton, *Brother of Girls*, 87.

10. Nellie Conroy was either one of the two "fallen girls" that Crittenton first told to "go and sin no more," or she was a sex worker brought to the Florence Crittenton Night Mission during its early years (probably the more likely version). Campbell and Knox, *Darkness and Daylight*, 240; "National Florence Crittenton Mission Records," SWHA, Box 1, Folder 5. On assumed names, see Wood's introduction to Washburn, *Underworld Sewer*, vi.

11. Campbell and Knox, *Darkness and Daylight*, 229.

12. Gilfoyle, *City of Eros*, 184. The 1903 *New York Charities Directory* listed the Crittenton Mission on Bleecker as a religious, missionary institution. *New York Charities Directory: A Classified and Description Directory to the Philanthropic, Educational and Religious Resources of the City of New York* (New York: Charity Organization Society, 1903), 212, 417.

13. L. Hereward, "A Famous Night Mission," *Westminster Review*, Vol. 140 (Sept. 1893): 273–280; Campbell and Knox, *Darkness and Daylight*, 227.

14. Campbell and Knox, *Darkness and Daylight*, 230

15. Crittenton, *Brother of Girls*, 217–219.

16. Washburn, *Underworld Sewer*, 293.

17. "A Visit to National Headquarters," *Florence Crittenton Magazine* Vol. 4, No. 11 (Jan. 1903): 342–344.

18. Campbell and Knox, *Darkness and Daylight*, 227.

19. "One From the Many," *Florence Crittenton Magazine*, Vol. 4, No. 12 (Feb. 1903): 391.

20. "How Girls Who Have Been With Us Feel Toward Us," *Florence Crittenton Magazine*, Vol. 4, No. 12 (Feb. 1903): 390.

21. Gordon, *Heroes of Their Own Lives*, 215. See also Broder, *Tramps, Unfit Mothers, and Neglected Children*, 117; Rosen, *Lost Sisterhood*, 161; Kunzel, *Fallen Women, Problem Girls*, 108–109; Pinzer, *Mamie Papers*, 193.

22. "President's Letter," *Florence Crittenton Magazine*, Vol. 4, No. 11 (Jan. 1903): 349–353.

23. Crittenton, *Brother of Girls*, 83.

24. "Chronology of Homes," SWHA, Box 1, Folder 4; Wilson, *Fifty Years' Work with Girls*, 36; Crittenton, *Brother of Girls*, 171.

25. Bordin, *Woman and Temperance*, 4.

26. Willard, *Glimpses of Fifty Years*, 428; Pivar, *Purity Crusade*, 116.

27. "The National Florence Crittenton Mission," *Florence Crittenton Magazine*, Vol. 1, No. 1

(Mar. 1899): 4; Crittenton, *Brother of Girls*, 201–202; Aiken, *Harnessing the Power of Motherhood*, 28–29; Pivar, *Purity Crusade*, 85.

28. Bordin, *Woman and Temperance*, 53–54; Bordin, *Frances Willard*, 131; Masson, "The Women's Christian Temperance Union 1874–1898"; Powell, et. al, "The Shame of America": 192–215.

29. Crittenton, *Brother of Girls*, 196; Pivar, *Purity Crusade*, 132–135.

30. Powell, et. al., "The Shame of America," 192–215.

31. B. O. Flower, "Lust Fostered by Legislation," *The Arena*, Vol. 11 (1895): 167–175; Edholm, *Traffic in Girls*, 128.

32. Edholm qtd. in Flower, "Lust Fostered by Legislation," 171.

33. Flower, "Lust Fostered by Legislation," 167–175.

34. Rosen, *Lost Sisterhood*, 137–145.

35. Alice Lee Moque, "On the Other Side," *Florence Crittenton Magazine*, Vol. 1 (Apr. 1899): 33.

36. Pivar, *Purity Crusade*, 255–256; D'Emilio and Freedman, *Intimate Matters*, 152.

37. Samuel Blackwell quoting Mrs. Charlton (Mary Grace) Edholm, "Responsibility of the Remonstrants," *Woman's Journal*, Vol. 27, No. 24 (June 13, 1896): 186.

38. Blackwell, "Responsibility of the Remonstrants," 186.

39. "Mr. Crittenton Here," *The Topeka State Journal*, July 11, 1902.

40. Frances E. W. Harper, "Social Purity," in Powell, *National Purity Congress*, 328–329; Pivar, *Purity Crusade*, 37–41.

41. Pivar, *Purity Crusade*, 18; D'Emilio and Freedman, *Intimate Matters*, 149.

42. Martha Schofield, "Slavery's Legacy of Impurity," in Powell, *National Purity Congress*, 178.

43. Harper, "Social Purity," in Powell, *National Purity Congress*, 328–329.

44. Harper, "Social Purity," 328.

45. Wood, *Freedom of the Streets*, 4.

46. Gardener, "What Shall the Age of Consent Be?," in "The Shame of America," by Powell et al., 196–197.

47. Willard and Gardener, "The Shame of America," 197.

48. Hamlin, *Free Thinker*, 139–140.

49. "Chronology of Homes, According to Affiliation with Florence-Crittenton," n.d., SWHA, Box 1, Folder 4.

CHAPTER 5. A LITTLE CHILD SHALL LEAD THEM

1. Moque, "On the Other Side," *Florence Crittenton Magazine*, Vol. 1, No. 2, (1899): 35.

2. Reference to the "millionaire evangelist" in "Work at Home," *Record of Christian Work*, Vol. 11, No. 1 (1892): 371; Wilson, *Fifty Year's Work with Girls*, 47.

3. For studies on the National Florence Crittenton Mission, see Aiken, *Harnessing the Power of Motherhood*; Kunzel, *Fallen Women, Problem Girls*, 17; Wilson, *Fifty Years' Work with Girls*.

4. Kate Waller Barrett, "Some Reminiscences," KWB, Box 3, Folder: Miscellaneous; Wilson, *Fifty Years' Work with Girls*, 146. See also, Jones-Rogers, *They Were Her Property*, chapter one: "Mistresses in the Making."

5. Letter from Kate Waller Barrett to Mrs. M. A. Thayer, June 6, 1906, SWHA, Box 1, Folder 1.

6. "A Pleasant Affair," *The Daily Dispatch*, Richmond, Va., Jan. 29, 1877; "Sudden Death," *The Daily Dispatch*, Richmond, Va., Aug. 5, 1874; Wilson, *Fifty Years' Work with Girls*, 152–153.

7. Hoffman, *Race, Class, and Power*, 88; Werber, *Report on Housing and Living Conditions*, 74.

8. See Hoffman, *Race, Class, and Power* for a discussion of postwar Richmond. See also Brown and Kimball, "Mapping the Terrain of Black Richmond," 66–113. For further discussions of disease and race, see Roberts, *Infectious Fear*; Hickey, *Hope and Danger*; Smith, *Sick and Tired*.

9. Kate Waller Barrett notes for article "Some Reminiscences," KWB, Box 3, Folder: Miscellaneous.

10. Kate Waller Barrett, "Maternity Work—Motherhood a Means of Regeneration," in *Fourteen Years' Work Among Erring Girls*, 52–62; Kate Waller Barrett, "Some Reminiscences," *Florence Crittenton Magazine*, Vol 1, No. 3 (1899): 62–66.

11. Waller Barrett, "Some Reminiscences," 62–66. On social purity reform and contemporary beliefs on who was a prostitute, see Rosen, *Lost Sisterhood*, 137–145; Pivar, *Purity Crusade*, 67–69, 78–195; Gilfoyle, *City of Eros*, 185.

12. Waller Barrett, "Some Reminiscences," 63.

13. Waller Barrett, "Some Reminiscences," 64.

14. Waller Barrett, "Some Reminiscences," 64.

15. Waller Barrett, "Maternity Work," 52–62.

16. Addams, *Twenty Years at Hull-House*, 87–88.

17. Kate Waller Barrett, "Some Reminiscences," 65; Wilson, *Fifty Years' Work with Girls*, 162. The Woman's Medical College of Georgia was organized in 1890 and graduated seven of ten students in its first class of 1891. By 1918 the school was closed, see Council on Medical Education and Hospitals, *Medical Colleges of the United States and of Foreign Countries 1918*, 7.

18. The 1910 Carnegie Foundation "Flexner Report" solidified preexisting trends to centralize medical institutions, enact higher admission and graduation standards, and decrease the number of medical schools in the United States. This resulted in the closure and consolidation of hundreds of medical schools, many of those who had once accepted African Americans and/or female students. Numbers of women admitted to medical schools began to rise in the 1970s as a result of Title IX amendments passed in 1972, and the Public Health Service Act of 1975, which outlawed discrimination based on gender. See Flexner, *Medical Education in the United States and Canada*; Morantz-Sanchez, *Sympathy and Science*, 234, 243; Walsh, *"Doctors Wanted*, 178–267; Aiken, *Harnessing the Power of Motherhood*, 36.

19. Wilson, *Fifty Years' Work with Girls*, 162.

20. Wilson, *Fifty Years' Work with Girls*, 162, 167; "Kate Waller Barrett, M.D., Sc. D. Nurse, Doctor and Sociologist," *The Trained Nurse and Hospital Review*, Apr. 1925, KWB, Box 3, Folder: Miscellaneous.

21. "Woman's World and Work," *Daily Picayune* [New Orleans, La.] Dec. 13, 1891, 18.

22. Hickey, *Hope and Danger in the New South City*, 6; Godshalk, *Veiled Visions*, 23; Hunter, *To 'Joy My Freedom*, 44–73.

23. Waller Barrett, "Some Reminiscences," 65.

24. Waller Barrett, "Some Reminiscences," 66; Wilson, *Fifty Years' Work with Girls*, 164; Aiken, *Harnessing the Power of Motherhood*, 37.

25. Waller Barrett, "Some Reminiscences, Part II," *Florence Crittenton Magazine*, Vol 1, No. 4 (1899): 84–87.

26. Another notable speaker was Booker T. Washington, who gave his first speech in front of a white southern audience at the event. Washington, *The Booker T. Washington Papers*, 199.

27. Waller Barrett, "Some Reminiscences, Part II," 86. For fears about the taint of rescue work, see Adda Flatbrush, *How She Was Lost*, 226; "Got the Money," *The Topeka State Journal*, Mar. 22, 1906; "Appeal to Women," *The Topeka State Journal*, Feb. 8, 1907.

28. Waller Barrett, "Some Reminiscences, Part II," 86; "Ladies Dined and Spoke," *The Washington Times*, Mar. 27, 1895; "Relics at the May Fete," *The Washington Times*, May 4, 1895; "Week in Washington," *The National Tribune*, Jan. 9, 1896.

29. "Chronology of Homes," SWHA, Box 1, Folder 4.

30. "Report on charitable and reformatory institutions of the District of Columbia 1898, Report of the Florence Crittenton Hope and Help Mission Washington, D.C. September 15, 1898," KWB, Box 1, Folder: Conference of Charities and Correction, 1908.

31. "A Letter from President C.N. Crittenton," *Florence Crittenton Magazine*, Vol. 1, No. 3 (1899): 66–67; Wilson, *Fifty Years' Work with Girls*, 130–131.

32. Address, Mrs. Kate Waller Barrett, Alexandria, Virginia, KWB, Box 3, Folder: National Florence Crittenton Mission.

33. Kate Waller Barrett, "Some Reminiscences," 63; Kunzel, *Fallen Women, Problem Girls*, 12.

34. "Home for Fallen Women," *The Morning Times* [Washington, D.C.], Jan. 5, 1896.

35. Pye Henry Chavasse, *Chavasse's Advice to a Mother on the Management of Her Children*, 15th ed. (New York: Routledge, 1898), 3.

36. Waller Barrett, *Some Practical Suggestions*, 47.

37. "Miscellaneous Questions and Problems" memo, n.d., SWHA, Box 1, Folder 4.

38. Letter from Charles Crittenton to Sue Anderson, Oct. 16, 1906, SWHA, Box 1, Folder 1.

39. "Report on charitable and reformatory institutions of the District of Columbia 1898, Report of the Florence Crittenton Hope and Help Mission Washington, D.C. September 15, 1898," KWB, Box 1, Folder: Conference of Charities and Correction, 1908.

40. Washburn, *The Underworld Sewer*, 263; "Twelfth Annual Report of the F.C. Hope and Help Mission, Washington, D.C.," SWHA, Box 2, Folder 1.

41. Congressional Charter, SWHA, Box 1, Folder 2. The congressional charter essentially made the NFCM a corporation and gave it the ability to sue and be sued, own and sell property, and have standing in a court of law as a stand-alone entity. This was the first such charter given to a charitable organization. Other entities that have congressional charters are the American Red Cross, Girl Scouts of the USA, and the National Park Service. Congress stopped granting congressional charters in 1992.

42. "Report on charitable and reformatory institutions of the District of Columbia 1898."

43. For a discussion of how women used personal connections in a political way before they had the vote see Ginzberg, *Women and the Work of Benevolence*, 74.

44. *Florence Crittenton Magazine*, "Women's Sphere," Vol. 1, No. 5 (July 1899): 117.

1. Miss. Marshall, "What Price Adoption?," n.d. (circa 1930), SWHA, Box 1, Folder 1, General Historical 1895–1932.

2. "Twelfth Annual Report of the F.C. Hope and Help Mission, Washington, D.C.," SWHA, Box 2, Folder 1.

3. "Home for Fallen Women," *The Morning Times* [Washington, D.C.], Jan. 5, 1896; Gordon, *Heroes of Their Own Lives*, 20. See also Fitzgerald, *Habits of Compassion*; Gordon, *The Great Arizona Orphan Abduction*; "Adoptions Folder," Children's Bureau Records, National Archives, Box 60, Folder 7346.

4. "Our Nursery," *Florence Crittenton Magazine*, Vol. 1, No. 9 (Nov. 1899): 191–193.

5. U.S. Children's Bureau, *Illegitimacy as a Child-Welfare Problem, Part 1*, 45–46; "Makes Plea for the Unmarried Mother," *The Daily Herald*, La Porte, Indiana, Oct. 19, 1917, clipping in KWB, Box 1, Folder: Bureau of Immigration.

6. U.S. Children's Bureau, *Illegitimacy as a Child-Welfare Problem, Part 1*, 35.

7. "Makes Plea for the Unmarried Mother."

8. Waller Barrett, "The Unmarried Mother and Her Child," speech given at the National Conference of Charities and Corrections in Saint Louis, Mo., Mar. 10, 1910, KWB, Box 3, Folder: Unmarried Mothers and Their Children.

9. "Our Nursery," 191; "Our Babies," *Florence Crittenton Magazine*, Vol. 5, No. 3 (May 1903): 89.

10. "Shall Girls Who are Able to Pay Be Received into Florence Crittenton Homes? If so, How Can We Prevent the Homes from Becoming Public Lying In Hospitals?" *Florence Crittenton Magazine*, Vol. 5, No. 4 (June 1903): 143; Aiken, *Harnessing the Power of Motherhood*, 78–79; Ladd-Taylor, *Raising a Baby the Government Way*, 38.

11. Letter from Charles Crittenton to Sue G. Anderson, Oct. 16, 1906, SWHA, Box 1, Folder 1.

12. Waller Barrett, *Some Practical Suggestions*, 7, 8.

13. Waller Barrett, *Some Practical Suggestions*, 17; "Like a New Place," *The Topeka State Journal*, Aug. 4, 1906.

14. "Twelfth Annual Report of the F.C. Hope and Help Mission, Washington, D.C."

15. Harriet Phillips, "Our Little Mothers," *Florence Crittenton Magazine*, Vol. 1, No. 11 (Jan. 1900): 232–234.

16. "Like a New Place"; "Colorado News Items," *Rocky Ford Enterprise*, Apr. 14, 1905.

17. Campbell and Knox, *Darkness and Daylight*, 227.

18. Freedman, *Their Sisters' Keepers*, 56.

19. Peiss, *Cheap Amusements*.

20. "A Salesgirl's Story," *The Independent*, Vol. 54 (July 1902): 1821.

21. Jane Addams, "Some Reflections on the Failure of the Modern City to Provide Recreation for Young Girls," *Charities and The Commons*, Vol. 21, (Dec. 1908): 365–368; Perry, "'The General Motherhood of the Commonwealth,'" 724.

22. T. Shelley Sutton, "Little Jane Smith," *Florence Crittenton Magazine*, Vol. 1, No. 6 (Aug. 1899): 134–137.

23. Kate Waller Barrett, "An Interesting Bit of Correspondence," *Florence Crittenton Magazine*, Vol. 11, No. 6 (Aug. 1908): 178.

24. Kunzel, *Fallen Women, Problem Girls*, 20–25; Broder, *Tramps, Unfit Mothers, and Neglected Children*, 129; Rosen, *Lost Sisterhood*, 99.

25. Rembis, *Defining Deviance*; Cahn, *Sexual Reckonings*, 46; Odem, *Delinquent Daughters*, 95–99.

26. Waller Barrett, *Some Practical Suggestions*, 48.

27. Waller Barrett, *Some Practical Suggestions*, 47.

28. "Twelfth Annual Report of the F.C. Hope and Help Mission, Washington, D.C."

29. "Miscellaneous Questions and Problems" memo, n.d., SWHA, Box 1, Folder 4; Rembis, *Defining Deviance*, 6.

30. "Reports from Homes," *Florence Crittenton Magazine*, Vol. 7, No. 9 (Feb. 1906): 445.

31. Anna Dugas Barrett, "What Love Can Do," *Florence Crittenton Magazine*, Volume 5, No. 2 (Apr. 1903): 41–42.

32. "For Civic Cleanliness," *Florence Crittenton Magazine*, Vol. 11, No. 1 (Mar. 1908): 18–19.

33. National Florence Crittenton Mission, Annual Report 1914, p. 136, SWHA, Box 2, Folder 4; Kunzel, *Fallen Women, Problem Girls*, 16.

34. Gordon, *Heroes of Their Own Lives*, 215–216; Odem, *Delinquent Daughters*, 100–101, 114–117; Broder, *Tramps, Unfit Mothers, and Neglected Children*, 119–120.

35. "Girl's Uncle is Father of Baby Left in Depot?," *The Topeka State Journal*, Mar. 21, 1918; "Local Mention," *The Topeka State Journal*, Apr. 6, 1918; "In Crittenton Home," *The Topeka State Journal*, Apr. 22, 1918.

36. Waller Barrett, "Motherhood A Means of Regeneration," pamphlet, n.d. (Washington: National Florence Crittenton Mission, n.d.), KWB, Box 3, Folder: Unmarried Mothers and their Children.

37. Marshall, "What Price Adoption?"

38. "Colorado Briefs," *The Elk Mountain Pilot*, Nov. 17, 1903.

39. Letter from Barrett to Thayer, June 6, 1906, SWHA, Box 1, Folder 1. "Wiping Out of Segregated Red Light Districts," memo, n.d., SWHA, Folder 1, Box 5.

40. Solinger, *Wake Up Little Susie*, 68; "Like a New Place."

41. "Our Colored Mission," *Florence Crittenton Magazine*, Vol. 1, No. 2 (Apr. 1899): 27–28.

42. Wilson, *Fifty Years' Work with Girls*, 466; Thomas A. Cox, *Blacks in Topeka*, 140; "Report from the President of the Colored F.C. Home, Topeka, Kansas," *Florence Crittenton Magazine*, Vol. 11, No. 6 (Aug. 1908): 186–187.

43. Wilson, *Fifty Years' Work with Girls*, 325–328; Solinger, *Wake Up Little Susie*, 68.

44. Harper, "Social Purity," in Powell, *National Purity Congress*, 328–329.

45. See Blight, *Race and Reunion*, 8.

46. Regina Kunzel mentions that only two Crittenton homes were integrated in *Fallen Women, Problem Girls*, 92; Gerda Lerner indicates the same in *The Female Experience*, 424; Ricky Solinger found the post–World War II NFCM highly exclusionary in *Wake Up Little Susie*, 51, 68, 72.

47. Aiken, *Harnessing the Power of Motherhood*, 131.

48. "Like a New Place"; quote in Aiken, *Harnessing the Power of Motherhood*, 135–137.

49. "Report From Homes," *Florence Crittenton Magazine*, Vol. 4, No. 12 (Feb. 1903): 413.

50. *Proceedings of the National Conference of Charities and Correction at the Twenty-fifth Annual Session held in the City of Richmond, Va. May 6–13th 1908,* "The Need of State Supervision for both Public and Private Charities" by Mrs. Kate Waller Barrett, M.D.D. S.C., KWB, Box 1, Folder: Conference of Charities and Correction, 1908

51. "National Council of Women," *Woman's Journal*, Vol. 27, No. 48 (Nov. 28, 1896): 380; "Executive Meeting National Council of Woman," *Woman's Journal*, Vol. 27, No. 48 (Nov. 28, 1896): 380; *History and Minutes of the National Council of Women of the United States*; "National Council of Women," *Child Welfare Magazine*, Vol. 10, No. 7 (Mar. 1916): 229; "National Council of Women," *Child Welfare Magazine*, Vol. 9, No. 4 (Dec. 1914): 128–129.

52. "27th Virginia State Conference," 1923, KWB, Box 2, Folder: DAR.

53. KWB Papers, Box 2, Folder: League of Women Voters, and Box 2, Folder: Federation of Women's Clubs.

54. "Our Study Table," *Florence Crittenton Magazine*, Vol. 1, No. 1 (Mar. 1899): 20–21.

55. "27th Virginia State Conference," 1923, KWB, Box 2, Folder: DAR.

CHAPTER 7. SISTER ARISE

1. Harper, "A Private Meeting," 772.

2. During the late nineteenth century and early twentieth century, the small but growing African American middle-class viewed itself as culturally and economically advanced enough to help working-class African Americans to be "uplifted" through their guidance. This movement was known as racial uplift.

3. Harper, *Iola Leroy*, 235; Borgstrom, "Face Value."

4. Andreá N. Williams, *Dividing Lines*, 26; McCaskill, "'To Labor … and Fight,'" 174.

5. William Still, *Underground Railroad*, 767.

6. Parker, "Frances Watkins Harper and the Search for Women's Interracial Alliances," 152; For temperance in *Iola Leroy*, see Harper, *Iola Leroy*, 158–160, 173–174, 185–186, 188.

7. "Middle-class" was more than an indicator of socioeconomic status; it also described men and women who considered themselves to be members of a collective group that believed morality, thrift, Christianity, education, and temperance were the basis of moral living and were the key to racial progress and uplift. When explaining class structures among Black reformers during this period, historian Michele Mitchell chose the term "aspiring class" to describe leading Black men and women in the late nineteenth and early twentieth century. Similarly, Glenda Gilmore points out that "middle-class" was a term never used by leading race men and women. However, "aspiring class" ignores the reality of many Black women who came from stable economic beginnings and education. Therefore, I have chosen to use the signifier "middle-class" as a way to denote a particular worldview common among Black reformers during the late nineteenth and early twentieth century. Mitchell, *Righteous Propagation*, 9; Gilmore, *Gender and Jim Crow*, xix.

8. Higginbotham, *Righteous Discontent*, 187.

9. Talbert, "Did the American Negro Make, in the Nineteenth Century, Achievements Along the Lines of Wealth, Morality, Education, etc., Commensurate with His Opportunities? If so, What Achievements Did He Make?," in Culp, ed., *Twentieth Century Negro Literature*, 21. The Niagara Movement was a precursor to the 1909 formation of the National Association for the Advancement of Colored People (NAACP).

10. Smith, *Sick and Tired*, 18; Gordon, "Black and White Visions," 579.

11. In her article "Black and White Visions of Welfare Activism, 1890–1945," Linda Gordon attempted to alter the historical parameters of welfare by exploring how ideologies of whiteness and accessibility to power shape the limitations of welfare. Gordon found that white women's reform work during the Gilded Age and Progressive Era had a large impact

on the state, but Black women's work did not. Gordon, "Black and White Visions," 588. For Victorian sexual morality, see Simmons, "African Americans and Sexual Victorianism," 61.

12. Notes from Circle No. 1, HBDP—Harry and Bertha Dandridge Papers (hereafter HBDP), Kansas Collection, RHMS625, Box 1, Folder 37; "Report from the President of the Colored F.C. Home, Topeka, Kansas," *Florence Crittenton Magazine*, Vol. 11, No. 6 (Aug. 1908): 186–187.

13. Higginbotham, *Righteous Discontent*, 202.

14. Rosetta Douglass Sprague, "What Role Is the Educated Negro Woman to Play in the Uplifting of Her Race?," in D. W. Culp, ed., *Twentieth Century Negro Literature*, 170.

15. Not all "girls" in Crittenton homes were pregnant or unwed mothers. Sometimes unruly or "wayward" girls were sent to the homes by court matrons or juvenile court judges. However, this was done with the intention of preventing such girls from having illegitimate children. "Reports from Homes," *Florence Crittenton Magazine*, Vol. 7, No. 9 (Feb. 1906): 440–446.

16. Thomas A. Cox, *Blacks in Topeka*, 140.

17. "Chronology of Homes," in "General Historical Notes– 1899–1910," SWHA, Box 1, Folder 4.

18. "Report from the President," 186.

19. W. E. B. Du Bois, ed., *Efforts for Social Betterment Among Negro Americans*, 103; "Crittenton Home Drive," *The Topeka State Journal*, Feb. 28, 1919.

20. Thomas A. Cox, *Blacks in Topeka*, 63; Painter, *Exodusters*, 147. The U.S. Census of 1880 shows Sarah and Balie living in Tennessee with Balie's sisters and brothers. The Kansas State Census of 1885 shows Sarah and Balie living in Topeka in their own home with daughter Ellen, age 4, and son Henry, age 3. U.S. Census Bureau, 1880; Kansas State Census, 1885.

21. Painter, *Exodusters*, 146–147.

22. Woods, "Integration, Exclusion, or Segregation?," 132; Thomas A. Cox, *Blacks in Topeka*, 34.

23. "Negro Immigration," *New West Monthly* (Apr. 1879): 131, qtd. in Woods, "Integration, Exclusion, or Segregation?," 130.

24. Qtd. in Thomas A. Cox, *Blacks in Topeka*, 49.

25. Doretha K. Williams, "Kansas Grows the Best Wheat and the Best Race Women," 59.

26. J. Silone Yates and A. H. Jones, "News from the Clubs: Kansas City. Women's League," *The Women's Era*, Vol. 1, No. 1 (Mar. 24, 1894): 2–3.

27. Thomas A. Cox, *Blacks in Topeka*, 107, 138–139; Doretha K. Williams, "Kansas Grows the Best Wheat and the Best Race Women," 68.

28. Thomas A. Cox, *Blacks in Topeka*, 89.

29. Knupfer, "'Toward a Tenderer Humanity'"; Lerner, "Early Community Work." In her analysis of Black women's organizing and activism, historian Deborah Gray White wrote that Black women "proclaimed the advent of the 'women's era' and came forth with a plan that made Black women the primary leaders of the race." White, *Too Heavy a Load*, 40.

30. Leslie Brown, *Upbuilding Black Durham*, 264.

31. Until 1912, Kansas politicians courted the Black male vote; Kansas women achieved the right to vote in 1912. Woods, "Integration, Exclusion, or Segregation?," 132; Thomas A. Cox, *Blacks in Topeka*, 132–133.

32. Thomas A. Cox, *Blacks in Topeka*, 138

33. "Report from the President," 8; Woods, "Integration, Exclusion, or Segregation?," 132; Thomas A. Cox, *Blacks in Topeka*, 136–137.

34. "Report of The National Florence Crittenton Mission and Its Affiliated Branches for the Year 1918–1919," SWHA, Box 2, Folder 6; "Report from the President," 186; "Topeka, Kansas," *Florence Crittenton Magazine*, Vol. 11, No. 12 (Feb. 1909): 410; "Asks Topeka To Help," *The Topeka State Journal*, Mar. 10, 1919.

35. "Reports from Homes, Mrs. Malone, Topeka, Kansas (Colored)," *Girls*, Vol. 13 (Nov. 1913): 190.

36. W. E. B. Du Bois, *The Negro Family*, 41.

37. Cahn, *Sexual Reckonings*, 20–26; Higginbotham, *Righteous Discontent*, 185–229; Salem, *To Better Our World*, 181–197; White and White, *Sylin'*, 283–85. A sample of ministers, teachers, and middle-class African Americans feared that parents were losing control of their children who were succumbing to "vicious" attractions, W. E. B. DuBois, "Morals and Manners," 34.

38. See Wolcott, *Remaking Respectability*, 6.

39. Name is changed to protect privacy.

40. "Record Card, Baby Born Jan. 3, 1913," HBDP, Box 1, Folder 6.

41. "Report of the National Florence Crittenton Mission and its Affiliated Branches for the Year 1918 to 1919."

42. Ida B. Wells, *Southern Horrors*; Lerner, *The Majority Finds Its Past*, 56.

43. Eleanor Tayleur, "The Negro Woman: Social and Moral Decadence," *The Outlook*, Vol. 76, No. 5 (Jan. 1904): 266–271.

44. W. E. B. Du Bois, *The Negro American Family*, 37; Mitchell, *Righteous Propagation*, 85; Higginbotham, *Righteous Discontent*, 187–188.

45. Schoen, *Choice and Coercion*; Larson, *Sex, Race, and Science*; Kline, *Building a Better Race*; Reilly, *The Surgical Solution*.

46. Mitchell, *Righteous Propagation*, 81–86.

47. Simmons, "African Americans and Sexual Victorianism," 55; Simmons, *Making Marriage Modern*, 21–24; Higginbotham, *Righteous Discontent*, 189–190.

48. Qtd. in Cahn, *Sexual Reckonings*, 81.

49. "In the Senate," *The Topeka State Journal*, Jan. 27, 1909; "Laid on the Shelf," *The Topeka State Journal*, Mar. 4, 1909.

50. "Hands Out Funds," *The Topeka State Journal*, Aug. 21, 1915.

51. "Retain State Aid," *The Topeka State Journal*, July 14, 1914.

52. Aiken, *Harnessing the Power of Motherhood*, 135.

53. "Report of the National Florence Crittenton Mission and its Affiliated Branches for the Year 1919 to 1920," SWHA, Box 2, Folder 6. Money received included state funds, charitable funds, and board from paying girls.

54. "It Has $3.45 Left," *The Topeka State Journal*, Aug. 10, 1915. Malone told the NFCM in 1918 that a majority of women and girls in the "colored" home were homeless: "Report of The National Florence Crittenton Mission and Its Affiliated Branches for the Year 1918–1919."

55. Hine, *Black Women in America*, 671; Aiken, *Harnessing the Power of Motherhood*, 237.

56. W. E. B. Du Bois, ed., *Efforts for Social Betterment*, 29; Gordon, *Pitied but Not Entitled*, 114.

57. "Topeka, Kansas," *Florence Crittenton Magazine*, Volume 11, No. 12 (Feb. 1909): 409.

58. "In Need of Funds," *The Topeka State Journal*, Dec. 12, 1917; "Asks Topeka to Help."

59. "Report of The National Florence Crittenton Mission and Its Affiliated Branches for the Year 1918–1919."

60. "Negroes in Campaign," *The Topeka State Journal*, Mar. 6, 1919.

61. "Asks Topeka to Help."

62. "Inmates Not Girls," *The Topeka State Journal*, Dec. 16, 1915.

63. "Mrs. Barrett on the program of the National Conference of Charities and Corrections in Topeka. Put in touch with the proprietor of Topeka Capital; he deeded property for an FC home." Later the home is listed as beginning "From Mrs. Barrett's work." "Chronology of Homes," SWHA, Box 1, Folder 4.

64. "Twelfth Annual Report of the F.C. Hope and Help Mission, Washington, D.C.," SWHA, Box 2, Folder 1.

65. Kansas Board of Control of State Charitable Institutions, *First Annual and Biennial Report*, 454.

66. A. W. Hunton, "The National Association of Colored Women," *The Crisis*, Vol. 2, No. 1 (May 1911): 17–18.

67. Hunton, "National Association of Colored Women," 17–18.

68. Gilmore, *Gender and Jim Crow*, 50–51.

69. For biographical information on Lugenia Burns Hope and the Neighborhood Union, see Rouse, *Lugenia Burns Hope*; Hickey, *Hope and Danger in the New South City*.

70. Rouse, *Lugenia Burns Hope*, 106.

71. Qtd. in Gatewood, *Aristocrats of Color*, 195.

72. Waller Barrett, "Some Preventive Measures," *Girls*, Vol. 17 (1914): 97.

73. "Minutes of the Annual Conference," *Reports of the National Florence Crittenton Mission and Its Affiliated Branches for the Year 1926*, p. 39, SWHA, Box 2, Folder 7; Aiken, *Harnessing the Power of Motherhood*, 105.

74. "Topeka, Kansas," *Girls*, Vol. 16 (1913): 113.

75. "Minutes of Conference of the National Florence Crittenton Mission, Held at Atlantic City, New Jersey, May 30–31, 1919, *Affiliated Branches, 1918–1919*, p. 106, SWHA, Box 2, Folder 6.

76. Gordon, "Black and White Visions of Welfare," 583–586.

77. Smith, *Sick and Tired of Being Sick and Tired*, 3; Gordon, *Pitied but Not Entitled*, 121.

78. *Girls*, Vol. 13 (1910): 172; Aiken, *Harnessing the Power of Motherhood*, 144–147.

79. "Snap Shots," *The Topeka State Journal*, Mar. 3, 1915.

80. "Three Pass Rigid Examination for Police Women," *The Chicago Defender*, Jan. 15, 1916; "Policewomen," *The Chicago Defender*, Apr. 13, 1918.

81. Freedman, *Maternal Justice*, particularly chapters 5, 6; Freedman, *Their Sisters' Keepers*, 46–66.

82. Clapp, "Welfare and the Role of Women"; Freedman, *Their Sisters' Keepers*, 154–155.

83. "A Home of Merit," *The Topeka State Journal*, July 18, 1914.

84. "Program of the Fiftieth Anniversary of the Florence Crittenton Work," HBDP, Box 1, Folder 37.

85. Minutes of Florence Crittenton Circle No. 1, HBDP, Kansas Collection, RHMS625, Box 1, Folder 37; Record Book 1928–1933, HBDP, no folder.

86. U.S. Census Bureau, 1920, 1930.

87. "Minutes of Conference of the National Florence Crittenton Mission," p. 106.

CHAPTER 8. THE NEIGHBORHOOD UNION

1. Lugenia Burns Hope Speech, n.d., NU, Box 1, Folder 24.

2. Lugenia Burns Hope Speech, n.d., NU, Box 1, Folder 25.

3. "Charter for the Neighborhood Union, 1911," NU, Box 2, Folder 1.

4. Hickey, *Hope and Danger*, 82; "Chronology of Homes," SWHA Box 1, Folder 4.

5. "Neighborhood Union Minute Book 1908–1918," NU, Box 4, Folder 1.

6. Neighborhood Union brochure, n.d., NU, Box 13, Folder 3.

7. "Annual Report of the Neighborhood Union, 1913–1914," reported in the *Spelman Messenger*, NU, Box 5, Folder 7.

8. Hickey, *Hope and Danger*, 83–84.

9. Hickey, *Hope and Danger*, 236n.15.

10. Letter from Jane Addams to Lugenia Burns Hope, June 3, 1908, NU, Box 1, Folder 8; Rouse, *Lugenia Burns Hope*, 16–17.

11. Lugenia Burns Hope, n.d., "Research Notes 1909–1933," NU, Box 13, Folder 47.

12. Rouse, *Lugenia Burns Hope*, 19–26.

13. Bradford, "Occasion and Purpose of the Conference," 7.

14. New South: An urban southern movement among white city leaders calling for a modernization of southern cities based on industrialization and a growing economy. It was an attempted rejection of the economy and traditions of the Old South and the slavery-based plantation system of the antebellum period. See Ayers, *The Promise of the New South*, 6.

15. Hunter, *To 'Joy My Freedom*, 45–46; Rouse, *Lugenia Burns Hope*, 29, 60–64; Galishoof, "Germs Know No Color Line," 26–27; Bayor, "The Civil Rights Movement as Urban Reform," 289.

16. A few examples from individual cities: Baltimore—Roberts, *Infectious Fear*, 83; Kansas—Woods, "Integration, Exclusion, or Segregation?," 130; Atlanta—Bayor, "Civil Rights Movement as Urban Reform," 289.

17. W. E. B. Du Bois, ed. "The Health and Physique of the Negro American," 88.

18. Mitchell, *Righteous Propagation*, 10; Smith, *Sick and Tired*, 10–11.

19. H. R. Butler, "Negligence a Cause of Mortality," in *Mortality Among Negroes in Cities*, 18.

20. W. E. B. Du Bois, "The Health and Physique of the Negro American," 88. For a definition of "infantile marasmus" as a general term for digestive ailments, see James B. Bell, *Homoeopathic Therapeutics*, 7.

21. Bush-Banks, "Heart-Throbs," 486.

22. "Mrs. Thompson Speaks on Children," *The Chicago Defender*, July 27, 1912.

23. Countless women reformers opened kindergartens for the children of working mothers across the country. A few examples: kindergartens for Mexican American children in Texas—Masarik, "Por la Raza, Para la Raza," 291; The Sheltering Arms Association for white children in Atlanta—Hickey, *Hope and Danger*, 86; day nurseries and kindergarten for immigrant children—Sklar, *Florence Kelley and the Nation's Work*, 189–191.

24. "The Story of the Gate City Free Kindergarten Association," NU, Box 12, Folder 25; Rouse, *Lugenia Burns Hope*, 28. Grace Town Hamilton, whose mother worked for the Gate City Kindergarten, said in an oral interview with Jacquelyn Hall in 1974 that Burns Hope

was not a founding member of the kindergarten association but was involved with it: Oral History Interview with Grace Towns Hamilton, July 19, 1974, Interview G-0026. Southern Oral History Program Collection (#4007), Wilson Library, University of North Carolina at Chapel Hill.

25. "Gate City Free Kindergarten," NU, Box 12, Folder 24.

26. "Great Need for More Kindergartens," The Chicago Defender, Oct. 5, 1912; "Kindergartens in Chicago," The Chicago Defender, Feb. 28, 1914.

27. "Mrs. Thompson Speaks on Children," The Chicago Defender, July 27, 1912.

28. Selena Sloan Butler, "Need of Day Nurseries," in Social and Physical Condition of Negroes in Cities, 63–65.

29. "Mrs. Thompson Speaks on Children."

30. "Mrs. Thompson Speaks on Children."

31. "The 'N' Street Day Nursery," The Crisis, Vol. 3, No. 4 (Feb. 1912): 165–166.

32. Baker, Following the Color Line, 5; Godshalk, Veiled Visions, 35–38; Hunter, To 'Joy My Freedom, 136.

33. Rouse, Lugenia Burns Hope, 43.

34. Qtd. in Rouse, Lugenia Burns Hope, 42–44.

35. Lugenia Burns Hope speech, NU, Box 1, Folder 24; "Charter for the Neighborhood Union, 1911."

36. Hickey, Hope and Danger, 100.

37. Gordon, "Black and White Visions of Welfare," 566.

38. "Annual Report of the Neighborhood Union, 1913–1914."

39. Organization 1926, NU, Box 2, Folder 8; "Atlanta Thanks College Women for Community Service Center," The Chicago Defender, Oct. 31, 1935; Smith, Sick and Tired, 30.

40. "Charter for the Neighborhood Union in 1911."

41. Minutes, Sept. 9, 1909, "Neighborhood Union Minute Book 1908–1918," NU, Box 4, Folder 1.

42. Minutes, Oct. 14, 1909.

43. Minutes, Feb. 1911.

44. Elsa Barkley Brown, "Imagining Lynching," 108.

45. "Charter for the Neighborhood Union in 1911."

46. Lugenia Burns Hope, transcript of speech, NU, Box 1, Folder 24.

47. "Constitution 1908," NU, Box 2, Folder 5.

48. "Organization 1926," NU, Box 2, Folder 8.

49. Black people were hungry for health knowledge, even if they eschewed the morality that came along with it. Dr. Wilberforce Williams wrote a weekly column in the Chicago Defender, covering a broad range of health topics from syphilis to infant mortality to proper toenail care. He was often attacked for discussing topics like sexually transmitted diseases in frank detail, but the longevity of his column and letters that poured in each week proved that the Defender's readers were hungry for information about healthcare. "Dr. Wilberforce Williams Talks On: Preventative Measures First Aid Remedies Hygienics and Sanitation," The Chicago Defender, Jan. 22, 1916; Stovall, "The 'Chicago Defender' in the Progressive Era."

50. Minutes, Oct. 1, 1908; Smith, Sick and Tired, 31; Rouse, Lugenia Burns Hope, chap. 4.

51. "The Neighborhood Union A Survey," 1926, NU, Box 2, Folder 8.

52. "Georgia: Atlanta, Ga.", *The Chicago Defender*, May 3, 1924; Smith, *Sick and Tired*, 30; Rouse, *Lugenia Burns Hope*, chap. 4.

53. Minutes, Oct. 1, 1908; Survey by the department of Social Research of Morehouse College, NU, Box 7, Folder 10; Neighborhood Union Report, Mar. 18, 1924, NU, Box 5, Folder 9.

54. Smith, *Sick and Tired*, 33.

55. Rouse, *Lugenia Burns Hope*, 81; Smith, *Sick and Tired*, 30–31.

56. Qtd. in Smith, *Sick and Tired*, 40–41; Hickey, *Hope and Danger*, 112.

57. Qtd. in Hickey, *Hope and Danger*, 112.

58. Judson, "Civil Rights and Civic Health," 94; Hickey, *Hope and Danger*, 118.

59. "Annual Report of the Neighborhood Union, 1913–1914"; Hickey, *Hope and Danger*, 118; Rouse, *Lugenia Burns Hope*, 80.

60. Minutes, May 28, 1909; Rouse, *Lugenia Burns Hope*, 82–83.

61. "Annual Report of the Neighborhood Union, 1913–1914.

62. Petition to Board of Education, 1913, NU, Box 2, Folder 20.

63. "Annual Report of the Neighborhood Union, 1913–1914."

64. "The Story of the Gate City Press Kindergarten Association," NU, Box 12, Folder 25.

65. Rouse, *Lugenia Burns Hope*, 48, 92–94, 98–103; Giddings, *When and Where I Enter*, 151–154; Gilmore, *Gender and Jim Crow*, 192–195; Hall, *Revolt Against Chivalry*, 84–86. The YWCA did not become fully committed to racial equity until 1946.

66. Frances E. W. Harper to William Still, Mar. 29, 1871, in Harper, "A Private Meeting with the Women," 773.

CHAPTER 9. THE WOMEN'S WELFARE NETWORK

1. Helen C. Putnam, M.D., "Department of Hygiene," *Child Welfare Magazine*, Volume 9, No. 4 (Dec. 1914): 121–123.

2. Letter from Jane Addams to Lugenia Burns Hope, June 3, 1908, NU, Box 1, Folder 8; Rouse, *Lugenia Burns Hope*, 17; letter from Kate Waller Barrett to Julia Lathrop, Mar. 13, 1925, KWB, Box 2, Folder: Department of Labor.

3. Jane Addams, *20 Years at Hull-House*; Muncy, *Creating a Female Dominion*, 30–34.

4. Edward Soja argues that the equitable distribution of resources, services, and access is a basic human right and the geographies people live within allow and/or disallow them to access those basic rights. Soja, *Seeking Spatial Justice*.

5. Sklar, *Florence Kelley and the Nation's Work*.

6. Elizabeth Morgan, qtd. in Sklar, *Florence Kelley and the Nation's Work*, 209.

7. Lindenmeyer, *A Right to Childhood*, 9.

8. Muncy, *Creating a Female Dominion*, 33, 47; Miriam Cohen, *Julia Lathrop*, 35–56.

9. Sklar, *Florence Kelley and the Nation's Work*, 229, 278; Sklar, "Hull-House Maps and Papers," 111–147; Muncy, *Creating a Female Dominion*, xii.

10. Duke, *Infant Mortality*; Richmond and Hall, *A Study of Nine Hundred and Eighty-Five Widows*; "It is Mothers' Problem: Infant Mortality Must Be Solved by Them, Says Wilbur Phillips," *New York Times*, Nov. 11, 1910. For a study of the birth certificate, see Pearson, *The Birth Certificate*.

11. Lindenmeyer, *A Right to Childhood*, 15–18.

12. Theodore Roosevelt, Committee on the District of Columbia, Proceedings of the Conference on the Care of Dependent Children, S. Doc. No. 60-721, at 5 (1909).

13. Roosevelt, Committee on the District of Columbia, Proceedings of the Conference on the Care of Dependent Children, S. Doc. No. 60-721, at 5, 36 (1909). For mothers' pensions, see Mink, *The Wages of Motherhood*, 34; Michel, "The Limits of Maternalism: Policies Toward American Wage-Earning Mothers During the Progressive Era," in *Mothers of the New World*, ed. Koven and Michel, 279; Fitzgerald, *Habits of Compassion*, 188; Skocpol, *Protecting Soldiers and Mothers*, part III.

14. Jane Addams, Committee on the District of Columbia, Proceedings of the Conference on the Care of Dependent Children, S. Doc. No. 60-721, at 11 (1909). See also Nelson, "The Origins of the Two-Channel Welfare State," 123–151. For an analysis of transnational Progressivism, see Rodgers, *Atlantic Crossings*.

15. Committee on the District of Columbia, Proceedings of the Conference on the Care of Dependent Children, S. Doc. No. 60-721, at 6 (1909).

16. Mrs. John M. Glenn (Mary Wilcox Glenn), Committee on the District of Columbia, Proceedings of the Conference on the Care of Dependent Children, S. Doc. No. 60-721, at 168 (1909); Hanson, "Mary Wilcox Glenn (1869–1940)," in *Social Welfare History Project*.

17. Lillian Wald, Committee on the District of Columbia, Proceedings of the Conference on the Care of Dependent Children, S. Doc. No. 60-721, at 170 (1909).

18. Homer Folks, Committee on the District of Columbia, Proceedings of the Conference on the Care of Dependent Children, S. Doc. No. 60-721, at 173 (1909).

19. James E. West, *Proceedings of the Conference on the Care of Dependent Children*, S. Doc. No. 60-721, at 174 (1909).

20. Mrs. Frederic Schoff (Hannah Kent Schoff), Committee on the District of Columbia, Proceedings of the Conference on the Care of Dependent Children, S. Doc. No. 60-721, at 170 (1909); Ladd-Taylor, *Mother-Work*, 48.

21. Wald, Committee on the District of Columbia, Proceedings of the Conference on the Care of Dependent Children, S. Doc. No. 60-721, at 201 (1909).

22. Committee on the District of Columbia, Proceedings of the Conference on the Care of Dependent Children, S. Doc. No. 60-721, at 68, 183, 185–186 (1909).

23. "Opposed to Federal Children's Bureau: Proposed New Government Department Not Needed, Say Child Welfare Workers," *New York Times*, Jan. 28, 1912.

24. Lillian Wald, "New Children's Bureau: Miss Wald Describes to Opposing Gerry Society Officials Its Purpose," *New York Times*, Feb. 1, 1912.

25. Organizational and Topical Material, 1912, Women's Trade Union League and Its Leaders: Margaret Dreier Robins Papers; Muncy, *Creating a Female Dominion*, 40; Lindenmeyer, *A Right to Childhood*, 18; Meckel, *Save the Babies*, 140, 151.

26. "Work of Children's Bureau," New York Times, Sept. 29, 1912; "Woman Heads Child Bureau," *Chicago Defender*, May 4, 1912.

27. Muncy, *Creating a Female Dominion*, 47.

28. U.S. Children's Bureau, *Birth Registration: An Aid in Protecting the Lives and Rights of Children*, Monograph No. 1, Second Edition (Washington: Government Printing Office, 1914), 6.

29. "Record Your Baby's Birth," *The Chicago Defender*, Oct. 10, 1914.

30. U.S. Children's Bureau, *First Annual Report of the Chief*, 12

31. "150,000 Babies May Be Saved Each Year," *New York Times*, Dec. 21, 1912; Ladd-Taylor, *Mother-Work*, 85–86.

32. U.S. Children's Bureau, *First Annual Report of the Chief*, 10.

33. U.S. Children's Bureau, *Third Annual report of the Chief*, 367–368.

34. Letter from Mrs. Frederic Schoff to Julia Lathrop, Nov. 1916, CB—Records of the Children's Bureau (hereafter CB),Box 35, Infant Mortality, 4-13-1; Ladd-Taylor, *Mother-Work*, 85–86.

35. Letter to Dr. B. L. Lewis from Dr. Anna E. Rude, Director, Children's Bureau Division of Hygiene, Sept. 30, 1919, CB, Box 23, Record Group 102, 4-0; Bradbury, *Five Decades of Action for Children*; Ladd-Taylor, *Mother-Work*, 86; Skocpol, *Protecting Soldiers and Mothers*, 489; Muncy, *Creating a Female Dominion*, 58–59.

36. U.S. Children's Bureau, *Fourth Annual report of the Chief*, 7.

37. "Safety First For Mothers," Notes from the Twenty-first Child Welfare Conference, Department of Obstetrics, Dr. Mary Sherwood, chairman, "What Women Can Do to Hasten Obstetrical Care?," *Child Welfare Magazine*, Vol. 11, No. 10 (June 1917): 285–290.

38. U.S. Children's Bureau, *Fourth Annual report of the Chief*, 8.

39. "Anecdotes from the Third Annual report of the Chief, Children's Bureau," *Reports of the Department of Labor 1915: Report of the Secretary of Labor and Reports of Bureaus*, (Washington: Government Printing Office, 1916), 367–368; U.S. Children's Bureau, *Fifth Annual Report of the Chief*, 23.

40. U.S. Children's Bureau, *Infant Mortality: Montclair, N.J.*, 11–19; U.S. Children's Bureau, *Third Annual report of the Chief*, 363.

41. U.S. Children's Bureau, *First Annual Report of the Chief*, 8; Muncy, *Creating a Female Dominion*, 52.

42. U.S. Children's Bureau, *Third Annual Report of the Chief*, 363.

43. *Third Annual Report of the Chief*, 363.

44. U.S. Children's Bureau, *Infant Mortality: Montclair, N.J.*, 8, 28; U.S. Children's Bureau, *First Annual Report of the Chief*, 8.

45. U.S. Children's Bureau, *Fifth Annual Report of the Chief*, 14–15, 45.

CHAPTER 10. DOING THE WORK

1. Mrs. Frederic Schoff, "The Evolution of Mothers Pensions, *Child Welfare Magazine*, Vol. 9, No 4 (Dec. 1914): 113–117.

2. "Mothers' Pensions' Greatest Victory," *Child Welfare Magazine*, Vol. 9, No. 9 (May 1915); Schoff, "Evolution of Mothers Pensions," 113–117.

3. Schoff, "Evolution of Mothers Pensions," 113–117; Skocpol, *Protecting Soldiers and Mothers*, 445–465.

4. Letter from Katharine Felton, General Secretary Associated Charities of San Francisco, to Julia Lathrop, Oct. 6, 1915, CB, Box 60, Mothers' Pensions, 7311; Memo to English Parliament from Frederick C. Potter, roughly 1915–1916 based on other correspondence in folder, CB, Box 60, Mothers' Pensions, 7311; Gordon, *Pitied but not Entitled*, 37–43.

5. Breckinridge, *Family Welfare Work*, 634–642, 634n.1.

6. Breckinridge, *Family Welfare Work*, 634–642.

7. Breckinridge, *Family Welfare Work*, 634–642.

8. Schoff, "Evolution of Mothers Pensions," 113–117. Thomas Krainz explores how mothers' pension payments in Colorado differed county to county in Krainz, *Delivering Aid*.

9. "From the President's Desk," *Child Welfare Magazine*, Vol. 9, No. 9 (May 1915): 285–288.

10. Mink, *The Wages of Motherhood*, 181; Patterson, *America's Struggle Against Poverty*, 69–70; Nelson, "The Origins of the Two-Channel Welfare State."

11. Ida D. Gilpin, "Mothers' Assistance in Philadelphia," *Child Welfare Magazine*, Volume 9, No. 8 (Apr. 1915): 264–266.

12. Gilpin, "Mothers' Assistance in Philadelphia."

13. P. McIntosh, "Mothers' Pension in Oregon," *Child Welfare Magazine*, Vol. 9, No. 6 (Feb. 1915): 196–198.

14. "Mothers' Pensions' Greatest Victory," *Child Welfare Magazine*, Vol. 9, No. 9 (May 1915): 299.

15. "Mothers' Pension Releases 2000 Children from Institutions," *Child Welfare Magazine*, Vol. 10, No. 8 (Apr. 1916): 265.

16. Letter from Sophie Gudden, Vice President, Wisconsin Consumers League, to Julia Lathrop, Jan. 30, 1915, CB, Box 60, Mothers' Pensions, 7311.

17. U.S. Children's Bureau, *Fifth Annual Report of the Chief*, 6.

18. U.S. Children's Bureau, *Third Annual Report of the Chief*, 8.

19. The ten states included "the New England States, Maryland, New York, Pennsylvania, Michigan, and Minnesota." Julia Lathrop, "Birth Registration—A message to the Mothers' Congress," *Child Welfare Magazine*, Vol 11, No. 6 (Feb. 1916): 173–174; U.S. Children's Bureau, *Fourth Annual Report of the Chief*, 17.

20. U.S. Children's Bureau, *Fifth Annual Report of the Chief*, 23.

21. Gordon, *Pitied But Not Entitled*, 24; Kleinberg, *Widows and Orphans First*, 118.

22. U.S. Children's Bureau, *Fourth Annual report of the Chief*, 21.

23. U.S Children's Bureau, *Fourth Annual report of the Chief*, 22.

24. Qtd. in Muncy, *Creating a Female Dominion*, 56.

25. Muncy, *Creating a Female Dominion*, 57.

26. U.S Children's Bureau, *Third Annual Report of the Chief*, 25; U.S. Children's Bureau, *Fifth Annual Report of the Chief*, 28; U.S. Children'd Bureau, *Eighth Annual Report of the Chief*, 6; Ladd-Taylor, *Raising a Baby the Government Way*, 2.

27. Mrs. W. M. to Julia Lathrop, Mar. 29, 1915, qtd. in, Ladd-Taylor *Raising a Baby the Government Way*, 162–163.

28. Julia C. Lathrop, "Income and Infant Mortality," *American Journal of Public Health*, Vol. 9, No. 4 (Apr. 1919): 270–274.

29. Letter from Mrs. W. D. to Julia Lathrop, June 22, 1918, qtd. in Ladd-Taylor, *Raising a Baby the Government Way*, 118.

30. Letter to Children's Bureau from Th. Schwarz, of Jersey City, N.J., Oct. 27, 1914, CB, Box 24, Sex Education, 4-0-6-1.

31. "Dr. A. Wilberforce Williams Talks on Preventative Measures, First Aid Remedies, Hygienics and Sanitation: Some Things from '1,000 Things Mothers Should Know,'" *Chicago Defender*, Mar. 1, 1919.

32. D'Emilio and Freedman, *Intimate Matters*, 155–156; Pivar, *Purity and Hygiene*, 48–50.

33. Letter from Mrs. Geo. H. Kelley II to Julia Lathrop, June 22, 1918, CB, Box 24, Record Group 201, 4-0-2; Letter from Julia Lathrop to Mrs. Geo. H. Kelley II, June 26, 1918, CB, Box 24, Record Group 201, 4-0-2.

34. Miriam Cohen, *Julia Lathrop*, 99; U.S. Children's Bureau, *Seventh Annual Report of the Chief*, 17.

35. Letter from Mrs. L. C. Smith to Julia Lathrop, May 8, 1917, CB, Box 24, Record Group 201, 4-0-2; Letter from Julia Lathrop to Mrs. L. C. Smith, May 11, 1917, CB, Box 24, Record Group 201, 4-0-2.

36. U.S. Children's Bureau, *First Annual Report of the Chief*, 13.

37. Letter from M. P. Clarke to the Children's Bureau, May 25, 1915, CB, Box 23, Record Group 102, 4-0-1.

38. U.S. Children's Bureau, *First Annual Report of the Chief*, 13; Withycombe, *Lost*, 69–71; Lindenmeyer, *A Right to Childhood*, 70.

39. U.S. Children's Bureau, *Third Annual Report of the Chief*, 365; U.S. Children's Bureau, *Fourth Annual Report of the Chief*, 25; U.S. Children's Bureau, *Fifth Annual Report of the Chief*, 28.

40. Laura Clarke Rockwood (Chairman of Child-Welfare Department, Electra Circle of King's Daughters, Iowa City, Iowa), "A Child-Welfare Station in Iowa: How A Group of Women Developed a Form of Community Service," *Child Welfare Magazine*, Vol. 11, No. 3 (Nov. 1916): 76–79.

41. U.S. Children's Bureau, *Third Annual Report of the Chief*, 365–366.

42. U.S. Children's Bureau, *Fourth Annual Report of the Chief*, 5, 12; Lindenmeyer, *A Right to Childhood*, 71.

43. U.S. Children's Bureau, *Fourth Annual Report of the Chief*, 5.

44. U.S. Children's Bureau, *Third Annual Report of the Chief*, 359–360; Muncy, *Creating a Female Dominion*, 63–64.

45. U.S. Children's Bureau, *Fourth Annual Report of the Chief*, 25; U.S. Children's Bureau, *Sixth Annual Report of the Chief*, 578.

46. "National Council of Women," *Child Welfare Magazine*, Vol. 10, No. 7 (Mar. 1916): 229; A. W. Hunton, "The National Association of Colored Women," *The Crisis*, Vol. 2, No. 1 (May 1911): 17–18; "Biennial Convention of the National Council of Women, Washington, D.C., Dec 9–12," *Child Welfare Magazine*, Vol. 22, No. 5 (June 1918): 67.

47. *Reports of the Department of Labor 1915*, 79; U.S Children's Bureau, *Fourth Annual Report of the Chief*, 20.

48. Interview, Dec. 12, 1916, with Miss Sadie American, Head of Field Work, Lakeview Home, New York City, CB, Box 68, Institutions, 7441.

49. "Minutes of the Conference of the National Florence Crittenton Mission Held at Atlantic City, New Jersey, May 30–31, 1919," *Affiliated Branches, 1918–1919*, p. 118, SWHA, Box 2, Folder 6; Aiken, *Harnessing the Power of Motherhood*, 186.

50. Letter from Julius Levy, Director, City of Newark Department of Health, to Helen B. Welsh, Supervisor, Maternity Hospital, Minneapolis, Minn., Feb. 24, 1920, CB, Box 68, Institutions, 7441.

51. U.S. Children's Bureau, *Illegitimacy as a Child-Welfare Problem*, pt. 3, 154.

52. "Illegitimacy Legislation (New York, Etc.)," memo dated July 12, 1918, CB, Box 108, Illegitimacy, 10.002.12; U.S. Children's Bureau, *Eighth Annual Report of the Chief*, 16.

53. Letter from Helen B. Welsh, Supervisor, The Maternity Hospital, Minneapolis, Minn., to Julia Lathrop, Director, Children's Bureau, Dec. 23, 1919, CB, Box 68, Institutions, 7441.

54. Qtd. in Broder, *Tramps, Unfit Mothers, and Neglected Children*, 175; Michel, "The Limits of Maternalism," in *Mothers of the New World*, ed. Koven and Michel, 277–320.

55. "The Day Nursery Discussed by Miss Addams," *Charities and the Commons*, Vol. 15 (1905): 411, qtd. in Michel, "The Limits of Maternalism," 291; Gordon, *Pitied But Not Entitled*, 23.

56. Broder, "Child Care or Child Neglect?," 128–148.

57. Reagan, *When Abortion Was a Crime*, 298n.8; see also Pivar, *Purity and Hygiene*, 58.

58. Report by the Juvenile Protective Association, "Some Facts about the Survey of Uncertified Homes Where Children Are Boarded Apart from Their Parents," Apr. 6, 1917, CB, Box 60, Baby Farms, 7349.1.

59. Memorandum from Miss Lathrop, July 19, 1916, CB, Box 60, Baby Farms, 7349.1.

60. Report by the Juvenile Protective Association, "Some Facts about the Survey of Uncertified Homes Where Children Are Boarded Apart from Their Parents;" Apr. 6, 1917, CB, Box 60, Baby Farms, 7349.1; Broder, "Child Care or Child Neglect?," 128–148.

61. Letter from Rollin Linder Hartt to Helen L. Sumber of the Children's Bureau, May 10, 1915, CB, Box 60, Adoptions, 7346.

62. U.S. Children's Bureau, *Fifth Annual Report of the Chief*, 30; U.S. Children's Bureau, *Sixth Annual Report of the Chief*, 574; Lindenmeyer, *A Right to Childhood*, 71–72.

63. Lathrop, "The Children's Bureau," 114.

64. Gould, *The Mismeasure of Man*, chapt. 5; Mink, *The Wages of Motherhood*, 15, 23.

65. S. Josephine Baker, "The Relation of the War to the Nourishment of Children," *New York Medical Journal*, Vol. 107, No. 7 (Feb. 16, 1928): 289–292; Mink, *The Wages of Motherhood*, 58–59.

66. "State Quotas of Babies to Be Saved During Children's Year" *Child Welfare Magazine*, Vol 22, No. 8 (Apr. 1918): 142–143.

67. U.S. Children's Bureau, *Sixth Annual Report of the Chief*, 574; Mrs. Sumner Whitten, "Attention Mothers," *Child Welfare Magazine*, Vol. 22, No. 10, (June 1918): 193.

68. U.S. Children's Bureau, *Eighth Annual Report of the Chief*, 11.

69. Kate Waller Barrett, Report of the President, American Legion Auxiliary, n.d., KB, Lib Congress, Box 1, American Legion Auxiliary.

70. Qtd. in Lindenmeyer, *A Right to Childhood*, 71–73 from "Report to Council of National Defense," May 25, 1917; Grace L. Meigs, "Memorandum on Report of the Committee to the Council of National Defense" CB, Box 47, 4-16-01.

71. U.S. Children's Bureau, *Fifth Annual Report of the Chief*, 21.

72. U.S. Children's Bureau, *Fifth Annual Report of the Chief*, 41.

73. Emma O. Lundberg, "The Illegitimate Child and War Conditions," Federal Children's Bureau publication, reprinted from the *American Journal of Anthropology*, Vol. 1, No. 3, 1918, KWB, Box 2, Folder: Illegitimate Children; U.S. Children's Bureau, *Fifth Annual Report of the Chief*, 40.

74. U.S. Children's Bureau, *Standards of Legal Protection for Children Born out of Wedlock*; U.S. Children's Bureau, *Tenth Annual Report of the Chief*, 25–26; Aiken, *Harnessing the Power of Motherhood*, 186.

75. U.S. Children's Bureau, *Ninth Annual Report of the Chief*, 22; U.S. Children's Bureau, *Eighth Annual Report of the Chief*, 16.

1. Florence Kelley, testifying before the Senate Committee on Public Health and National Quarantine, "S. 3259, Protection of Maternity and Infancy," 66th Cong., 2nd sess., May 12, 1920, 51–53.

2. Charles A. Selden, "The Most Powerful Lobby in Washington."

3. *Protection of Maternity and Infancy: Hearing on S. 3259, Before the Committee on Public Health and National Quarantine*, 66th Cong., 2nd sess. (1920) (statement of Mary Stewart, representative of the Women's National Republican Executive Committee), 42.

4. Selden, "The Most Powerful Lobby in Washington."

5. *Protection of Maternity and Infancy* (statement of Mrs. Henry W. Keyes [Frances Parkinson Keyes], author and wife of senator Henry W. Keyes), 23.

6. *Hygiene of Maternity and Infancy: Hearings on H.R. 12634 Before the House Committee on Labor*, 65th Cong., 3rd sess. (1919) (statement of Rep. Jeanette Rankin (R–Mont.)), 7.

7. *Hygiene of Maternity and Infancy* (statement of Dr. Anna E. Rude, director, Children's Bureau Division of Hygiene), 33.

8. *Hygiene of Maternity and Infancy* (statement of Dorothy Reed Mendenhall, Children's Bureau), 29.

9. *Hygiene of Maternity and Infancy* (statement of Florence Kelley, secretary, Consumers' League), 34.

10. *Protection of Maternity And Infancy* (statement of Mrs. Josephus Daniels [Addie Worth Bagley Daniels], National Democratic Committee), 22.

11. *Protection of Maternity and Infancy* (statement of Anne Martin, National Women's Party), 20.

12. *Protection of Maternity: Hearings on S. 1039 before the Senate Committee on Education and Labor*, 67th Cong., 1st sess. (1921) (statement of Dr. Alfred H. Quessy of Fitchburg, Massachusetts), 96; Lindenmeyer, *A Right to Childhood*, 85–86.

13. "Woman Assails Maternity Bill: Miss Robertson Denounces the Methods of Supporters of the Measure," *New York Times*, Aug. 11, 1921.

14. *Protection of Maternity And Infancy* (exchange between Florence Kelley and Sen. Joseph Ransdell (D–La.), 51–53.

15. *Protection of Maternity And Infancy* (statement of Frances Parkinson Keyes, author and wife of senator Henry W. Keyes), 53.

16. Selden, "The Most Powerful Lobby in Washington," 93–95.

17. U.S. Children's Bureau, *Tenth Annual Report of the Chief*, 5; Lindenmeyer, *A Right to Childhood*, 88–92.

18. U.S. Children's Bureau, *Tenth Annual Report of the Chief*, 6; Lindenmeyer, *A Right to Childhood*, 88–92.

19. U.S. Children's Bureau, *The Promotion of the Welfare and Hygiene of Maternity and Infancy for the Fiscal Year Ending June 30, 1929*, 27; Mink, *The Wages of Motherhood*, 71.

20. Nelson, "The Origins of the Two-Channel Welfare State"; Klein, *For All These Rights*, 11, 25.

21. Katznelson, *When Affirmative Action was White*, 42–46; Patterson, *America's Struggle Against Poverty*, 69–70; Muncy, *Creating a Female Dominion*, 151–154.

22. Muncy, *Creating a Female Dominion*, 160.

23. U.S. Children's Bureau, *Eighth Annual Report of the Chief*, 13.

24. For example, see "Women, Infants, and Children," *Catholic Charities*, accessed Feb. 28, 2020, https://www.ccwny.org/wic.

25. Ginzberg, *Women and the Work of Benevolence*, 74.

26. *National Center for Education Statistics*, "Characteristics of Public School Teachers"; Tikkanen et al., "Maternal Mortality and Maternity Care."

27. Salzberg et al., "The Social Work Profession"; U.S. Bureau of Labor Statistics, "Education Pays, 2021."

28. Historian Molly Ladd-Taylor demonstrates the darkest results of this type of resentment toward social welfare spending in her study of eugenic sterilization in Interwar Minnesota, where she argued lack of funds and political expediency fueled the drive to sterilize or incarcerate society's most vulnerable people. Ladd-Taylor warns against simple explanations of eugenic sterilization as "pseudoscience and an intrusive state" and argues instead that the legacy of eugenic sterilization is "a disturbing tale of political expediency and taxpayer stinginess" that can easily happen again. Ladd-Taylor, "The 'Sociological Advantages' of Sterilization," 281–299.

29. *Protection of Maternity and Infancy* (statement of Mrs. Henry W. Keyes [Frances Parkinson Keyes], author and wife of senator Henry W. Keyes), 23.

30. Ely and Driscoll, "Infant Mortality in the United States"; Centers for Disease Control and Prevention, "Infant Mortality."

31. R. B. Ince, "Too Late," *Child Welfare Magazine*, Vol. 9, No. 4 (Dec. 1914): 117.

BIBLIOGRAPHY

ARCHIVES

CB—Records of the Children's Bureau. Record Group 102. United States National Archives.

HBDP—Harry and Bertha Dandridge Papers. Kansas Collection, Kenneth Spencer Research Library, University of Kansas Libraries, Lawrence, Kans.

KWB—Kate Waller Barrett Papers. Manuscript Division, Library of Congress, Washington, D.C.

"19th Century Mourning." Permanent exhibit, National Museum of Funeral History, Houston, Texas.

NU—Neighborhood Union Papers. Atlanta University Center Robert W. Woodruff Library, Atlanta, Ga.

Organizational and Topical Material. 1912. Women's Trade Union League and Its Leaders: Margaret Dreier Robins Papers. Arthur and Elizabeth Schlesinger Library on the History of Women in America, Harvard University. *Women's Studies Archive.* Accessed May 10, 2019. https://www.gale.com/c/womens-trade-union-league-and-its-leaders.

Southern Oral History Program Collection (04007G), Wilson Library, University of North Carolina at Chapel Hill.

SWHA—Social Welfare History Archives. Florence Crittenton Collection, University of Minnesota, Anderson Special Collections, Minneapolis, Minn.

PRIMARY SOURCES

Addams, Jane. *Twenty Years at Hull-House with Autobiographical Notes.* New York: MacMillan, 1911.

American Tract Society. *The Child's Anti-Slavery Book: Containing a Few Words about American Slave Children. And Stories of Slave-Life.* New York: American Tract Society, 1859.

Baker, Ray Stannard. *Following the Color Line: An Account of Negro Citizenship in the American Democracy.* New York: Doubleday Page, 1908.

Beecher, Catherine. *A Treatise on Domestic Economy: For the Use of Young Ladies at Home, and at School.* Boston: Thomas H. Webb, 1843.

Bell, James B. *The Homoeopathic Therapeutics of Diarrhoea, Dysentery, Cholera Morbus, Chol-*

era Infantum, and all Other Loose Evacuations of the Bowels. Philadelphia: F. E. Boericke, Hahnemann, 1888.

Bradford. George G. "Occasion and Purpose of the Conference." In *Mortality Among Negroes in Cities: Proceedings of the Conference for Investigation of City Problems, Held at Atlanta University, May 26–27, 1896*, 7–12. Atlanta: Atlanta University Press, 1896.

Breckinridge, Sophonisba. *Family Welfare Work in a Metropolitan Community: Selected Case Records*. Chicago: The University of Chicago Press, 1924.

Bush-Banks, Olivia Ward. "Heart-Throbs." In *Before Harlem: An Anthology of African American Literature from the Long Nineteenth Century*, edited by Ajuan Maria Mance, 486. Knoxville: University of Tennessee Press, 2016.

Butler, H. R. "Negligence a Cause of Mortality." In *Mortality Among Negroes in Cities: Proceedings of the Conference for Investigation of City Problems, Held at Atlanta University, May 26–27, 1896*, 20–25. Atlanta: Atlanta University Press, 1896.

Butler, Selena Sloan. "Need of Day Nurseries." In *Social and Physical Condition of Negroes in Cities: Report of an Investigation Under the Direction of Atlanta University: And Proceedings of the Second Conference for the Study of Problems Concerning Negro City Life Held at Atlanta University, May 25–26, 1897*. Atlanta University Publications, No. 2. Atlanta: Atlanta University Press, 1897.

Campbell, Helen, and Thomas Wallace Knox. *Darkness and Daylight: Or, Lights and Shadows of New York Life*. Hartford, Conn.: Hartford Publishing Company, 1895.

Centers for Disease Control and Prevention. "Infant Mortality." Accessed Aug. 2020. https://www.cdc.gov/reproductivehealth/maternalinfanthealth/infantmortality.htm.

Committee of Fifteen. *The Social Evils with Special Reference to Conditions Existing in the City of New York: A Report Prepared (in 1902) Under the Direction of the Committee of Fifteen*. 2nd ed., Edwin R. A. Seligman, ed. New York: G. P. Putnam's Sons, 1912.

Council on Medical Education and Hospitals. *Medical Colleges of the United States and of Foreign Countries*. American Medical Association, 1918.

Crapsey, Edward, and Benno Loewy. *The Nether Side of New York: Or, the Vice, Crime and Poverty of the Great Metropolis*. New York: Sheldon, 1872.

Crittenton, Charles Nelson. *The Brother of Girls: The Life Story of Charles N. Crittenton as Told by Himself*. New York: World's Events, 1910.

Culp, Daniel Wallace. *Twentieth Century Negro Literature*. Toronto: J. L. Nichols, 1902.

Du Bois, W. E. B. *Efforts for Social Betterment among Negro Americans*. Atlanta University Publications, No. 14. Atlanta: Atlanta University Press, 1909.

———, ed. "The Health and Physique of the Negro American." In *Report of a Social Study Made Under the Direction of Atlanta University*. Atlanta: Atlanta University Press, 1906.

———. "Morals and Manners among Negro Americans." In *Report of a Social Study Made Under the Direction of Atlanta University*. Atlanta: Atlanta University Press, 1914.

———. *The Negro American Family*. Atlanta: Atlanta University Press, 1908.

———. *The Negro Family*, Atlanta University Publications, No. 13. Atlanta: University of Atlanta Press, 1909.

Duke, Emma. *Infant Mortality: Results of a Field Study in Johnstown, Pa Based on Births in One Calendar Year*. Washington: Government Printing Office, 1915.

Edholm, Mrs. Charlton (Mary Grace). *Traffic in Girls and Work of Florence Crittenton Missions*. Chicago: The Woman's Temperance Publishing Association, 1893.

Ely, Danielle M., and Anne K. Driscoll. "Infant Mortality in the United States, 2019: Data from the Period Linked Birth/Infant Death File." *U.S. Department of Health and Human Services National Vital Statistics Reports*, Vol. 70, No. 14 (2021).

Flatbrush, Adda. *How She Was Lost; Or, Methods and Results of Rescue Work.* Kansas City: Hudson-Kimberly, 1904.

Flexner, Abraham. *Medical Education in the United States and Canada: A Report to the Carnegie Foundation for the Advancement of Teaching.* Bulletin No. 4. New York City: Carnegie Foundation for the Advancement of Teaching, 1910.

Gardener, Helen Hamilton. *Is This Your Son, My Lord?* 2nd ed. Boston: Arena, 1894.

———. *Pray You, Sir, Whose Daughter?* Boston: Arena, 1892.

Gibbons, Abby Hopper. *Life of Abby Hopper Gibbons: Told Chiefly through Her Correspondence.* New York: Putnam, 1897.

Harper, Frances E. W. *Iola Leroy: Or, Shadows Uplifted.* Philadelphia: Garrigues, 1893.

———. "A Private Meeting with the Women," Letter from Frances E. W. Harper to William Still, Greenville, Georgia, 1870, printed in William Still, *The Underground Railroad.* 1871. Reprint, New York: Arno, 1968.

History and minutes of the National Council of Women of the United States, Organized in Washington, D.C., Mar. 31, 1888. Boston: E. B. Stillings, 1898.

Jacobs, Harriet. *Incidents in the Life of a Slave Girl, Written by Herself.* Boston: Thayer & Eldridge, 1861.

Lathrop, Julia C. "The Children's Bureau." Speech given at the Fifty-Seventh Annual Meeting of the National Education Association of the United States, Milwaukee, Wisconsin, June 28–July 5, 1919, https://www.google.com/books/edition/Proceedings_Abstracts_of _Lectures_and_a/_ZReAAAAIAAJ?hl=en&gbpv=0.

National Center for Education Statistics. "Characteristics of Public School Teachers." Retrieved Aug. 2022. https://nces.ed.gov/programs/coe/indicator/clr.

Phelps, Elizabeth Stuart. *Chapters from a Life.* New York: Houghton, Mifflin, 1900.

———. *The Gates Ajar.* Boston: Ticknor & Fields, 1868.

———. *Three Spiritualist Novels.* Introduction by Nina Baym. Urbana: University of Illinois Press, 2000.

Pinzer, Mamie. *The Mamie Papers: Letters from an Ex-Prostitute.* Eds. Sue Davidson and Ruth Rosen. New York: Feminist Press, 1997.

Powell, Aaron, ed. *The National Purity Congress: Its Papers, Addresses, Portraits. An Illustrated Record of the Papers and Addresses of the First National Purity Congress, Held Under the Auspices of the American Purity Alliance, In the Park Avenue Friends' Meeting House, Baltimore, October 14, 15 and 16, 1895.* New York: American Purity Congress, 1896.

Powell, Aaron M., et.al. "The Shame of America—The Age of Consent Laws in the United States: A Symposium." *The Arena, Vol.* 11 (1895): 192–215.

Richmond, Mary E., and Fred S. Hall. *A Study of Nine Hundred and Eighty-Five Widows: Known to Certain Charity Organizations in 1910.* New York: Charity Organization Department of the Russell Sage Foundation, 1913.

Rowson, Susanna. *Charlotte Temple: A Tale of Truth.* Ed. Cathy Davidson. New York: Oxford University Press, 1986.

Salzberg, Edward, et.al. "The Social Work Profession: Findings from Three Years of Surveys of New Social Workers." In *A Report to The Council on Social Work Education and the National Association of Social Work.* Aug. 2020. https://www.socialworkers.org/LinkClick .aspx?fileticket=1_j2EXVNspY%3D&portalid=0.

Sanger, William. *The History of Prostitution: Its Extent, Causes, and Effects Throughout the World. Being an Official Report to the Board of Alms-House Governors of the City of New York.* New York: Harper, 1858.

Selden, Charles E. "The Most Powerful Lobby in Washington: It Is the Public Welfare Lobby Backed by Seven Million Organized Women." *The Ladies Home Journal* (Apr. 1922): 5, 93–96.

Still, William. *The Underground Railroad: A Record of Facts, Authentic Narratives, Letters &c., Narrating the Hardships, Hair-breadth Escapes, and Death Struggles of the Slaves in Their Efforts for Freedom, as Related by Themselves and Others Or Witnessed by the Author: Together with Sketches of Some of the Largest Stockholders and Most Liberal Aiders and Advisers of the Road.* Philadelphia: Porter & Coates, 1872.

Stowe, Harriet Beecher. "The Mourning Veil." *The Atlantic,* No. 1 (Nov. 1857): 63–70.

———. *Uncle Tom's Cabin: Or, Life Among the Lowly.* Cleveland: Ohio: Jewett, Proctor, & Worthington, 1852.

Tikkanen, Roosa, et al. "Maternal Mortality and Maternity Care in the United States Compared to 10 Other Developed Countries." Issue Brief, The Commonwealth Fund, Nov. 18, 2020. https://doi.org/10.26099/411v-9255.

Truth, Sojourner. *Narrative of Sojourner Truth: A Bondswoman of Olden Times.* New York: Arno, 1968.

Ufford, Walter S. "Possible Improvements in the Care of Dependent Children." *Charities,* Vol. 7, No. 5 (1901): 125.

U.S. Bureau of Labor Statistics. "Education Pays, 2021." *Career Outlook,* May 2022. https://www.bls.gov/careeroutlook/2022/data-on-display/education-pays.htm.

Waller Barrett, Kate. "Maternity Work—Motherhood a Means of Regeneration." In *Fourteen Years' Work Among Erring Girls,* 52–62. Washington, D.C.: National Florence Crittenton Mission, 1897.

———. *Some Practical Suggestions on the Conduct of a Rescue Home.* Washington, D.C.: National Florence Crittenton Mission, 1903.

Washburn, Josie. *The Underworld Sewer: A Prostitute Reflects on Life in the Trade, 1871–1909.* Introduction by Sharon E. Wood. Lincoln: Bison, 1997.

Washington, Booker T. *The Booker T. Washington Papers.* Vol. 1, *The Autobiographical Writings,* edited by Louis Harlan and John Blassingame. Champaign: University of Illinois Press, 1972.

Wells, Ida B. *Southern Horrors: Lynch Law in All Its Phases.* New York: New York Age, 1892.

Willard, Frances. *Glimpses of Fifty Years: The Autobiography of an American Woman.* Chicago: Woman's Temperance Publication Association, 1889.

GOVERNMENT DOCUMENTS

Bradbury, Dorothy E. *Five Decades of Action for Children: A History of the Children's Bureau.* U.S. Department of Health, Education, and Welfare. Washington, D.C.: U.S. Government Printing Office, 1962.

Committee on the District of Columbia. Proceedings of the Conference on the Care of Dependent Children. S. Doc. No. 60-721 (1909).

Hygiene of Maternity and Infancy: Hearings on H.R. 12634 Before the House Committee on Labor. 65th Cong., 3rd sess. Washington, D.C.: Government Printing Office, 1919.

Kansas Board of Control of State Charitable Institutions. *First Annual and Biennial Report of the Board of Control of the State Charitable Institutions of Kansas.* Topeka: Kansas Publishing House, 1906.

Kansas State Census. 1885. *Ancestry.com.* Kansas, U.S., State Census Collection, 1855–1925.

U.S. Children's Bureau. *Illegitimacy as a Child-Welfare Problem,* edited by Emma O. Lundberg and Katharine F. Lenroot. 3 pts. Washington, D.C.: Government Printing Office, 1920.

Protection of Maternity and Infancy: Hearing on S. 3259: A Bill for the Public Protection of Maternity and Infancy and Providing a Method of Cooperation between the Government of the United States and the Several States Before the Senate Committee on Public Health and National Quarantine. 66th Cong., 2nd sess. Washington, D.C.: Government Printing Office, 1920.

Protection of Maternity: Hearings on S. 1039 Before the Senate Committee on Education and Labor. 67th Cong., 1st sess. Washington, D.C.: Government Printing Office, 1921.

Reports of the Department of Labor 1915: Report of the Secretary of Labor and Reports of Bureaus. Washington, D.C.: Government Printing Office, 1916.

Werber, Gustavus A. *Report on Housing and Living Conditions in the Neglected Sections of Richmond, Virginia.* Richmond: Whittet & Shepperson Printers, 1913.

U.S. Children's Bureau. *Birth Registration: An Aid in Protecting the Lives and Rights of Children.* Monograph No. 1. Washington, D.C.: Government Printing Office, 1913.

———. Department of Commerce and Labor. *Establishment of the Children's Bureau.* Washington, D.C.: Government Printing Office, 1912.

———. *Infant Mortality: Montclair, N.J.: A Study of Infant Mortality in a Suburban Community.* Washington, D.C.: Government Printing Office, 1915.

———. *Annual Report[s] of the Chief, Children's Bureau to the Secretary of Labor.* Washington, D.C.: Government Printing Office, 1913–1921.

———. *The Promotion of the Welfare and Hygiene of Maternity and Infancy for the Fiscal Year Ending June 30, 1929.* U.S. Children's Bureau Publication No. 203. Washington, D.C.: Government Printing Office, 1931.

———. *Standards of Legal Protection for Children Born out of Wedlock: A Report of Regional Conferences Held under the Auspices of the U.S. Children's Bureau and the Inter-City Conference on Illegitimacy.* U.S. Children's Bureau Publication No. 77. Washington Printing Office, 1920.

U.S. Census Bureau. 1880. *FamilySearch.org.* https://www.familysearch.org/search /collection/list#page=1&recordType=Census.

———. 1920. *FamilySearch.org.* https://www.familysearch.org/search/collection/list#page =1&recordType=Census.

———. 1930. *FamilySearch.org.* https://www.familysearch.org/search/collection/list#page =1&recordType=Census.

MAGAZINES AND JOURNALS

American Journal of Public Health

The Annals of the American Academy of Political and Social Science

The Arena

The Atlantic

Charities and the Commons

Child Welfare

The Crisis

Florence Crittenton Magazine

Girls

The Independent
Mother's Journal and Family Visitant
New Outlook
New York Medical Journal
The New-York Weekly Magazine: Or,
  Miscellaneous Repository

The Pharmaceutical Era
Record of Christian Work
Westminster Review
The Woman's Era
Woman's Journal

NEWSPAPERS

The Chicago Defender, Chicago, Ill.
The Daily Dispatch, Richmond, Va.
The Daily Herald, La Porte, Ind.
The Daily Picayune, New Orleans, La.
The Elk Mountain Pilot, Irwin, Colo.
The Morning Times, Washington, D.C.

The National Tribune, Washington, D.C.
The New York Times, New York, N.Y.
Rocky Ford Enterprise, Rocky Ford, Colo.
The Topeka State Journal, Topeka, Kans.
The Washington Times, Washington, D.C.

SECONDARY SOURCES

Aiken, Katherine G. *Harnessing the Power of Motherhood: The National Florence Crittenton Mission, 1883–1925*. Knoxville: University of Tennessee Press, 1998.

Andrews, William L., and Mitch Kachum, eds. "Editor's Introduction." In *The Curse of Caste: Or, The Slave Bride: A Rediscovered African American Novel by Julia C. Collins*. New York: Oxford University Press, 2006.

Ayers, Edward L. *The Promise of the New South: Life After Reconstruction*. New York: Oxford University Press, 1992.

Baker, Paula. "The Domestication of Politics: Women and American Political Society, 1780–1920." *American Historical Review*, Vol. 89 (June 1984): 621–632.

Balkansky, Arlene. "Sojourner Truth's Most Famous Speech," *Library of Congress Blog*. Accessed Jan. 12, 2022. https://blogs.loc.gov/headlinesandheroes/2021/04/sojourner -truths-most-famous-speech/.

Balogh, Brian. *The Associational State: American Governance in the Twentieth Century*. Philadelphia: University of Pennsylvania Press, 2015.

———. *A Government Out of Sight: The Mystery of National Authority in Nineteenth-Century America*. Cambridge: Cambridge University Press, 2009.

Barthes, Roland. *Camera Lucida: Reflections of Photography*. Translated by Richard Howard. New York: Hill & Wang, 1991.

Bayor, Ronald H. "The Civil Rights Movement as Urban Reform: Atlanta's Black Neighborhoods and a New 'Progressivism.'" *The Georgia Historical Quarterly*, Vol. 77, No. 2 (Summer 1993): 286–309.

Bender, Thomas. "The Rural Cemetery Movement: Urban Travail and the Appeal of Nature." *The New England Quarterly*, Vol. 47, No. 2 (June 1974): 196–211.

Ben-Moshe, L., C. Chapman, and A. Carey, eds. *Disability Incarcerated: Imprisonment and Disability in the United States and Canada*. New York: Palgrave Macmillan, 2014.

Blair, Cynthia. *I've Got to Make My Livin': Black Women's Sex Work in Turn-of-the-Century Chicago*. Chicago: The University of Chicago Press, 2010.

Blight, David. *Race and Reunion: The Civil War in American Memory*. Boston: Belknap, 2002.

Bordin, Ruth. *Frances Willard: A Biography*. Chapel Hill: University of North Carolina Press, 1986.

———. *Woman and Temperance: The Quest for Power and Liberty, 1873–1900*. Philadelphia: Temple University Press, 1981.

Borgstrom, Michael. "Face Value: Ambivalent Citizenship in 'Iola Leroy.'" *African American Review*, Vol. 40, No. 4 (Winter, 2006): 779–793.

Boydston, Jeanne. "The Woman Who Wasn't There: Women's Market Labor and the Transition to Capitalism in the United States." *Journal of the Early Republic*, Vol. 16 (Summer 1996): 183–206.

Braude, Ann. *Radical Spirits: Spiritualism and Women's Rights in Nineteenth-Century America*. Bloomington: Indiana University Press, 2001.

Brinkley, Alan. *The End of Reform: New Deal Liberalism in Recession and War*. New York: Knopf, 1995.

Broder, Sherri. "Child Care or Child Neglect? Baby Farming in Late-Nineteenth-Century Philadelphia." *Gender and Society*, Vol. 2, No. 2 (June 1988): 128–148.

———. *Tramps, Unfit Mothers, and Neglected Children: Negotiating the Family in Nineteenth-Century Philadelphia*. Philadelphia: University of Pennsylvania Press, 2002.

Brown, Elsa Barkley. "Imagining Lynching: African American Women, Communities of Struggle, and Collective Memory." In *African American Women Speak Out on Anita Hill–Clarence Thomas*, edited by Geneva Smitherman, 100–124. Detroit, Mich.: Wayne State University Press, 1995.

Brown, Elsa Barkley, and Gregg D. Kimball. "Mapping the Terrain of Black Richmond." In *The New African American Urban History*, edited by Raymond Mohl and Kenneth W. Goings, 66–113. Chicago: University of Chicago Press, 2009.

Brown, Gillian. *Domestic Individualism: Imagining Self in Nineteenth-Century America*. Berkeley: University of California Press, 1990.

Brown, Kathleen. *Foul Bodies: Cleanliness in Early America*. New Haven, Conn.: Yale University Press, 2009.

Brown, Leslie. *Upbuilding Black Durham: Gender, Class, and Black Community Development in the Jim Crow South*. Chapel Hill: University of North Carolina Press, 2008.

Burns, Stanley B. *Sleeping Beauty III: Memorial Photography: The Children*. New York: Burns Archive, 2010.

Butler, Anne M. *Daughters of Joy, Sisters of Misery: Prostitutes in the American West, 1865–90*. Urbana: University of Illinois Press, 1985.

Cahn, Susan K. *Sexual Reckonings: Southern Girls in a Troubling Age*. Cambridge, Mass.: Harvard University Press, 2012.

Carby, Hazel. *Reconstructing Womanhood: The Emergence of the Afro-American Woman Novelist*. New York: Oxford University Press, 1987.

Chauncy, George. *Gay New York: Gender, Urban Culture, and the Making of the Gay Male World, 1890–1940*. New York: Basic Books, 1994.

Clapp, Elizabeth J. "Welfare and the Role of Women: The Juvenile Court Movement." *Journal of American Studies*, Vol. 28, No. 3 (Dec. 1994): 359–383.

Cohen, Miriam. *Julia Lathrop: Social Service and Progressive Government*. Boulder, Colo.: Westview, 2017.

Cohen, Patricia Cline. *The Murder of Helen Jewett*. New York: Knopf, 1999.

Cothran, James R., and Erica Danylchak. *Grave Landscapes: The Nineteenth-Century Rural Cemetery Movement*. Columbia: University of South Carolina Press, 2008.

Cott, Nancy. *The Bonds of Womanhood: "Women's Sphere" in New England, 1780–1835*. New Haven, Conn.: Yale University Press, 1977.

Cox, Robert S. *Body and Soul: A Sympathetic History of American Spiritualism*. Charlottesville: University of Virginia Press, 2003.

Cox, Thomas A. *Blacks in Topeka, Kansas, 1865–1915: A Social History*. Baton Rouge: Louisiana State University Press, 1982.

Cross, Whitney. *The Burned-over District: The Social and Intellectual History of Enthusiastic Religion in Western New York, 1800–1850*. New York: Harper Torchlight, 1950.

Davidson, Cathy N. *Revolution and the Word: The Rise of the Novel in America*. New York: Oxford University Press, 2004.

Day, Carolyn A. *Consumptive Chic: A History of Beauty, Fashion, and Disease*. New York: Bloomsbury, 2017.

D'Emilio, John, and Estelle B. Freedman. *Intimate Matters: A History of Sexuality in America*. 2nd ed. Chicago: University of Chicago Press, 1997.

DeWolf, Rebecca. *Gendered Citizenship: The Original Conflict over the Equal Rights Amendment, 1920–1963*. Lincoln: University of Nebraska Press, 2021.

Douglas, Ann. *The Feminization of American Culture*. New York: Knopf, 1977.

———. "Introduction." In *Uncle Tom's Cabin*, by Harriet Beecher Stowe. New York: Viking, 1981.

Edwards, Rebecca. *Angels in the Machinery: Gender in American Party Politics from the Civil War to the Progressive Era*. New York: Oxford University Press, 1997.

Doane, Mary Ann. *The Desire to Desire: The Woman's Film of the 1940s*. Bloomington: Indiana University Press, 1987.

Doyle, Laura. "The Folk, the Nobles, and the Novel: The Racial Subtext of Sentimentality." *Narrative*, Vol. 3, No. 2 (1995): 161–187.

Doyle, Nora. *Maternal Bodies: Redefining Motherhood in Early America*. Chapel Hill: University of North Carolina Press, 2018.

DuBois, Ellen Carol. *Woman Suffrage and Women's Rights*. New York: New York University Press, 1998.

Earls, Averill. "Locked Up and Poxxed: THE Venereal Disease and Women who Sold Sex in the Victorian British Empire." *Dig: A History Podcast*. Accessed Dec. 14, 2019. https://digpodcast.org/2019/03/10/locked-up-poxxed-syphilis/.

Epstein, Barbara Leslie. *The Politics of Domesticity: Women, Evangelism, and Temperance in Nineteenth-Century America*. Middletown, Conn.: Wesleyan University Press, 1981.

Faust, Drew Gilpin. *This Republic of Suffering: Death and the American Civil War*. New York: Vintage, 2009.

Ferguson, Philip M. *Abandoned to Their Fate: Social Policy and Practice Toward Severely Retarded People in America, 1820–1920*. Philadelphia: Temple University Press, 1994.

Fitzgerald, Maureen. *Habits of Compassion: Irish Catholic Nuns and the Origins of New York's Welfare System, 1830–1920*. Urbana: University of Illinois Press, 2006.

Freedman, Estelle B. *Maternal Justice: Miriam Van Waters and the Female Reform Tradition*. Chicago: University of Chicago Press, 1996.

———. "Separatism as Strategy: Female Institution Building and American Feminism, 1870–1930." *Feminist Studies*, Vol. 5, No. 3 (1979): 512–529.

———. *Their Sisters' Keepers: Women's Prison Reform in America, 1830–1930.* Ann Arbor: The University of Michigan, 1984.

Gaines, Kevin K. *Uplifting the Race: Black Leadership, Politics, and Culture in the Twentieth Century.* Chapel Hill: University of North Carolina Press, 1996.

Galishoff, Stuart. "Germs Know No Color Line, Black Health and Public Policy in Atlanta, 1900–1918." *Journal of the History of Medicine and Allied Sciences*, Vol. 40 (1985): 22–41.

Gatewood, Willard B. *Aristocrats of Color: The Black Elite, 1880–1920.* Fayetteville: University of Arkansas Press, 2000.

Giddings, Paula. *When and Where I Enter: The Impact of Black Women on Race and Sex in America.* New York: HarperCollins, 1996.

Gilfoyle, Timothy. *City of Eros: New York City, Prostitution, and the Commercialization of Sex, 1790–1920.* New York: W. W. Norton, 1994.

———. *A Pickpocket's Tale: The Underworld of Nineteenth-Century New York.* New York: W. W. Norton, 2007.

Gilmore, Glenda Elizabeth. *Gender and Jim Crow: Women and the Politics of White Supremacy in North Carolina, 1896–1920.* Chapel Hill: University of North Carolina Press, 1996.

Ginzberg, Lori. *Women and the Work of Benevolence: Morality, Politics, and Class in the Nineteenth-Century United States.* New Haven, Conn.: Yale University Press, 1992.

Gleeson, Muin Sara. "Feminizing Grief: Victorian Women and the Appropriation of Mourning." PhD diss., University of Missouri-Kansas, 2016. ProQuest Order No. 10250362.

Godshalk, David Fort. *Veiled Visions: The 1906 Atlanta Race Riot and the Reshaping of American Race Relations.* Chapel Hill: University of North Carolina Press, 2005.

Goffman, Erving. *Asylums: Essays on the Social Situation of Mental Patients and Other Inmates.* New York: Doubleday Anchor, 1961.

Gordon, Linda. "Black and White Visions of Welfare Activism, 1890–1945." *The Journal of American History*, Vol. 78, No. 2 (1991): 559–590.

———. "Gender, State and Society: A Debate with Theda Skocpol." In *Debating Gender, Debating Sexuality.* New York: New York University Press, 1996.

———. *The Great Arizona Orphan Abduction.* Cambridge, Mass.: Harvard University Press, 2001.

———. *Heroes of Their Own Lives: The Politics and History of Family Violence—Boston, 1880–1960.* Champaign: University of Illinois Press, 1989.

———. *The Moral Property of Women: A History of Birth Control Politics in America.* Champaign: University of Illinois Press, 2002. Kindle.

———. *Pitied But Not Entitled: Single Mothers and the History of Welfare, 1890–1935.* Cambridge, Mass.: Harvard University Press, 1994.

———, ed. *Women, the State, and Welfare.* Madison: University of Wisconsin Press, 1990.

Gould, Stephen Jay. *The Mismeasure of Man.* New York: W. W. Norton, 1981.

Grob, Gerald N. *From Asylum to Community: Mental Health Policy in Modern America.* Princeton, N.J.: Princeton University Press, 2016.

Hall, Jacquelyn Dowd.

———. *Revolt Against Chivalry: Jessie Daniel Ames and the Women's Campaign Against Lynching.* New York: Columbia University Press, 1993.

Hamlin, Kimberly A. *Free Thinker: Sex, Suffrage, and the Extraordinary Life of Helen Hamilton Gardener*. New York: W. W. Norton, 2020.

Hanson, J. E. "Mary Wilcox Glenn (1869–1940)." *Social Welfare History Project*. Virginia Commonwealth University. Accessed Oct. 18, 2019. http://socialwelfare.library.vcu.edu /eras/great-depression/glenn-mary-wilcox.

Hart, Emma. "Work, Family and the Eighteenth-Century History of a Middle Class in the American South." *The Journal of Southern History*, Vol. 79, No. 3 (Aug. 2012): 551–578.

Hawley, Ellis W. "Herbert Hoover, the Commerce Secretariat, and the Vision of an 'Associative State,' 1921–1928." *The Journal of American History*, Vol. 61, No. 1 (1974): 116–140.

Hemphill, Katie M. *Bawdy City: Commercial Sex and Regulation in Baltimore, 1799–1915*. New York: Cambridge University Press, 2020.

Hendler, Glenn, María Carla Sánchez, and Jennifer Travis. "Twentieth-Anniversary Reflections on *The Culture of Sentiment: Race, Gender, and Sentimentality in Nineteenth-Century America* edited by Shirley Samuels." *Legacy: A Journal of American Women Writers*, Vol. 31, No. 1 (2014), 122–128.

Hickey, Georgina. *Hope and Danger in the New South City: Working-Class Women and Urban Development in Atlanta, 1890–1940*. Athens: University of Georgia Press, 2005.

Higginbotham, Evelyn Brooks. *Righteous Discontent: The Women's Movement in the Black Baptist Church, 1880–1920*. Rev. ed. Cambridge, Mass.: Harvard University Press, 1994.

Hine, Darlene Clark, ed. *Black Women in America: An Historical Encyclopedia*. Brooklyn, N.Y.: Carlson, 1993.

Hobson, Barbara Meil. *Uneasy Virtue: The Politics of Prostitution and the American Reform Tradition*. New York: Basic, 1987.

Hoffman, Steven. *Race, Class, and Power in the Building of Richmond, 1870–1920*. Jefferson, N.C.: McFarland, 2004.

Hunter, Tera. "*To 'Joy My Freedom": Southern Black Women's Lives and Labors After the Civil War*. Cambridge, Mass.: Harvard University Press, 1997.

Jalland, Pat. *Death in the Victorian Family*. Oxford: Oxford University Press, 2000.

Jones-Rogers, Stephanie E. *They Were Her Property: White Women as Slave Owners in the American South*. New Haven, Conn.: Yale University Press, 2019.

Joseph, Gerhard, and Herbert F. Tucker. "Passing On: Death." In *A Companion to Victorian Literature and Culture*, edited by Herbert F. Tucker, 110–123. Oxford: Blackwell, 1999.

Judson, Sarah. "Civil Rights and Civic Health: African American Women's Public Health Work in Early Twentieth-Century Atlanta." *NWSA Journal*, Vol. 11, No. 3 (1999): 93–111.

Katz, Michael B. *The Undeserving Poor: America's Enduring Confrontation with Poverty*. 2nd ed. Oxford: Oxford University Press, 2013.

Katznelson, Ira. *When Affirmative Action was White: An Untold History of Racial Inequality in Twentieth-Century America*. New York: W. W. Norton, 2006.

———. *Fear Itself: The New Deal and the Origins of Our Time*. New York: Liveright, 2013.

Kerber, Linda. *Women of the Republic: Intellect and Ideology in Revolutionary America*. Chapel Hill: University of North Carolina Press, 1980.

Kessler-Harris, Alice. "Designing Women and Old Fools: The Construction of the Social Security Amendments of 1939." In *U.S. History as Women's History*, edited by Linda Kerber, 87–106. Chapel Hill: University of North Carolina Press, 1995.

Klein, Jennifer. *For All These Rights: Business, Labor, and the Shaping of America's Public-Private Welfare State*. Princeton, N.J.: Princeton University Press, 2006.

Kleinberg, S. J. *Widows and Orphans First: The Family Economy and Social Welfare Policy, 1880–1939*. Urbana: University of Illinois Press, 2006.

Kline, Wendy. *Building a Better Race: Gender, Sexuality, and Eugenics from the Turn of the Century to the Baby Boom*. Berkeley: University of California Press, 2002.

Koven, Seth, and Sonya Michel, eds. *Mothers of the New World: Maternalist Politics and the Origins of Welfare States*. New York: Routledge, 1993.

Knupfer, Anne Meis. "'Toward a Tenderer Humanity and a Nobler Womanhood': African-American Women's Clubs in Chicago, 1890 to 1920." *Journal of Women's History*, Vol. 7, No. 3 (1995): 58–76.

Krainz, Thomas. *Delivering Aid: Implementing Progressive Era Welfare in the American West*. Albuquerque: University of New Mexico Press, 2005.

Kunzel, Regina. *Fallen Women, Problem Girls: Unmarried Mothers and the Professionalization of Social Work, 1890–1945*. New Haven, Conn.: Yale University Press, 1995.

Ladd-Taylor, Molly. *Mother-Work: Women, Child Welfare, and the State, 1890–1930*. Urbana: University of Illinois Press, 1994.

———, ed. *Raising a Baby the Government Way: Mothers' Letters to the Children's Bureau 1915–1932*. New Brunswick, N.J.: Rutgers University Press, 1986.

———. "The 'Sociological Advantages' of Sterilization." In *Mental Retardation in America: A Historical Reader*, edited by Stephen Noll and James Trent, 281–299. New York: New York University Press, 2004.

Laderman, Gary. *The Sacred Remains: American Attitudes Toward Death, 1799–1883*. New Haven, Conn.: Yale University Press, 1999.

Larson, Edward. *Sex, Race, and Science: Eugenics in the Deep South*. Baltimore: Johns Hopkins University Press, 1995.

Lehuu, Isabelle. "Sentimental Figures: Reading *Godey's Lady's Book* in Antebellum America." In *Culture of Sentiment: Race, Gender, and Sentimentality in Nineteenth-Century America*, edited by Shirley Samuels, 73–91. New York: Oxford University Press, 1992.

Lerner, Gerda. "Early Community Work of Black Club Women." *The Journal of Negro History*, Vol. 59, No. 2 (Apr. 1974): 158–167.

———. *The Female Experience: An American Documentary*. Indianapolis: Bobbs-Merrill, 1977.

———. *The Majority Finds Its Past: Placing Women in American History*. New York: Oxford University Press, 1979.

Leuchtenburg, William E. *Franklin D. Roosevelt and the New Deal: 1932–1940*. New York: Harper Perennial, 2009.

Levine, Philippa. "Venereal Disease, Prostitution, and the Politics of Empire: The Case of British India." *Journal of the History of Sexuality*, Vol. 4, No. 4 (Apr. 1994): 579–602.

Lindenmeyer, Kristen. *A Right to Childhood: The U.S. Children's Bureau and Child Welfare, 1912–46*. Urbana: University of Illinois Press, 1997.

Linden-Ward, Blanche. *Silent City on a Hill: Picturesque Landscapes of Memory and Boston's Mount Auburn Cemetery*. Amherst: University of Massachusetts Press, 2007.

Lyons, Clare A. *Sex Among the Rabble: An Intimate History of Gender and Power in the Age of Revolution, Philadelphia, 1730–1830*. Chapel Hill: The University of North Carolina Press, 2006.

MacKell, Jan, and Thomas J. Noel. *Red Light Women of the Rocky Mountains*. Albuquerque: University of New Mexico Press, 2011.

Masarik, Elizabeth Garner. "Por la Raza, Para la Raza: Jovita Idar and Progressive-Era Mexicana Maternalism along the Texas–Mexico Border." *Southwestern Historical Quarterly.* Vol. 122, No. 3 (Jan. 2019): 278–299.

Masson, Erin M. "The Women's Christian Temperance Union 1874–1898: Combating Domestic Violence." *William and Mary Journal of Race, Gender, and Social Justice,* Vol. 3, No. 1 (1997): 163–188.

Mathers, Helen. *Patron Saint of Prostitutes: Josephine Butler and the Victorian Sex Scandal.* Stroud, U.K.: History Press, 2014.

Matthews, Glenna. *The Rise of the Public Woman: Woman's Power and Woman's Place in the United States, 1630–1970.* New York: Oxford University Press, 1992.

McCaskill, Barbara. "'To Labor . . . and Fight on the Side of God': Spirit, Class, and Nineteenth-Century African American Women's Literature." In *Nineteenth-Century American Women Writers: A Critical Reader,* edited by Karen L. Kilcup, 164–183. Malden, Mass.: Blackwell, 1998.

Meckel, Richard. *Save the Babies: American Public Health Reform and the Prevention of Infant Mortality, 1850–1929.* Baltimore: Johns Hopkins University Press, 1990.

Mink, Gwendolyn. *The Wages of Motherhood: Inequality in the Welfare State, 1917–1942.* Ithaca, N.Y.: Cornell University Press, 1995.

Mintz, Steven. *Moralists and Modernizers: America's Pre–Civil War Reformers.* Baltimore: Johns Hopkins University Press, 1995.

Mitchell, Michele. *Righteous Propagation: African Americans and the Politics of Racial Destiny after Reconstruction.* Chapel Hill: University of North Carolina Press, 2004.

Morantz-Sanchez, Regina. *Sympathy and Science: Women Physicians in American Medicine.* Chapel Hill: University of North Carolina Press, 1999.

Mott, Frank Luther. *Golden Multitudes: The Story of Best Sellers in the United States.* New York: Macmillan, 1947.

Muncy, Robyn. *Creating a Female Dominion in American Reform, 1890–1935.* New York: Oxford University Press, 1994.

Nelson, Barbara J. "The Origins of the Two-Channel Welfare State: Workman's Compensation and Mothers' Aid." In *Women, the State, and Welfare,* edited by Linda Gordon, 125–151. Madison: University of Wisconsin Press, 1990.

Noble, Marianne. *The Masochistic Pleasures of Sentimental Literature.* Princeton, N.J.: Princeton University Press, 2000.

Novak, William. "The Myth of the 'Weak' American State." *The American Historical Review,* Vol. 113, No. 3 (2008): 752–772.

———. *New Democracy: The Creation of the Modern American State.* Cambridge, Mass.: Harvard University Press, 2022.

Odem, Mary. *Delinquent Daughters: Protecting and Policing Adolescent Female Sexuality in the United States, 1885–1920.* Chapel Hill: University of North Carolina Press, 1995.

Painter, Nell. *Exodusters: Black Migration to Kansas after Reconstruction.* New York: Alfred A. Knopf, 1977.

Parker, Alison M. "Frances Watkins Harper and the Search for Women's Interracial Alliances." In *Susan B. Anthony and the Struggle for Equal Rights,* edited by Christine L. Ridarsky and Mary M. Huth, 145–171. Rochester, N.Y.: University of Rochester Press, 2012.

Parsons, Elaine Frantz. *Manhood Lost: Fallen Drunkards and Redeeming Women in the Nineteenth-Century United States.* Baltimore: Johns Hopkins University Press, 2009.

Patterson, James T. *America's Struggle Against Poverty in the Twentieth Century*. 4th ed. Cambridge, Mass.: Harvard University Press, 2000.

Patton, Venetria K. *Women in Chains: The Legacy of Slavery in Black Women's Fiction*. Albany: State University of New York Press, 2000.

Pearson, Susan J. *The Birth Certificate: An American History*. Chapel Hill: University of North Carolina Press, 2021.

Peiss, Kathy. *Cheap Amusements: Working Women and Leisure in Turn-of-the-Century New York*. Philadelphia: Temple University Press, 1986.

Perry, Elizabeth. "'The General Motherhood of the Commonwealth': Dance Hall Reform in the Progressive Era." *American Quarterly*, Vol. 37, No. 5 (Winter 1985): 719–733.

Pivar, David. *Purity and Hygiene: Women, Prostitution, and the "American Plan," 1900–1930*. Westport, Conn.: Greenwood, 2002.

———. *Purity Crusade: Sexual Morality and Social Control, 1868–1900*. Westport, Conn.: Praeger, 1973.

Quadagno, Jill. *The Color of Welfare: How Racism Undermined the War on Poverty*. New York: Oxford University Press, 1996.

Reagan, Leslie. *When Abortion Was a Crime: Women, Medicine, and Law in the United States, 1867–1973*. Berkeley: University of California Press, 1997.

Reilly, Philip. *The Surgical Solution: A History of Involuntary Sterilization in the United States*. Baltimore: Johns Hopkins University Press, 1991.

Rembis, Michael. *Defining Deviance: Sex, Science, and Delinquent Girls, 1890–1960*. Urbana: University of Illinois Press, 2013.

Roberts, Samuel Kelton Jr. *Infectious Fear: Politics, Disease, and the Health Effects of Segregation*. Chapel Hill: The University of North Carolina Press, 2009.

Rodgers, Daniel. *Atlantic Crossings: Social Politics in a Progressive Age*. Cambridge, Mass.: Harvard University Press, 1998.

Rosen, Ruth. *The Lost Sisterhood: Prostitution in America, 1900–1918*. Baltimore: Johns Hopkins University Press, 1982.

Ross, Herbert. *The Sentimental Novel in America, 1789–1860*. Durham, N.C.: Duke University Press, 1940.

Rothman, Sheila M. *Living in the Shadow of Death: Tuberculosis and the Social Experience of Illness in American History*. Baltimore: Johns Hopkins University Press, 1995.

Rouse, Jacqueline Anne. *Lugenia Burns Hope: Black Southern Reformer*. Athens: University of Georgia Press, 1989.

Ruby, Jay. *Secure the Shadows: Death and Photography in America*. Cambridge, Mass.: MIT Press, 1995.

Rust, Marion. *Prodigal Daughters: Susanna Rowson's Early American Women*. Chapel Hill: University of North Carolina Press, 2008.

Ryan, Mary P. *Cradle of the Middle Class: The Family in Oneida County, New York, 1790–1865*. New York: Cambridge University Press, 1981.

———. *The Empire of the Mother: American Writing About Domesticity, 1830–1860*. New York: Haworth, 1982.

Salem, Dorothy. *To Better Our World: Black Women in Organized Reform, 1890–1920*. Philadelphia: Carlson, 1990.

Samuels, Shirley, ed. *The Culture of Sentiment: Race, Gender, and Sentimentality in Nineteenth-Century America*. New York: Oxford University Press, 1992.

——."Sentimentalism and Domestic Fiction." *Oxford Bibliographies*. Accessed Feb. 6, 2018. http://www.oxfordbibliographies.com/view/document/obo-9780199827251/obo -9780199827251-0015.xml.

Sánchez-Eppler, Karen. *Dependent States: The Child's Part in Nineteenth-Century American Culture*. Chicago: University of Chicago Press, 2005.

——. *Touching Liberty: Abolition, Feminism, and the Politics of the Body*. Berkeley: University of California Press, 1993.

Sante, Luc. *Low Life: Lures and Snares of Old New York*. New York: Macmillan, 2003.

Schoen, Johanna. *Choice and Coercion: Birth Control, Sterilization, and Abortion in Public Health and Welfare*. Chapel Hill: University of North Carolina Press, 2005.

Seeman, Erik R. *Speaking with the Dead in Early America*. Philadelphia: University of Pennsylvania Press, 2019.

Sellers, Charles. *The Market Revolution: Jacksonian America, 1815–1846*. New York: Oxford University Press, 1991.

Simmons, Christina. "African Americans and Sexual Victorianism in the Social Hygiene Movement, 1910–1940." *Journal of the History of Sexuality*, Vol. 4, No. 1 (July 1993): 51–75.

——. *Making Marriage Modern: Women's Sexuality from the Progressive Era to World War II*. Oxford: Oxford University Press, 2009.

Sklar, Kathryn Kish. *Florence Kelley and the Nation's Work: The Rise of Women's Political Culture, 1830–1900*. New Haven, Conn.: Yale University Press, 1995.

——. "Hull-House Maps and Papers: Social Science as Women's Work in the 1890s." In *The Social Survey in Historical Perspective, 1880–1940*, edited by Martin Bulmer, Kevin Bales, and Katherine Kish Sklar, 111–147. Cambridge: Cambridge University Press, 1991.

Skocpol, Theda. *Protecting Soldiers and Mothers: The Political Origins of Social Policy in the United States*. Cambridge, Mass.: Belknap, 1992.

Smith, Susan L. *Sick and Tired of Being Sick and Tired: Black Women's Health Activism in America, 1890–1950*. Philadelphia: University of Pennsylvania Press, 1995.

Soja, Edward W. *Seeking Spatial Justice*. Minneapolis: University of Minnesota Press, 2010.

Solinger, Ricki. *Wake Up Little Susie: Single Pregnancy and Race Before Roe V. Wade*. New York: Routledge, 1992.

Stanley, Amy Dru. "Histories of Capitalism and Sex Difference." *Journal of the Early Republic*, Vol. 36, No. 2 (June, 2016): 343–350.

Stannard, David E. *The Puritan Way of Death: A Study in Religion, Culture, and Social Change*. Oxford: Oxford University Press, 1979.

Stansell, Christine. *City of Women: Sex and Class in New York, 1789–1860*. New York: Knopf, 1986.

Stovall, Mary E. "The 'Chicago Defender' in the Progressive Era." *Illinois Historical Journal*, Vol. 83, No. 3 (1990): 159–172.

Tagg, John. *The Burden of Representation: Essays on Photographies and Histories*. Minneapolis: University of Minnesota Press, 1988.

Tomes, Nancy. *The Gospel of Germs: Men, Women, and the Microbe in American Life*. Cambridge, Mass.: Harvard University Press, 1998.

Tompkins, Jane. *Sensational Designs: The Cultural Work of American Fiction, 1790–1860*. New York: Oxford University Press, 1986.

Wagner, Roland Richard. "Virtue Against Vice: A Study of Moral Reformers and Prostitution in the Progressive Era." PhD diss., University of Wisconsin, 1971.

Walkowitz, Judith. *Prostitution and Victorian Society: Women, Class, and the State.* Cambridge: Cambridge University Press, 1982.

Walsh, Mary Roth. *"Doctors Wanted: No Woman Need Apply": Sexual Barriers in the Medical Profession, 1835–1975.* New Haven, Conn.: Yale University Press, 1977.

Welke, Barbara Young. *Law and the Borders of Belonging in the Long Nineteenth Century United States.* New York: Cambridge University Press, 2010.

Wells, Robert V. *Facing the "King of Terrors": Death and Society in an American Community, 1750–1990.* New York: Cambridge University Press, 2000.

Welter, Barbara. "The Cult of True Womanhood, 1820–1860." Pt. 1. *American Quarterly,* Vol. 8, No. 2 (Summer 1966): 151–174.

Werble, Amy. *Lust on Trial: Censorship and the Rise of American Obscenity in the Age of Anthony Comstock.* New York: Columbia University Press, 2018.

Wexler, Laura. *Tender Violence: Domestic Visions in an Age of U.S. Imperialism.* Chapel Hill: University of North Carolina Press, 2000.

———. *Too Heavy a Load: Black Women in Defense of Themselves, 1894–1994.* New York: W. W. Norton, 1999.

White, Shane, and Graham White. *Sylin': African American Expressive Culture from Its Beginnings to Zoot Suit.* Ithaca, N.Y.: Cornell University Press, 1998.

Wilkinson, Patrick. "The Selfless and the Helpless: Maternalist Origins of the U.S. Welfare State." *Feminist Studies,* Vol. 25, No. 3 (Autumn 1999): 571–597.

Williams, Andreá N. *Dividing Lines: Class Anxiety and Postbellum Black Fiction.* Ann Arbor: University of Michigan Press, 2013.

Williams, Doretha K. "Kansas Grows the Best Wheat and the Best Race Women: Black Women's Club Movement in Kansas 1900–30." PhD diss., University of Kansas, 2011. https://kuscholarworks.ku.edu/handle/1808/10685.

Williams, Greg. *The Liberty Ships of World War II: A Record of the 2,710 Vessels and Their Builders, Operators and Namesakes.* Jefferson, N.C.: McFarland, 2014.

Williamson, Jennifer. *Twentieth-Century Sentimentalism: Narrative Appropriation in American Literature.* New Brunswick, N.J.: Rutgers University Press, 1995.

Willis, Deborah. *Reflections in Black: A History of Black Photographers 1840 to the Present.* New York: W. W. Norton, 2000.

Wilson, Otto. *Fifty Years' Work with Girls, 1883–1933.* Alexandria, Va.: National Florence Crittenton Mission, 1933.

Withycombe, Shannon. *Lost: Miscarriage in Nineteenth-Century America.* New Brunswick, N.J.: Rutgers University Press, 2019.

Wolcott, Victoria. "'Bible, Bath, and Broom': Nannie Helen Burroughs National Training School and African American Racial Uplift." *Journal of Women's History,* Vol. 9, No. 1 (Spring 1997): 88–110.

———. "The Culture of the Informal Economy: Numbers Runners in Inter-War Black Detroit." *The Radical History Review,* No. 69 (Fall 1997): 46–75.

———. *Remaking Respectability: African American Women in Interwar Detroit.* Chapel Hill: University of North Carolina Press, 2001.

Wood, Sharon E. *The Freedom of the Streets: Work, Citizenship, and Sexuality in a Gilded Age City.* Chapel Hill: University of North Carolina Press, 2005.

Woods, Randall B. "Integration, Exclusion, or Segregation?: The 'Color Line' in Kansas, 1878–1900." In *African Americans on the Western Frontier*, edited by Monroe Lee Billington and Roger D. Hardaway. Niwot: University of Colorado Press, 1998.

Yellin, Jean Fagan. Introduction. In *Incidents in the Life of a Slave Girl*, by Harriet Jacobs. New York: Civitas, 2005.

Zaeske, Susan. *Signatures of Citizenship: Petitioning, Antislavery, and Women's Political Identity*. Chapel Hill: University of North Carolina Press, 2003.

INDEX

———————◦⊙⟨⊙⟩⊙◦———————

motherhood, 10– 11, 21, 70, 99, 144, 165; as empowering, 94, 121, 155–156; ideals of, 17–18, 78, 141; universality of, 8, 19, 21, 78; as impetus for reform, 65, 72–73, 83, 121; protection of 9, 73, 65–67, 142–143; as avenue to salvation, 78–79, 86–87, 95

mothers' pensions, 131, 141, 142–146, 154–157, 160–161

mourning, 10, 26, 27, 28, 29, 37–38

Muncy, Robyn, 130, 169

National Association of Colored Women's Clubs (NA-CWC), 98, 101, 153

National Association of Colored Women (NACW), 108–109

National Child Labor Committee, 1, 135

National Conference of Charities and Correction, 83, 135

National Congress of Mothers, 93, 94, 131, 133–134, 142, 144, 147, 153, 163

National Council of Women (NCW), 93, 108–109, 135, 153, 172

The National Era, 20

National Florence Crittenton Mission (NFCM), 11–13, 42, 88–92, 94–95, 114, 184n41; matrons of the, 84, 89, 90, 188n15; as precursor to Children's Bureau, 169–170; relationship to the Colored NFCM (Topeka, Kan.) 99–100, 102–103, 106–107, 111–112; role in women's welfare network, 40, 134, 153–155, 157, 161; transformation of, 76–80, 82–84, 86–87

National Negro Health Week, 123–124

National Purity Congress, 66

National Woman Suffrage Association, 93–94

Neighborhood Union (Atlanta), 12, 114–115, 121–126, 128

New Deal, 8–9, 168–169

"New South," 71, 75, 116

New West Monthly, 100

New York City, 33, 54, 57; Crittenton's social life in, 41–46; mortality in, 26, 130–131; mothers' pensions in, 145–146

New York Committee for the Prevention of State Regulation of Vice, 52

New York Female Moral Reform Society, 39, 50

New York Raines Law, 55

New York Society for the Prevention of Contagious Diseases, 51

New York Times, 135, 165

New-York Weekly Magazine, 25

orphans, 84, 131–132, 147

The Outlook, 4, 93, 104

Pall Mall Gazette, 63

patriarchy, 19, 38, 55, 73, 101, 105, 118

Peiss, Kathy, 86

Pettey, Sarah Dudley, 5

Pierce Parent-Teachers' association, 108

Plaindealer, 109

Poems on Miscellaneous Subjects, 97

policing, 50, 51, 53–54, 61, 75, 89; of behavior, 42, 87, 172; matrons of, 54–55, 111

politics, 93–95, 101, 128; as a male domain, 130, 163, 168

poverty, 103, 131–132, 142, 152, 169; awareness of, 127–128, 130; and sex work, 44, 65, 72, 87; studies of, 73, 138–140, 146–147, 149

Pray You, Sir, Whose Daughter?, 23, 64

pregnancy, 72–73, 89, 105, 149–150, 161

the press, 75, 93, 120, 130, 156, 166; coverage of Children's Bureau, 140, 147–148

prison, 13, 51, 54, 58, 63, 67, 145

Progressive Era, 2–3, 57, 87–88, 102, 127, 164

Progressivism, 3, 78, 93–94, 147–148; of maternalists, 10, 13, 155–156, 166

prostitution, 10–11, 55–56, 63–65, 101, 115; as consequence of "the fall," 14, 38–39, 73–74; increased visibility of, 41–42, 43–45, 71–72, 75; reform movements aimed at, 18–19, 42, 50–53, 59; and rescue work 60–61, 79–80, 89–90, 99. *See also* sex worker

Protestantism, 20, 48, 95, 131; and death, 26, 28–29, 30; of reform organizations, 59, 62, 63, 79, 145; evangelism within, 41, 43, 59, 70, 73, 77

public action, 70, 81, 138, 172

public health, 7, 13, 51, 140, 152, 162; data collection about, 136–139; inequities of, 71–72, 116–117, 129–130

public schools, 170; for black children, 107, 125

publicity, 75, 82–84, 93, 133–134, 148–149, 152

racial uplift, 12, 22, 96–99, 103–106, 117, 187n2

race, 19, 22, 66–67, 70, 104, 120–121, 169; as a factor in aid, 91–92, 144; reformers as

working class (*continued*)
child care for the, 120, 156–157; culture of, 43–45, 55, 57–58; exploitation of, 52, 60, 103, 110, 115; respectability of, 5, 65, 98–99, 110–111; vulnerability of, 23, 67, 84, 99, 116, 118–121, 123

working mothers, 79, 118, 140–141, 156, 159–160, 191n23

Young Women's Christian Association (YWCA), 102, 109, 125, 163, 193n65

Printed in the United States
by Baker & Taylor Publisher Services